EQUITY IN SCIENCE

EQUITY IN SCIENCE

*Representation, Culture, and
the Dynamics of Change in
Graduate Education*

Julie R. Posselt

Stanford University Press
Stanford, California

Stanford University Press
Stanford, California

Printed in the United States of America on acid-free, archival-quality paper

Library of Congress Cataloging-in-Publication Data

Names: Posselt, Julie R., author.

Title: Equity in science : representation, culture, and the dynamics of change in graduate education / Julie R. Posselt.

Description: Stanford, California : Stanford University Press, [2020] | Includes bibliographical references and index.

Identifiers: LCCN 2019051524 (print) | LCCN 2019051525 (ebook) | ISBN 9781503608702 (cloth) | ISBN 9781503612716 (paperback) | ISBN 9781503612723 (ebook)

Subjects: LCSH: Science—Study and teaching (Graduate)—Social aspects. | Minorities—Education (Graduate)—Social aspects. | Minorities in science—United States. | Diversity in the workplace—United States.

Classification: LCC Q183.3.A1 P67 2020 (print) | LCC Q183.3.A1 (ebook) | DDC 507.1/1—dc23

LC record available at https://lccn.loc.gov/2019051524

LC ebook record available at https://lccn.loc.gov/2019051525

Cover design: Amanda Weiss
Cover image: iStock
Typeset by Newgen in 10/14 Minion

To the students and scholars who have persisted
in science despite its slow evolution

A time for retooling has arrived.

    —*Thomas Kuhn*, The Structure of Scientific Revolutions

Contents

Preface

This book brings together case studies of equity and inclusion work in scientific disciplines to identify strategies for changing the interactions, organizations, and institutions that shape how science is carried out. I focus on graduate education in science for two reasons: First, it is the most important site for the selection and socialization of the next generation of scientists. The very nature of institutions is to resist change and reproduce themselves, and graduate education is where this reproduction happens in the disciplines. Second, in spite of the tendency toward reproduction, there is currently significant activity dedicated to diversifying graduate education in science, technology, engineering, and mathematics (STEM). Without attention to what may be learned from prior efforts, this movement is all but certainly doomed to repeat past mistakes. Analyzing how real organizations manage the tension between the forces of reproduction and change is therefore the intellectual aim of this book.

Different visions and strategies drive change agents and the work that they carry out. Even within small groups engaged in the same equity project, people interpret the work and bring varied motivations to it. In one project, a white man worked to change patterns represented in a bar graph representing African Americans' degree attainment in physics, so that the bars would not get progressively shorter from BS to MS to PhD. Another on the team, a Black woman, dedicated herself to deepening her colleagues' discourse about the reasons so few Black undergraduates go on to graduate school. Variation in how we define the vision (e.g., equity, diversity, inclusion), goals (e.g., degree attainment, learning, satisfaction), scale (e.g., individual experiences, organizational practices, group outcomes), and work (e.g., personal, organizational, institutional) add to the layers of complexity within equity efforts that must be negotiated if "the work" is to succeed. Shared language, it turns out, matters just as much as shared metrics.

This is hard work, for which few in STEM have training. And because of the very inequalities they are working against, initiatives for equity, diversity, and inclusion are often led by people who have been personally sheltered from barriers that come with being a person of color and/or a woman in science—that is, people who identify as white and/or as men. Learning therefore needs to be a central aspect of this activity for those engaged in it, particularly for those who enter it with limited personal or professional background knowledge.

I enter this research as a white woman, which comes with imperatives for learning of its own. In social science, we use the word *positionality* to describe how a researcher is personally related to the phenomenon they are studying. Disclosing one's positionality is believed to promote quality in research through transparency about how one's perspective may lead them to frame a research issue and interpret data about it in particular ways. In my case, research and engagement with STEM communities have taught me much, and also changed my view of myself as a scholar. As a social scientist and education professor, I will never have the credentials or credibility to enter a lab as an insider; however, as a full participant and leader in a few recent projects on science equity, I have obtained an unexpectedly clear and close view of everyday realities in these communities. As a white person, I have not been the target of racist behaviors, although I have observed them and have seen how racism is quietly institutionalized in everyday practices. As a straight, cis-gendered person, gender identity and sexual orientation were never barriers to my sense of connection to the communities I engaged with for the research here.

However, the universe conspired to ensure that, while writing a book about equity work in science, as a woman I would endure sexual harassment and assault firsthand—some at the hands of scientists. I have therefore also experienced firsthand the pangs that come from seeing respect accorded to people whom you know to act differently behind closed doors. I have breathed the same quiet determination that women of all backgrounds and people of color breathe every day to maintain professionalism in the face of crude, rude, and otherwise demeaning behavior. I have felt sinking disappointment when those whom I thought of as allies chose to stay silent or chose the path of least resistance. But I have also developed close, rewarding friendships with experts in subfields that I did not know existed as specialties a decade ago. I have developed deeper respect for those who speak up and act on behalf of women of all backgrounds and racially minoritized groups.

Along the way, I got tenure from the University of Southern California, a powerful research university that is recovering from scandals related to sexual harassment and assault by its employees. Both responding to my own experiences with harassment and assault and witnessing how USC tries to recover from failure to protect its own "Trojan family" from the same have provided me with an education of its own. I therefore complete this manuscript with deeper conviction of solidarity with communities working to create worlds in higher education and science where students and scholars from those marginalized communities do not just reluctantly stay but also lead and thrive.

These are serious issues, making it all the more important that our efforts to make scientific communities more inclusive involve laughing and learning together, and setting expectations to listen and care for one another. How we handle the mistakes that will inevitably be made—both those we make and those that others make that hurt us—play an important role in going forward, together. Indeed, I have come to believe that the longevity and success of efforts that imagine changing culture will be contingent on key players staying in the conversation long enough to trust one another. That trust has to be earned, especially by people whose past behavior or social identities predispose them to judgments of untrustworthiness.

And so although people socialized to disciplines that privilege data may be most comfortable using the language of statistics to talk about equity work, and although we might need to execute that work in part with the same mundane, bureaucratic apparatus through which we get anything done at the office (i.e., there will be agendas, PowerPoint slides, and budgets to manage), the work will necessarily involve emotional, psychological, and moral dimensions as well. Those may be uncomfortable in part because people often deny their relevance at work and in part because science does not select people for self-awareness or social skills, but also because the work requires facing our involvement in systems of oppression that are often taboo to discuss.

A major theme of this book concerns the necessity and limits of both bottom-up and top-down change, and the necessity of combining these with inside-out change—that is, interrogating our inherited assumptions, acknowledging our identities, and learning what to do with the ways our identities are wrapped up in systems of power. Successful partnerships of diverse people seeking equity and inclusion goals involve more self-reflection and honest dialogue than is typical in the academy.

I am heartened by how many people I have met who want to be part of the solution and are working in grassroots efforts or quietly resisting and subverting academe's dominant paradigms. I am similarly heartened by growing support for this work among powerful organizations like the National Academies of Sciences, Engineering, and Medicine, as well as foundations, universities, and disciplinary societies. But just as graduate education grapples to negotiate forces of reproduction and change, the universities that serve graduate students are in many ways caught between regressive and progressive tendencies, making the future anything but certain. It is my hope that, in addition to contributing to the sociologies of education and science, this text's portraits of real struggles to define and seek equity will inform the development of more humane policy and partnerships across disciplinary boundaries.

Los Angeles
August 22, 2019

EQUITY IN SCIENCE

1   Equity Work as Science

U NDER BRIGHT LIGHTS ON THE STAGE OF A LARGE AUDITORIUM, A panel of PhD students spoke from their hearts: "I'm blessed to have my advisor," Christopher said. "I went to prison and spent most of my under-graduate years hiding from that history." He paused, his face a mix of anger, frustration, and sadness. "I knew if I went to grad school, that I didn't want to live like that. I wanted to be out as a felon. . . . So it's really important for you to seek out people who will accept you for who you are."

"Yeah," said the woman next to him. "There was this time I was having problems with the lab manager, who constantly gave me a hard time. . . . It didn't matter what I did, how I dressed, she always had something to say to me. So finally I talked to my advisor about it, and she worked it out."

Reina, who had been mostly quiet, spoke up: "My advisor is wonderful, but she has much better book knowledge on matters of diversity than lived experience and practical knowledge. We relate as women and she's really well read, but we'll never connect on race. I have to be OK with that and respect her efforts to learn."

In this short exchange and the longer discussion of which it was part, three doctoral students constructed their faculty advisors in three roles—one as a trusted mentor, another as an advocate, a third as a socially conscious learner. They fielded audience questions, talking about the worlds of science they had entered, how they were adjusting to those worlds and, in small ways, striving to change them. The professors did not need to be physically present for their influence to be felt.

Depending on the academic cultures in which a person has been trained and works, taking on the roles of mentor, advocate, or learner implied in this student panel may seem more or less natural. This book invites readers to learn from the successes and mistakes of faculty like them, a rarely examined group. How do scientists in predominantly and historically white, male disciplines work for equity, diversity, or inclusion? What role does graduate education play in creating equity in science? How can equity work be improved to create better outcomes and healthier academic communities for the present and next generations?

I define equity work as reconfiguring structures, cultures, and systems to empower marginalized groups and close disparities. I choose to set equity as the bar for the work that is needed instead of diversity or inclusion. Diversity and inclusion imply that the mere presence of difference suffices or that people can be allowed in, but on terms that maintain racial, gender, and other status hierarchies that subordinate historically marginalized groups. To close gaps and keep them closed means reckoning with multiple, intersecting power dynamics and empowering marginalized group members' voices, votes, and other forms of influence—to define the present and future of the community.

Equity work manifests variably in metrics, in movements, in everyday experiences, and in professional practice.[1] It is, at its most effective, a case of institutional change, defined as changing mindsets, policies, and practices across the multiple levels and cultures of a system, through collaboration across differences that typically separate us. With this systemic perspective in mind, I will argue that the dynamics of change aimed at equity, diversity, or inclusion in STEM can therefore be captured as well by ideas and metaphors from complex systems and quantum theory as those from the tidy predictability of classical dynamics. Institutional change can be messy, because we are working within—and are therefore affected by—the very systems of power and organizational structures that we are also trying to improve. We may find ourselves working with people, language, or knowledge that is new to us. Efforts are almost always partial and imperfect, and people within the same department or initiative may read the extent of progress quite differently. It's not easy work, making it all the more important to learn from the mistakes and successes of outliers in the academic community who are taking it seriously. We begin with one of the most important concepts in change efforts—culture—and how disciplinary cultures in science present barriers to equity.

Blinded by Culture in Science

It is no revelation that culture change of some sort is needed in science, and so widespread is this awareness that more and more people want to be associated with contributing to positive cultural changes. The trouble is, few within science have been socialized to recognize the cultures in their midst, much less what changing them entails. Having defined culture outside the core of necessary knowledge to be an effective scientist, knowledge and skills for improving culture are limited within the community. It may well be that more graduate students in STEM are trained in using techniques in the toolbox of spectrometry than those in the toolboxes of effective teaching, mentoring, leadership, or change management—four practices that reflect and reinforce culture.

Culture is a system of inherited values, goals, and language that provides members with a shared sense of who they are and a common purpose for action. A multifaceted concept, culture most simply put "is reflected in what is done, how it is done, and who is involved in doing it."[2] One can observe culture in an organization by noticing shared values and beliefs. Though values and beliefs are abstract, they surface in predictable ways: how a mission or goals are defined and applied, evaluative criteria and the socialization processes through which new members are inducted, priorities used for decision making, and expectations placed on members and leaders.[3] Culture is rarely unified or integrated. It can also be differentiated, as in groups with clear sub-cultures, and it can be fragmented when those sub-cultures are ambiguous or in tension. These are normal features of organizational life, and making space for people who think differently than those who have predominated is one of the surest paths to creativity and change in organizations.[4]

As people settle into a new group, especially one that aligns with their own values, they often cease to notice the culture. It is, to most people, like water to a fish—an essential medium, yet usually taken for granted unless we somehow get outside of it. In academe, we are usually so surrounded by people who think and act like we do that it becomes hard to distinguish, much less challenge, what is normal and necessary from that which simply reflects our local organizational culture.[5] As is the case for fish adapted to mildly toxic waters, those who stay in academia long enough may stop noticing the toxicity of the culture in which we work.

For example, it becomes easy to lose sight of the mismatch between our cultural beliefs of equal opportunity and impartiality with the realities of inequities and discrimination. Beliefs associated with meritocracy (i.e., distribution of opportunities on the basis of individual effort, talent, and achievement rather than by heredity or privilege) and objectivity (i.e., impartiality and a focus on evidence over personal preferences or feelings) are two powerful aspects of academic culture, especially within science and engineering fields. We use meritocracy and objectivity to justify our systems for allocating membership and honors and, more fundamentally, to define who and what should be deemed legitimate.[6] However, the strong commitment to these beliefs also obscures the ways we are responsible for creating and sustaining inequalities.[7]

For one, scholars who are accustomed to thinking that their achievements are earned, or who think of themselves as impartial, may be less vigilant against implicit bias and other forms of discrimination. Studies in economics have measured these tendencies. In an experiment with sixty-five men role-playing a game about hiring a factory manager, men primed to think of themselves as objective and logical were more likely to favorably rate a male-identified applicant with the same qualifications as one who is female.[8] Ironically, a strong belief in our objectivity as knowers may predispose us to be less objective, and more biased, in judging merit. When we acknowledge that our systems and practices for ensuring equal opportunity and access are broken, then unpacking misperceptions about merit and objectivity becomes a powerful strategy for cultural change. Good intentions to be objective do not immunize us from bias. They can, however, make us more wary of our own judgments.

Nominally "impartial" beliefs can also make it difficult to perceive our role in inequalities by rationalizing them—cloaking social wrongs in more attractive rationales. In social science this is called legitimation, and it is the process by which unpopular ideas like inequality become accepted as normal and legitimate. In previous research I found that leaders of selective graduate programs rationalized their low admission rates of Black applicants as a problem of that group's lower scores on the Graduate Record Examinations (GRE), which they thought of as more objective indicators of merit than the alternatives. Yet they were not attuned to the distributions and error on scores, or to their own tendencies to infer meanings from scores beyond those qualities that the Educational Testing Service (ETS) constructs the test to measure (i.e., reasoning and skills).[9] I found they read additional qualities into GRE scores, such as who is intelligent, who poses a risk, and who ultimately belongs.[10] Failure to apply the same scrutiny to the objectivity of our measures of merit that we place on other statistics has enabled academia to portray inequities in enrollment and completion as students' problem, not ours. That perspective, however, occludes generations of injustice in American education and also the fact that professors have a choice every year about whether or not to prioritize racialized metrics among the information they could solicit about applicants.

For too long, claiming an insufficient supply of "qualified" graduate student and faculty candidates has served as what organization theorists call a social defense: a spurious story that people tell to protect themselves from the discomfort of acknowledging how their behavior and thinking may be part of the very problem they wish to solve.[11] The uncomfortable truth is that the socialization that higher education presently provides into meritocratic and objectivist logics leads many scholars—in both the sciences and more broadly—not to see racial or gender inequalities produced in learning and work environments as a critical problem for them, in either an absolute sense or relative to other pressures.[12]

Additional refrains are also sung in minimizing the significance or urgency of inequities in science: Some do not see social identities and the perspectives that may come with them as relevant to them or to scientific work. Others dismiss higher education as too late to face inequities with origins in broader society or K–12 education. They may have inherited false information about what constitutes "risk" or the related falsehood that equity and excellence are mutually exclusive. Whole fields resist rethinking their course sequencing and prerequisites to enable a broader population to earn advanced degrees.

There are also structural forces in play. Doctoral students have long been positioned dually as students and employees, but the balance has shifted in many places toward the latter. Admissions and education have thus come to consist of hiring and supervising skilled employees as much as identifying talent and cultivating scholars. Therefore, judgments of "merit" often emphasize experience and achievements over potential. It is not hard for faculty to point to the structures in which they are situated—university policies and budget models, the pressures to publish and bring in grant funding, and a broader policy environment—as reasons not to elevate equity considerations.

Working Toward Solutions

Yet for every professor making excuses for inequalities or evading responsibility for them, there are others determined to be part of the solution. Scholars from myriad backgrounds are working hard to buck inertia and overcome resistance. They want to leave their department, their discipline, and the academic profession more humane than when they entered it. They want to do better and be better themselves. They want to push the diversity conversation into questions about climate and how the system we have created drives away talented students of *all* backgrounds. They want to talk seriously about shifting community norms and reward structures to be more amenable to scholars with families and more respectful of the contributions that people of color make. They want, somehow, for the jerks in their communities to be held accountable.

Some are doing much more than passionately holding such desires, good intentions, and visions of a better world. They are putting in serious time—often nights and weekends—on task forces, initiatives, or grants that their institutions and promotion criteria may or may not value. They are confronting the obstinate and doing science differently in the spaces in which they have authority. They are collecting and analyzing data about their programs, taking a hard look at their own behavior, and reforming policies and practices. I was struck by how many of the professors I interviewed used the analogy of work-life balance to describe the difficulty of balancing their scientific work with work related to demands for equity, diversity, and inclusion. The work is important to them and worthy of effort but poorly woven into the fabric of current academic expectations. They may not be fully confident in what they are doing or whether they are balancing their obligations appropriately, and they may disagree with colleagues on tactics. However, there are more people working on this than ever—and they want to get it right.

Thus, we have in academia both significant barriers and significant resources for cultural change. Academia is an institution, which means it is constituted not only by organizations but also by shared stories, values, and norms that regulate behavior, provide identity, and constrain change. Meritocracy and objectivity are two such values. However, we also have increasingly urgent calls for diversity, equity, and inclusion and some serious efforts toward these goals. What's more, investments from foundations and universities, experimentation with the rules of the game, and demographic trends all favor the interests of a more diverse society. Will harnessing these resources be enough to overcome—or even circumvent—the barriers?

Graduate Education: Its Importance and Inequities

Toward the visions of equity in science and a more inclusive system of higher education, graduate education is justifiably the target of a variety of reform efforts. Reports by the National Academies of Science, Engineering, and Medicine (NASEM) in 2005, 2011, and 2018 each called for graduate education as a site for intervention.[13] The 2005 report *Rising Above the Gathering Storm*, noted that demographic changes were outpacing improvements in the representation of people of color in sciences, including at the graduate level. Then, in 2011 *Expanding Underrepresented Minority Participation* identified the "transition to graduate education" as one of two key areas in which intervention was needed in order to broaden participation. Most recently, *Graduate STEM Education for the 21st Century* offered a suite of recommendations for making graduate education more equitable, diverse, and inclusive.[14] It asserted needs for fundamental changes to the cultures of STEM and STEM education, as well as to their incentive structures. These reports are hardly the first calls to address inequities in graduate education. Decades of research also indicate that graduate education is an important indicator of workforce preparation and that it has positive economic returns for individuals, but also that in many fields, students of color and women of all backgrounds enroll and graduate at rates lower than their shares of the population.

The NASEM reports' emphasis on the transition to graduate education is consistent with a major finding of the research in this book: in PhD programs that enrolled and graduated more women and underrepresented minority students than their field, every single one reformed admissions criteria and practices.[15] The process of collectively reexamining standard gatekeeping practices is powerful, because it surfaces and compels discussion of otherwise latent (but nonetheless powerful) cultural norms, priorities, and perceptions about who belongs in the organization and on what basis. Throughout higher education today, changing typical practices to recruit, admit, and educate graduate students hopes to broaden participation and reduce inequities in enrollment and degree attainment . Although there are important programs under way to increase access to graduate school (e.g., Meyerhoff Scholars Program, McNair Scholars Program), and organizations that support students of color in STEM fields (e.g., SACNAS), these are not my focus. Rather, I examine how historically white and/or male fields and departments are changing.

The Value of a Degree

A full third of college graduates today go on to earn postbaccalaureate degrees. Whereas once those degrees signaled distinction in a labor market saturated with bachelor's-degree recipients, graduate credentials are also increasingly required for certification in professions or expected as a prerequisite for careers involving research—and certainly for faculty positions. Much has been made of the declining share of PhD recipients who enter academia, opening a critical conversation about the appropriate size of graduate programs and the focus, skills, and knowledge that should be provided within them. In physics, for example, although the unemployment rate for PhDs has hovered around 2 percent since 1979, only about 11 percent of PhDs (including international students) obtain faculty positions.[16] How much should graduate programs reform their curriculum, mentoring, selection criteria, or dissertation expectations to accommodate the diverse career pathways in their fields? One problem in motivating reform is that those who direct and teach within graduate programs derive personal and professional value from their students going on to faculty life themselves, and most are unequipped to mentor students toward other careers.

Regardless, across employment sectors of academia, industry, and research labs, the economic returns to graduate credentials are substantial. They are rising at a faster rate than returns to undergraduate degrees, and they represent a growing portion of the overall returns to higher education.[17] Women aged 40–65 in 2012 received salaries from master's, doctoral, and professional degrees that were 25 percent, 60 percent, and 108 percent greater, respectively, than salaries of women with only bachelor's degrees. For men in the same age range, the benefits of advanced degrees over bachelor's degrees for median salaries were 17 percent, 30 percent, and 100 percent.[18] Graduate and professional degrees thus benefit both men and women relative to bachelor's degrees, but women appear to especially benefit from graduate education, at least financially.

Graduate education's importance is both economic and cultural. Students in graduate education are like canaries in the coal mine of the academy: many of the tensions that affect the lives of professors are first experienced by doctoral students who are making their way in departmental and disciplinary environments. When there is a competitive atmosphere; when senior scholars hold racist, sexist, or homophobic attitudes; or when norms for time at the lab bench blur the line between dedication and workaholism, it is those who are most vulnerable in our communities who will experience it most profoundly. We learn something about the quality of scientific work environments through the persistence and well-being of our graduate students. And when we neglect how the environments we create affect well-being, we are more likely not only to lose rising scholars from the academic track but also to neglect how the environments affect everyone in them.

Reform in graduate education thus offers a strategic intervention for cultural change in the disciplines. Graduate students both develop expertise in formal subject matter and pick up a vast amount of informal knowledge—such as unspoken rules and everyday practices—about what it means to be "good" scholars and professionals. The disciplines and professions persist and evolve partly through the socialization that graduate education provides.[19] Therefore, graduate education's socialization function could be used more strategically to instill norms, habits, and skills that would make the scientific enterprise more inclusive. Students educated within graduate programs that purposefully operate according to more equitable, inclusive cultural norms are likely to take on at least some of what they pick up as their own standards of thinking and behavior, and then go on to seed their workplaces with them. More mindful professional development of the next generation—be it within PhD programs, through graduate schools, or via disciplinary societies—offers a powerful, long-term intervention in both the well-being and equity of the scientific enterprise.

Slow Progress on Inequities in Graduate Education

Despite the importance of graduate education, many fields have stalled in closing gender and ethno-racial gaps between rates of doctoral degree attainment and representation in the population.[20] Of the 41,400 STEM PhDs awarded in US universities in 2012, only 8.5 percent went to Black, Latinx, and Native American students,[21] and there were twelve fields of study in 2017 in which not a single PhD was awarded to a person who identified as African American. At the program level, participation of Black, Latinx, and Native American students in STEM doctoral education is so very low that we have to be able to think about change one human at a time.[22] Women today earn doctoral and professional degrees across fields at close to the same rate as men, but within STEM, rates vary widely, from more than 50 percent awarded to women in biological sciences to less than 20 percent in physical sciences, mathematics, and engineering.[23]

A few schools of thought have emerged about the origins and persistence of these inequities.[24] Analyses of typical educational pathways for specific student populations offer one explanation. Within STEM, women, Black, and Latinx students disproportionately choose majors in fields where lower shares of undergraduates go on to pursue graduate degrees. Women have higher odds than men of majoring in biological sciences, for example, in which undergraduates are 25 percent as likely as students in other STEM fields to continue on to graduate education and careers.[25] Another school of thought goes even further back, focusing on K–12 schools and undergraduate education. How we select, educate, and advance graduate students in the United States is part of a broader educational system that, far from promoting large-scale social mobility or social transformation, tends to reproduce and even amplify inequalities. As such, graduate education receives and reflects society's gender, racial, and socioeconomic hierarchies and feeds them forward into the labor market. Within our grossly unequal education system, whether or not one happens to attend a well-resourced school, as wealthy and white children are more likely to do, confers a host of material and symbolic benefits in positioning children for college and adulthood.[26] Among other benefits, going to a well-resourced K–12 school is associated with attending more selective colleges and universities, which is associated with significantly higher odds of being admitted to graduate school and professional degree programs.[27]

These perspectives are well established empirically, and I outline them not as straw men to be taken down but as critical elements of a complex social phenomenon. However, analysis of student choices, typical pathways, and the aggregate outcomes that result cannot alone explain why, even in fields like the biological sciences, there is a precipitous drop from the percentages of bachelor's degrees, relative to master's degrees and PhDs, awarded to women and groups classified as underrepresented minorities (see Figures 1 and 2). Nor can work like this explain inequities in graduate student well-being. Graduate students of color from all ethno-racial groups except Pacific Americans have higher rates of depression than white graduate students.[28] And despite having higher grades, women graduate students are more likely to leave PhD

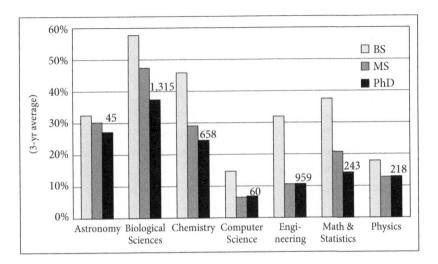

FIGURE 1. Percentages of degrees awarded to women by STEM field.

SOURCE: IPEDS Completion Survey.

NOTE: Numbers above PhD indicate absolute number of PhDs awarded per field to US women, averaged across three years.

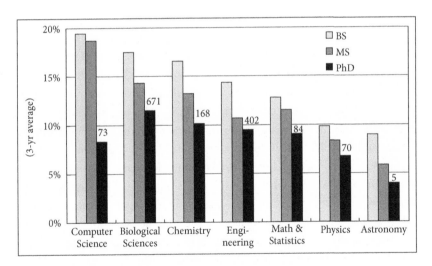

FIGURE 2. Percentages of degrees awarded to underrepresented minorities by STEM field.

SOURCE: National Center for Education Statistics and APS.

NOTE: Numbers above PhD indicate absolute number of PhDs awarded per field for underrepresented minority students, averaged across three years.

programs than male counterparts.[29] To understand the loss of students at this advanced stage and disparities in well-being among those enrolled, I focus not on student choices or on stratification in K–16 education, but rather on the organizational behavior of graduate programs and the practices of faculty within them.

Looking at the production of inequalities only before pursuit of graduate education detracts attention from the difference that stakeholders of graduate education can and do make. Qualities of graduate programs and of advisor-student relationships are among the most important factors shaping PhD student outcomes.[30] Research studies have also documented discrimination as a reality in graduate programs in a wide variety of institutional settings and fields.[31] In this book I investigate the subtle and not-so-subtle ways that routine paradigms and practices within graduate programs and disciplines are racialized and gendered, and how members are challenging the status quo.[32] It is my hope that by presenting these examples of organizations and faculty, that readers inside and outside of STEM will become better attuned to the need and potential to create more equitable systems.

Thinking Systemically

As the case studies in this book demonstrate, creating equity in graduate education requires thinking systemically about established areas of professional practice, as well as the relationships among those practices and the contexts in which they occur. Complex systems are, by definition, composed of many interrelated parts that have relationships, dependencies, and interactions, both internally and with their environment. In graduate education, recruitment, admission, curriculum, pedagogy, and mentoring are not independent but are rather an interconnected system with multiple feedbacks. As one example, professors' beliefs about whether brilliance is innate or cultivated, which affect how prospective students are assessed for admission, do not disappear when students enroll; these beliefs resurface in the classroom, in advising meetings, and in decisions about who merits which honors and opportunities. Who joins, thrives, or struggles in our organizations as a result of these processes shapes the character of a department and the climate therein, affecting both how future prospective students will judge their own "merit" and how we will judge theirs. The best outcomes therefore occur when leaders coordinate improvements in practice with one another and with their specific contexts and students in mind.

Complex systems are marked by interactions across spatial and temporal scales, and scientists find that what happens on small scales can sometimes influence what happens on larger spatial and longer timescales; other times large-scale changes manifest in small-scale phenomena. The relationship between weather and climate presents a straightforward example of the latter: Earth's climate is driven by large-scale (i.e., global) changes, with variations in the sun's intensity affecting the entire planet, and greenhouse gases tending to be long lived and well mixed in the atmosphere. The important responses to changes in the climate happen locally, however, in the form of weather events. We see them in the day to day through precipitation amounts and the occurrence and intensity of heat waves. In the social world, seemingly small-scale organizational changes at a single point in time can have ripple effects over decades, and large-scale policy changes can differentially effect small-scale organizational realities. In one research study that I conducted, the relatively small decision of a civil engineering department to add *environmental* to its name in the 1960s set in motion a rapid change in the interest that women students and faculty alike took in the department, such that by the 2010s, they found themselves close to gender parity. And we have seen in recent years how large-scale changes in federal immigration policy under the Trump administration almost immediately affected international students' applications to US graduate programs in physics and engineering, which tend to receive many applicants from Iran, but applications in some other fields barely nudged. We have to account for interactions with contexts of space and time when describing causes and effects in complex systems.

Feedback loops also highlight the importance of thinking and working systemically. I have observed a common feedback loop in elite doctoral programs I have studied: They may acknowledge a lack of gender or racial diversity, and may be willing to make exceptions to their rule, but they often want to leave much of how the select and interact with students unchanged: They may therefore admit a few students who "feel like a risk" but embody the diversity they seek. However, they often do not attend to how their climate, mentoring, and curriculum are experienced by students of color, leaving intact a graduate program culture riddled with threats to such students' likelihood of thriving. In subsequent years, when admitted students from similar backgrounds visit campus for a recruitment weekend, they cannot help but notice the lack of critical mass of students who share their identities, the cues of an elitist culture and impersonal climate that signal what their own experience would be. In some cases, the few students of color already enrolled would try to pull them aside for some real talk about life in the program. And therefore, admitted students ultimately enroll elsewhere, putting the department back where it started, agonizing over its lack of diversity.

The impressive frequency with which I have observed this pattern—and have heard it reiterated in sharing my research around the country—has made clear that PhD programs serious about remediating enrollment and degree attainment inequities cannot rely on a strategy of admitting a few people as "exceptions to the rule" who will flavor the status quo. Particularly in academic organizations, where annually we repeat the same cycle of activities in admitting and enrolling new groups of students, there is opportunity to fine-tune our systems not only by attending to the inputs but also by improving processes through which we serve students (that is, in systems talk, how we produce outputs).

How does this work in practice? The case studies in chapters that follow reveal change efforts involving activity on multiple scales and through a combination of top-down, bottom-up, and inside-out forces. These efforts involved intentionality, time, coordination, and honest self- analysis. Graduate education and the disciplines are decentralized and faculty hold incredible autonomy, so we need a movement from the bottom up that includes critique and advocacy from members of the community whose voices have historically been marginalized (including students). We also need individual scholars tweaking daily habits and routines, and putting pressure on leaders to change specific policies. Institutionalizing those new approaches depends on the coordination and resources that come with top-down administrative, governance, and managerial effort. Policy remains one of the most powerful tools at our disposal. Working bottom-up and top-down will fall short in the long term, however, without change that comes from within: we also need individual reflection and collective dialogue about the inherited norms and beliefs that can ultimately obscure our ability to perceive how inequities operate in our midst. The PhD programs in my research that realized enrollment and degree attainment gains *and* student satisfaction worked on policies and practices, as well as more subtle cultural cues such as who is in leadership and informal norms for interactions and decision making. And as people experiment with new values, policies, and practices, we need research and evaluation about their effectiveness.

Learning from Outliers

To understand the possibilities and limits of equity efforts in science, and to inform future efforts to this end, this book shares lessons from three research projects that used methods of cultural sociology to examine how scientists work to change aspects of graduate education in STEM disciplines. My goal is for readers to learn from organizational outliers, which have significantly higher shares of women and US-born students of color with respect to their gender and/or racial composition. I use an intersectional analytic approach where possible to consider how this work places distinctive burdens on multiply minoritized students and faculty.[33] Chapter 2 introduces the lenses through which I conducted my fieldwork, drawing on concepts from quantum physics, relational sociology, and organizational theory to understand the complexity of institutional change.[34] I then present six case studies over four chapters, beginning in Chapter 3 with an ethnographic case study of a geology field course in which I observed firsthand how threats to gender equity in science workplaces may begin in the smallest of interactions. The second research project was an ethnographic comparative case study, through which my research team and I compared the trajectories of high-diversity STEM graduate programs. Chapters 4 and 5 review results from this study, covering the mistakes, learning, and design features of psychology, chemistry, and applied PhD programs. Chapter 6 more deeply considers prospects for change in the physical sciences by examining and reflecting upon discipline-level equity and diversity efforts in astronomy and physics in which I have been a participant. Here we see how efforts aimed at diversity have cultures all their own, which deserve our attention like the cultures of science themselves. The narrative arc for the book thus builds from micro to macro contexts for institutional change, from everyday encounters in a single class to institutional change efforts by disciplinary societies.

My analysis presents a balance of positive and negative lessons that can be learned from equity efforts. I take this approach intentionally. We are likely to see more clearly both strengths and imperfections when we look closely at anything, and a balanced perspective is also crucial to improving future investments. My current home, Los Angeles, provides some inspiration for this. It is a city stereotyped as a hub for beautiful people, but if you look closely, it is also filled with contradictions. Person to person, house to house, street to street, and neighborhood to neighborhood, Los Angeles juxtaposes beauty and blight, wealth and poverty, lives of leisure and labor. It has one of the country's highest rates of homelessness and one of the country's highest median home prices. It's an amazing city where struggle and privilege are overlain, fractal-like. By similarly presenting a candid picture of the strengths and shortcomings of equity work, it is my hope that this book will embolden readers that they do not have to engage in total overhaul or get it perfect in order to get started. We may like to believe there are departments or universities that are doing it right, that have figured out or committed themselves to accomplishing something the rest of us have not. Or, perhaps, we think we've done a pretty good job with our own organization.

But I'm increasingly persuaded no such place exists. The closer we look and the longer we spend with any organization to understand what makes it tick, the more likely we are to find issues worthy of critique or ways it could be improved. For example, in Chapter 4, the psychology department's story may be interpreted as much of a cautionary tale as an exemplar, and one can think of the chemistry department counterpoint in that same chapter only as an exemplar with respect to reducing gender equity. They are just beginning to tackle racial inequalities in that department. We have a long way to go but more resources than ever available. How will we harness them?

A word about my focus on STEM and on high-status organizational contexts: I do not intend by focusing on these disciplines to replicate the pernicious and false narratives that they have greater value, that they are the only disciplines with equity and inclusion problems, or that only these fields have the resources required to make positive change. These myths have been consequential, undermining support for both policy and institutional initiatives. Rather, I focus on these contexts because if we can crack the prospects for change in the highly change-resistant environments of high-status STEM organizations, we are more likely to affect the system as a whole. The intellectual contributions that small-n studies like this can make are distinctive from that of controlled experiments or other quantitative research, but ethnographic case studies like the ones in this book are ideally suited for uncovering mechanisms behind social phenomena that may be present in a variety of contexts.[35] Many of the lessons emerging from the case studies here can be taken up across the disciplines and across our universities.

I will argue that institutional change involves revisiting practices and priorities we have been socialized to through our own training. Limitations in our vocabularies, knowledge, and skill sets will need to be acknowledged. Learning may be needed in functional areas ranging from curriculum design, to respectful communication, to recognizing and mitigating bias, to organizational change. Those whose own lives have sheltered them from realities of sexism and racism need some retooling with specific knowledge—maybe most fundamentally a more critical understanding of the varied ways that power works and is often abused in small behaviors and policies alike.[36] Although these ambitions may be grand, the work itself will be carried out with familiar apparatus—meetings to facilitate conversation and coordination among stakeholders, and presentations of statistics and stories. As academic incentive structures begin to hold scholars and other academic leaders to standards of professional performance that include work toward equity, diversity, and inclusion goals, those who design graduate programs and faculty development will also need to incorporate corresponding learning opportunities. For if graduate education's role is the formation of disciplinary stewards,[37] and the disciplines we want are more equitable and just, then the work will only progress through collective action and ongoing learning by all involved.

2 Managing Complexity
in Institutional Change

NEWTONIAN PHYSICS FORMED THE FOUNDATION OF CLASSICAL dynamics and mechanics, as well as causal inference models that predominate in the social sciences. However, evidence around the turn of the twentieth century from quantum research about the nature of light shook Western science's Newtonian foundation. Studies striving to resolve whether light behaves as a wave or a particle revealed that the measurement apparatus used in an experiment can affect which phenomena are observed.[1] That is, the act of measurement and the apparatus for measurement affect what we perceive to be objective reality. The continuous interactions among researcher, instrument, and phenomenon lead to observations and measures that are a function of both intrinsic properties of the phenomenon and the measurement process itself.

Karen Barad proposes philosophical implications of this tenet and others from quantum physics in her book, *Meeting the Universe Halfway*.[2] In it, she develops a philosophy she calls agential realism from two complementary, fundamental principles of quantum theory. These two principles, focused on complementarity and uncertainty, both challenged the strict determinism of Newtonian mechanics—that is, they challenged the assumption that given the initial conditions of a particle's position and momentum at a specific time point, anything about its trajectory could be calculated. Bohr's *Complementarity Principle* proposed that objects possess certain pairs of properties that cannot be measured simultaneously. For example, position and momentum, wave and particle properties, entanglement and coherence, and energy and duration are all complementary pairs whose observation depends on the technology being used for measurement. In short, "Not all aspects of a system can be viewed simultaneously."[3] Tools have specific and limited purposes, and generally, we can measure only one property at a time.[4] A piece of equipment sheds light on one property but cannot be used to measure others. Another apparatus might reveal a different characteristic of the same phenomenon. Although other disciplines had long recognized complementarity, classical physics had not; Bohr's observation enabled this principle to be adopted as more or less universal. Next, Heisenberg's uncertainty principle posited that if measurements cannot be made without affecting the system being measured, then there is inherently a trade-off in the certainty with which a pair of properties can simultaneously be known. The more we know about a particle's momentum, for example, the less we know about its position.

Perhaps paradoxically, quantum thinking launched the most audacious challenge to the intellectual pride of Western science by proposing that a more humble stance toward knowledge is warranted. Things are more complex than they seem because our representations of things are not the things themselves. Further, the boundary between a knower and what is known that is implied in objectivism is not what it seems, because our measurement instruments shape what we think of as objective knowledge. And as the makers of instruments, humans are part of the reality we strive to understand.

These insights from quantum theory hold fresh perspective for how we conceptualize key concepts—such as agency, continuity, and boundaries—in understanding stasis and change within complex organizations and systems. Two defining qualities of institutional change for equity are its complexity and the associated need for a systemic approach. Consider these layers of multiplicity that may need accounting for in a field that wants to improve graduate education:

- *Multiple possible goals:* Equity, diversity, inclusion, degree attainment, well-being, and more
- *Multiple contexts:* Labs, courses, field sites, PhD programs, departments, universities, disciplines
- *Multiple domains of faculty practice:* Recruitment, admissions, pedagogy, mentoring
- *Multiple levels of analysis:* Individual experiences, interpersonal interactions, organizational policies and practices, and academic culture

- *Multiple, intersecting systems of power:* Racism, sexism, nationalism, elitism, and more
- *Multiple stakeholders:* Faculty, administrators, students, foundations, professional societies

It is no wonder things seem so slow to change! Not only is there much to do, but activities also need to be mutually reinforcing. Rather than backing away from the complexity or denying the need to think and work systemically, I offer in this chapter perspectives for managing it, and then develop them empirically in the case studies that follow.

Small Wins

First, Karl Weick's theory of small wins in organizations suggests that when we focus on large-scale social problems or try to address them in all their complexity at one time, the difficulty of making a dent can become so daunting that we are unable to use our best problem-solving capacities. "When social problems are described this way," he writes, "efforts to convey their gravity disable the very resources of thought and action necessary to change them. . . . Processes such as frustration, arousal, and helplessness are activated."[5] Instead of focusing on resolving significant problems in their entirety, he and others have proposed that we can make real progress by reframing or redefining the problem on smaller, more manageable scales. Doing so has two major benefits: it stabilizes arousal to a level of intensity where it can be used as a resource, and the very work of redefining the problem can actually be part of the solution.[6]

Therefore, my analytic focus does not examine equity efforts at the scale and complexity of science in its entirety—or even of graduate education. Instead, I present critical analyses of organizational processes, which build from micro to macro contexts: improving communication in a geoscience field course, changing recruitment and admissions in psychology and chemistry PhD programs, designing a PhD program from scratch with inclusion in mind, and coordinating change via disciplinary societies in astronomy and physics. You may have noticed that each of those clauses begins with an activity—improving, changing, designing, coordinating—and I am intentional about this to emphasize that equity work need not be thought of as a monolithic, bureaucratic reform effort. Rather, it is a series of distinct but interconnected practices by and for real humans. Efforts have the greatest potential for impact when they are independently pursued and calibrated to both one another and the organizational contexts in which change is sought. That being said, transformative change often requires large-scale efforts, and in their design, there is much to be learned about the dynamics of change from relatively "small wins" that occur on smaller scales.

Frequently missing, however, is coordination across focused efforts. We may rethink admissions, for example, may try to improve mentoring; we may even go to great lengths to reconfigure established structures of education like the curriculum or qualifying exam in our PhD programs. But how often do we think systematically about how change on one of these fronts may produce opportunities and unintended consequences elsewhere? I am not talking here about mechanistic calibration, as if all that were needed is for doctoral education to become a better machine in processing shiny widgets that are comparable to humans. To the contrary, the institutions we are talking about involve real, complex humans whose relationships have power, social, psychological, and cultural dimensions. Unfortunately, the roots of most organizational theories of change in Newtonian conceptions of causes and effects have lacked ways of talking about, and therefore accounting for and managing, relational complexities. The mechanistic, managerial foundations of mainstream organizational change literature may help explain why reform efforts grounded in these theories often stall or fail to yield substantive gains.

Therefore, in the rest of this chapter I explore more deeply the implications of two relational theories whose implications, along with a small wins approach, can help explain and manage the inherent complexity of institutional change. I continue exploring quantum theory per Barad as a basis for rethinking the dynamics of change in graduate education; then, I link this with cultural and cognitive aspects of sociological boundary work theory. Applying relational perspectives like these can enable deeper, more sustainable gains by encouraging us to pay attention to both individual people and phenomena as well as the lines of interaction and relationships among them. They provide a useful entry into discussions of culture, they account for feedback loops and interactions, and they ensure that we attend to intersections of multiple identities and systems of power.

Quantum Insights for Institutional Change

Within physics, dynamics is a branch of mechanics concerned with the effects that forces have on objects' motion. And within dynamics, quantum theory has come to be viewed as a complement or counterpart to classical theory. So too can quantum theory complement views of organizational dynamics that are rooted in classical dynamics, for there are limits in our ability to hypothesize, predict, measure, and explain groups of both physical particles and of humans. I suggest several insights and concepts have particular salience in social and organizational contexts:

1. *Objects of change*: What increasingly need change in our organizations are not only how people think and act but also a variety of nonhuman technologies that affect mindsets and practices. A posthumanist framework for change is necessary.

2. *Process of change*: The concept of entanglement applied to the social world highlights dependencies and feedbacks in humans' intentions and actions. Structure, constraint, and agency are interdependent.

3. *Non-linearity of change*: The quantum discontinuity suggests that that the futures of lives, organizations, and institutions play out not linearly along predictable trajectories, but rather iteratively and conditionally. History is a dynamic force in the present and future.

4. *Embeddedness in change*: Perhaps most fundamentally, quantum theory's revelation that we are part of the reality that our science strives to understand makes salient that we are also part of the communities we are trying to change. Our identities and associated subjectivities are factors that have strong weights in the calculus of change.

Although assembled, described, and extended from the first time here via quantum dynamics, each of these four tenets has strong support in theory and empirical research about organizational change from interpretive, critical, and postmodern paradigms.[7]

A Posthumanist Foundation

While classical dynamics focuses solely on physical laws that exist apart from humans, quantum dynamics concerns itself both with describing the physical world and humans' knowledge of that world. Extending this view for the purposes of social philosophy, Barad proposes a posthumanist perspective as a foundation for conceptualizing reality (i.e., ontological foundation).[8] A post-humanist view does not deny the integral role of humans in shaping history or natural and social realities. However, it does draw attention to the fact that in today's world, both humans and nonhumans (e.g., technology, algorithms, programs, machines, natural phenomena) play a crucial role in what we know to be real in society and organizational life. I propose that a posthumanist ontological foundation is also relevant for creating equity within scientific organizations, in light of two simultaneous facts.

First, our institutions are populated and led by people, whose micro-level thinking and interactions aggregate to create meso-level organizational processes and macro-level structural and material realities.[9] Scientific institutions are thus inhabited institutions: science provides the raw material for collective work, but humans, in interaction with one another through bureaucratic organizations, propel the enterprise forward.[10] People carry out science and are ultimately the point of the entire movement for diversity, equity, and inclusion. A serious conversation about equity therefore should be informed by data about real people, without reducing people to mere numbers or statistics. Indeed, numbers are an incomplete language for capturing much of what makes humans tick, an idea that led Robert Ross of the California Endowment to quip: "No numbers without stories, and no stories without numbers."[11]

Alongside a recognition of human centrality, we need to grapple with the implications of more activities within organizations being turned over every year to technology, automation, and apparatuses that operate without direct human action. They focus our attention, condition our behavior, and constitute what we see as reality. Apparatuses include the data that feed algorithms and guide decisions, the technology and programs that privilege what information we see, and policies that condition behavior. Although they are value-neutral on their face, nonhuman organizational influences like these are not neutral in their effects.[12] In graduate admissions, for example, online application and enrollment management systems like Slate influence the information faculty have to judge admissibility and how they judge it. It is not just the information universities ask for, but also that which is displayed first in a person's online profile that anchors reviewer judgment about the person. At the organizational level, checklists of preconditions determine whether a campus building is "sustainable" and thus eligible for Leadership in Energy and Environmental Design (LEED) certification. Climate surveys and check-lists of criteria tell us whether a department or college is "inclusive."

At the macro level, we see ongoing sponsorship and entanglement of major scientific projects with broader political, economic, and social institutions and the likelihood that corporate interests will, in one way or another, influence science. Science also runs on organizations of our own making and maintenance, and it is a basic tenet of science and technology studies that scientific organizations are subject to the same power dynamics and power asymmetries as other organizations and reflect the same patterns of racism and sexism within society.[13] The National Institutes of Health (NIH) and the National Science Foundation (NSF) make awards to research organizations, not to individual people. Universities produce not only new scientists and knowledge but also inventions and products subject to technology transfer.

Indeed, human inventions—both conceptual and technical—form the foundation of modern science. With the exception of natural phenomena, nonhuman influences still result from human design, which should compel inclusive, universal design practices as the norm.[14] A posthumanist view of change must therefore concern itself with both the justice and care reflected in individual mindsets, decisions, and behaviors that run science today as well as with the values evinced in the varied institutionalized organizational apparatus through which many decisions and behaviors play out.

Entangled Intentions and Actions

Quantum entanglement occurs when groups or pairs of particles interact such that the quantum state of each cannot be described without reference to the others, regardless of the time and space that separate them. What Einstein dismissed as "spooky action at a distance" has since been demonstrated in objects that are almost large enough to observe with the human eye.[15] This view is well suited in providing language to understand the intertwining of human actions within complex organizations and systems, in which small or apparently random changes can yield surprisingly consequential outcomes. Just as it was hypothesized that the flapping of a butterfly's wings could set initial conditions that shape the formation and path of a tornado weeks later, very small actions can have untold, profound effects.

With a quantum, posthumanist perspective comes a distinctive view of agency, defined as one's ability to frame situations, see options, and take action to advance goals. This view centers on entanglement in how people act and make choices. Conventional views claim that people have separate free-doms and separate constraints, both of which affect how they are likely to in-teract with others. However, a quantum perspective suggests that one person's agency actually represents the entanglement of that person's agency with oth-ers' agency. We may see a person making choices, but those choices are condi-tioned by structures and situations of which they are part, which affect others as well.[16] Crucially, the forces affecting a person's choices include the perceived freedoms and constraints enacted by people in one's circle, as well as envi-ronmental factors such as the reward structure and normative environment.[17]

If as humans our intentions and actions are not separate but entangled, we may not even realize the subtle ways in which small actions have ripple effects on those around us, affecting what appear downstream as their independent "choices" (or the choices of others with whom they associate). One person's choice to speak up or not, in particular ways to particular people, at particu-lar moments in an organization or an initiative may condition the thoughts, actions, and intentions of myriad others who follow.

There may be rare cases when indicators of equity emerge over time as unintended ripple effects of actions that had been taken in the interest of other goals. I mentioned in Chapter 1 the civil engineering department that, by taking the small step of adding the word *environmental* to the department's title, saw a jump in women's participation. The first ripple effect of the name change was an increase in women faculty applicants studying biological and environmental implications of engineering projects. A secondary effect of several women's subsequent hiring was a surge of women undergraduate and graduate students, who were attracted to a department where women mentors would not be an exception to the rule.[18]

Finally, it bears noting that a view of intentions and actions as entangled also contributes to the quiet debate about whether one's professional actions or personal motivations should determine that individual's credibility as a change agent.[19] A view that highlights entanglement would suggest we ought to focus on actions and limit our judgments' of others' intentions, for there is no way for us to know the matrix of freedoms and constraints in which another person operates.

Continuity Is Not What It Seems
Quantum theory permits new views of continuity and change, in addition to shaping how we think about reality and agency. Underlying dominant models

of organizational change in higher education are metaphors for dynamics that derive from classical physics. As noted earlier, language like *trajectory, momentum, acceleration,* and *inertia* rests on Newtonian determinism, with its orderly, predictable universe in which continuity is a given. Quantum entanglement of physical matter with sociocultural, technological, and scientific practice interrupts this tidiness and continuity. Views of causality are themselves interrupted by the recognition that the unfolding of human action is caught up in the actions of those who surround them. Just as William Faulkner wrote, "The past is never dead. It's not even past,"[20] the quantum discontinuity suggests that we never fully leave behind the past. It is never fully finished and the future will not appear as a neat progression from of the moment in which we find ourselves presently. Lives, organizations, and institutions play out iteratively, conditionally, and processes of change are better described as a matter of becoming than one of determining. In that becoming, the past and future are enfolded as forces and participants, and much is contingent on small actions that are inherently social.[21]

"We Are a Part of That Nature Which We Seek to Understand"

Consciousness and the emotional or affective dimensions of the human experience distinguish people from particles, and they become especially salient in change work, which humans both affect and are affected by. Quantum physics asserts that "we are a part of that nature which we seek to understand," and the truth of this principle applies both to scientists' research and to their engagement in changing communities of which they are members.[22] The perspectives and knowledge we each bring to equity efforts (and those knowledge and perspectives that we don't have) constitute an apparatus, for engagement in it. They have roots in our most formative social identities and contexts; yours are different from mine, but everyone's is inherently partial and will come with a mix of strengths and weaknesses for the task at hand. Being part of a common system, and yet with individual knowledge on these matters that is inherently incomplete, means that the likelihood of institutional change depends in part on the willingness of everyone involved to engage in continuous learning.

With the recognition that our perspective and knowledge are by definition partial, a change becomes more natural in how we see ourselves—not with the pride of an expert, as academia typically rewards, but rather with humility of a learner. Cultural humility is an emerging idea that highlights the ability to maintain openness to others, engage in self-critique, redress power asymmetries, and work in partnerships to advocate for others.[23] We may never develop full "cultural competency" (or the more recent discursive shift to a language of cultural and racial literacy) to perfectly behave with grace in the full range and combinations of backgrounds that we encounter; however, developing cultural humility through critical self-reflection and dialogue ensures that when we do engage, we will not be inclined to see ourselves as superior to others or to dominate.[24] Inner work that cultivates humility—alongside skills of literacy and competency—increases the chances that we will be effective equity practitioners in a variety of settings and with a variety of colleagues.

Seeing ourselves as learners and admitting that our knowledge is partial also enables us to appreciate the value of disciplinary perspectives that are different from our own. Most scientists working to reduce barriers to access to or unhealthy climates would benefit from knowledge that has historically been centered in the social sciences, for example, but on the margins of natural sciences. Without knowing the range of ways that racism manifests in organizations, for example, people are unlikely to recognize racist behavior (i.e., their own and their colleagues'), how racism is institutionalized in norms and practices, or why racial inequities persist. And how can we expect people to change complex organizations without some knowledge about organizational change? Scientists are great problem solvers in their areas of training, and they know the theories of their fields inside and out. The reality is, however, that few institutions educate scientists about the social dimensions of scientific practice, nor do they select for scientists who hold that knowledge or require that they demonstrate or develop it. As with its meritocratic and objectivist beliefs, this quality of STEM culture—that is, the failure to socialize members to social knowledge relevant to the scientific enterprise—currently presents a fundamental barrier to remediating inequities.

The insight that we are entangled in the scientific reality we strive to understand and the organizational realities we strive to change draws our attention to ways that the scientific enterprise is of our own making.[25] Indeed, it runs on a host of socially constructed relationships, roles, rules, and resources. The scientific method is, itself, socially constructed.[26] For example, the observations that feed applications of the scientific method are measurements, whose units are also of our own making and that are defined and standardized through human-designed technologies and the policies of a massive bureaucracy, the National Institute of Standards and Technology.[27] This is not to say that scientists and engineers are embedded in a purely social enterprise, or that we are not ever converging on more precise and expansive understanding of natural laws and phenomena. However, social activity is inherent to scientific activity, shaping what we strive to know, how we know it, and who constitutes this "we."[28]

Presently, knowledge and skills to help broaden the "we" of science— either through micro-level interactions or through large-scale policies and structural change—are part of neither socialization for scholarly roles nor institutional expectations for fulfilling them. That such knowledge and skill are perceived to be largely separate from the knowledge it takes to be a "good scientist" has been driven home to me by the number of times I heard the phrase "that diversity stuff" in the course of my research.[29] And it is no surprise: PhD programs often struggle to make space for training scholars to teach their subject matter with the depth they would like, much less to mentor, lead, manage projects, or carry out other activities of scholarly life with cultural literacy or with equity in mind.

We have, therefore, a chicken-egg dilemma: Unless the next generation of scholars comes to see the social dimensions of our work as intrinsic to our science and builds skills in those areas, we are unlikely to enact more inclusive, equitable scientific practices. And without institutionalizing them as expected and normal, we are unlikely to make space for systematically developing capacities in this area within PhD programs, especially amid pressures to reduce both expenditures per student and time to degree.[30] Negotiating priorities and the definition of what "counts" as scientific knowledge and skill is needed, as is retooling to build new competencies.

Symbolic Boundaries and Boundary Work in Science

The conversation that enables such reform rests on a recognition that access to, and honors and opportunities within, academic organizations go to those who best embody or "fit" a community's treasured cultural ideals. Thus, definitions of shared values like excellence, merit, collegiality, and even "good" science operate as symbolic boundaries,[31] defined as "conceptual distinctions made by social actors to categorize objects, people, practices, and even time and space."[32] For their use in distributing opportunities, resources, and status, boundaries are cultural tools that help justify inclusion and exclusion— in key moments of gatekeeping and in everyday interactions. They provide grounds for what sociologists call social closure, the protection of a group by the exclusion of people who do not possess some desired quality. Closure is ubiquitous and promotes group identity by envisioning "others" who do not share the same core characteristics as insiders.[33]

Symbolic boundaries on the meaning of core values have been conceived of in ways that disproportionately include certain demographic groups and exclude others. With respect to merit, for example, even well-intentioned professors often operationalize the idea in ways that undermine espoused racial diversity and gender equity goals, because present definitions result from historically unfolding systems of power.[34] Jerome Karabel wrote that how a culture defines merit "expresses underlying power relations and tends, accordingly, to reflect the particular cultural ideals" of the groups most influential in shaping the culture.[35]

To put a finer point on it, definitions of many professional, intellectual, and cultural boundaries in science have privileged white, male, wealthy interests, for those groups founded today's scientific organizations and wrote the rules by which academia proceeds. We need to understand how mainstream academics think to undermine gendered and racialized logics of inclusion and exclusion.[36] Meanwhile, listening to and learning from people in our communities who have been on the margins, or excluded altogether, enables new ways of thinking and acting. What may seem like a fragmented culture is also one with resources for creativity and change, if managed with care.

Just as socialization to meritocratic and objectivist thinking can obscure our roles in in sustaining inequities, socialization can obscure the essential arbitrariness of the symbolic boundaries that define any group.[37] That said, the fact that they are constructed and arbitrary also means that they are subject to management and change. For this reason, disciplines have been likened to "tribes and territories" and to "imagined communities."[38] Over centuries, they established their professional authority and legitimacy by distinguishing their work and values from what neighbors do. For example, science drew rhetorical boundaries of utility, empiricism, skepticism, and objectivity to distinguish itself from religion; and boundaries regarding progress, experimentation, theory, and discovery distinguished the authority of science over mechanics.[39]

Drawing boundaries is not the only sort of boundary work, though. Scholars have also written about the power to change dynamics of inclusion and exclusion by spanning, erasing, relocating, redefining, and subverting boundaries, or in some cases, creating or activating new ones altogether.[40] Because how we define boundaries has powerful implications for inclusion and exclusion, and because understanding across current boundaries and differences is so important for effective collaborations toward equity, I add to the conversation about boundary work by proposing the importance of translation across boundaries and differences as an additional means of managing change in complex organizations.

Managing Change amid Complexity Through Cultural Translation

I discussed at the start of this chapter the benefit of redefining large, complex challenges like inequality on smaller, more cognitively manageable scales. In such situations, arousal does not overwhelm but rather can be used as a resource.[41] Weick wrote that a second benefit for institutional change of seeking small wins is that the very work of redefining the problem can be part of the solution. When scholars are challenged to negotiate their viewpoints and values for the purposes of defining a common mission or activity, the understanding they build becomes a resource for moving forward. Therefore, a core finding of my research is the need to create spaces for communication that make our personal and professional differences intelligible—that facilitate shared understanding. In addition to learning, mentoring, and advocacy as key activities for scholars in practicing equity, another practice is *cultural translation*, defined as sustained effort to decode, comprehend, and appreciate cultural knowledge outside the worldviews and roles into which we have been socialized.

Cultural translation enables equity work by improving communication and collaboration across disciplinary, organizational, social identity, and other perspectives. For example, C. P. Snow's *The Two Cultures* may have oversimplified the differences between natural sciences and those that are humanistic and social, but he was right about one thing: scholars are trained to speak different languages, just as racial, ethnic, and gender socialization lead us to see and experience the world differently.[42] The format of most social science research articles alone does not help natural scientists digest relevant scholarship, and it ultimately reifies the "two cultures" divide. Few scientists have the time or desire to read thirty pages of what can seem like jargon-laced theory! In addition to a need for learning on the part of practitioners in the natural sciences, then, an obligation also sits with those of us in the social sciences, education, and science studies to communicate with more care: to reach beyond our usual audiences, publication venues, and styles of discourse to make our expertise meaningful on their terms.[43]

Importantly, bell hooks wrote, "If I do not speak in a language that can be understood, there is little possibility of dialogue."[44] And indeed, observations of natural scientists in meetings, professional development, conferences, and informal gatherings has revealed this to me: The ability to use their own disciplinary language and metaphors when talking about social issues enables a sense of familiarity, understanding, and comfort with social issues and knowledge that may otherwise seem foreign, controversial, or simply uncomfortable to discuss. A physics admissions committee, for example, repeatedly referred to concepts from classical mechanics. The committee members justified a decision to accept one student who felt like a risk in terms of "maintaining momentum" on diversity and rationalized changing the GRE policy, in part, in terms of "resisting inertia" of traditional selection.[45] Disciplinary language also enables learning about key ideas from social science. A geology student I spoke with had an "aha" moment about the meaning of social stratification when I compared it to the stratification of vertically arranged rock layers. We may be trained into different languages, but with translational support, those same languages can provide tools for understanding.

Theoretical physicist Carlo Rovelli wrote: "Science begins with a vision. Scientific thought is fed by the capacity to 'see' things differently than they previously have been seen."[46] To improve how we train the next generation of scientists, we need a vision of how scholars of all backgrounds can come together and work on multiple scales, activities, goals, and populations. With small wins, quantum theoretical insights, and boundary work introduced as three, interrelated angles for managing the complexity of institutional change, the chapters that follow will provide concrete examples of equity efforts at different scales and in different contexts. It is my hope that, by revealing the dynamics of this work in the detail that case studies permit, those who work in higher education will more thoughtfully design and carry out such work themselves.

3 Eroded Boundaries and Everyday Interactions in Geoscience Fieldwork

Mid-afternoon, the sun is harsh, with no clouds or shade in sight. The student and teaching assistant sit down beside each other on a rock, both clearly exhausted. The TA takes a drink of water, and he hands her the water bottle. She gulps, and they peer at a map together. She points at the next ridge over, the one that the group is mapping, and from which they've just climbed up. He leans in very close to her, makes eye contact, and gives her a half smile. She fidgets with the water bottle, awkwardly hands it back to him, stands up quickly, and says she has to go back to the group.

THREATS TO GENDER EQUITY IN SCIENCE WORKPLACES MAY BEGIN IN the smallest of interactions. In the episode described here, do you perceive any of the interactions as problematic? Is sharing a rock or a water bottle at the end of a long day of hiking a natural thing to do, or is it inappropriately intimate for a TA and student? Has the TA's behavior violated boundaries of professionalism? There are no simple answers to questions like these. They require a full consideration of the context and views of those involved. Yet sexually charged encounters are just the tip of the iceberg as we think about the types of gendered interactions that merit our attention in creating more inclusive learning and research environments. I argue in this chapter that we need to take everyday norms and communication patterns seriously as both the microfoundations of larger structural arrangements and for their pervasiveness in research settings across the disciplines. For the window that they provide into scientific culture, and harassment and assault within it, I invite you to examine with me the everyday interactions that take place in scientific fieldwork.

In navigating the inevitable gray areas around the boundaries of interactions that most agree are either acceptable or problematic, we need more than just descriptions of situations. We also need the perspectives of the people involved. Individual experiences have to be understood for two reasons: first, they shape whether those who find themselves in similar situations will read them as appropriate, welcome, or hostile—which shapes how they will act. Second, hearing how people other experience everyday interactions may also affect whether we encourage, tolerate, or resist such behavior in others—and when we choose to speak up on behalf of others.

How we interact ourselves and how we respond to interactions occurring around us determine what becomes engrained in us as routine and habit. Cultural sociologists and anthropologists pay a lot of attention to interactions, routines, and habits because they reflect shared understandings of typical behavior,[1] which are both powerful for their ripple effects and for how they drive future behavior. Yet they almost always require observational data because, being part of the culture in which insiders swim, interactions, routines, and habits often seem invisible and taken for granted to insiders themselves.

To improve science workplaces and learning environments, we must attend to the routine interactions and norms to which rising scholars are exposed, for learning the ways of science that trained scientists take for granted—"the way we do things around here"—is the hidden curriculum of graduate education. That curriculum is largely cultural knowledge. It is socially constructed and the result of a process through which people are socialized to see some behaviors as normal and within bounds—and other behaviors not. At some point in history, for example, it became customary for geoscientists to work through the weekends when they are in the field, instead of taking a day or two off. At some point, it became typical for them to drink alcohol through seminars and poster sessions at conferences, although it might be more common on campus or in other disciplines to wait to have a drink until after those activities are done.

The place of gender in the hidden curriculum of science merits urgent attention. In their call for faculty and researchers to respond to distressing rates of sexual harassment and assault in the sciences, St. John, Riggs, and Mogk argue that geoscientists' behavior in settings ranging from the field, to the lab, to the classroom conveys their character and values as people and a community. The behaviors they choose and those they tolerate in others are powerful in setting the tone for work together and modeling to students what is acceptable.[2]

The extent of harassment and assault in the geosciences and the need to intervene in field culture has been clarified in two recent studies. In a survey of 666 field scientists in the physical, life, and social sciences (77.5 percent of whom were women), Clancy and colleagues found that 72.4 percent of respondents "directly observed or had been told about" incidents in their most recent field site involving inappropriate or sexual remarks.[3] A majority (64 percent) reported personally experiencing sexual harassment, and 21.7 percent had personally been sexually assaulted. Unsurprisingly, women were much more likely than men to have experienced harassment and assault. However, there was another key gender difference: when men experienced harassment and assault, perpetrators tended to be peers, whereas among women victims, perpetrators were superiors. The authors go on to connect these patterns to the absence of codes of conduct and sexual harassment policy for fieldwork. They argue for a need for clarity about what constitutes acceptable behavior, and for intervening in the absence of and unawareness about mechanisms for reporting harassment and assault when they occur.

In another recent study designed to examine women's major choice and persistence in geology, Sexton and colleagues found clear evidence that women experience sexist behavior in both fieldwork and classroom settings.[4] In all six departments in their study, undergraduate women reported having experienced sexist behavior in the field, with a higher number of sexist incidents per person reported in departments with lower proportions of women students. Following these experiences, some women changed subdisciplines to avoid fieldwork; others left geology entirely.

Understanding the Cultural Foundations of Fieldwork

Addressing these patterns requires action above and beyond calling them out. We need to understand and address their cultural foundations, and indeed, this has been the goal of the NSF-funded project Fieldwork Inspiring Expanded Leadership for Diversity (FIELD). FIELD includes two parts: ethnographic research about the cultural dynamics of learning and inclusion in geoscience fieldwork at the undergraduate and graduate levels, and a professional development institute in which field leaders from across the country came together to learn how they might improve the inclusiveness of field experiences for which they have responsibility. This chapter reports one set of findings from FIELD's research.

Ethnographic studies of scientific fieldwork are necessary and timely. Most cultural analyses of scientific research focus on work in lab settings of various sorts. We know far less about the nature of scientific work outside those controlled environments. Science also takes researchers to the world's tallest mountain ranges, the ocean's depths, and everywhere in between. It is important in its own right as a context for work, and within the sciences, fieldwork holds cultural significance as a potent means of recruitment and a rite of passage. As one oceanography student in my research noted: "Ship experiences are life changing! After my first one, I was like, 'Sign me up for life.'" And while decades of research have examined labs and classrooms as workplaces and learning environments with "chilly" climates and toxic cultures for women, very little research has examined the field as a site that may have similar climate and culture problems. In the summer of 2017, I was fortunate to be a participant-observer in a graduate-level, interdisciplinary field course on the West Coast of the United States. I followed the course in its three sites: a week in field sites in the Sierra Nevada, two weeks on a university campus, and two weeks at a coastal field station. I slept in the same facilities as the group, shared all my meals with the student researchers and instructors, joined the group in daily field excursions and exercises to observe their work together, and sat in on their nightly seminars. In the final stretch of the course, I also individually interviewed each of the seventeen students and six instructors about their experience in this and other field settings. The same summer, my colleague Anne-Marie Núñez conducted similar research for the FIELD project in an undergraduate field camp in the Rocky Mountains.[5]

Our case studies, individually and together, highlight how geoscience's disciplinary culture may be used either for or against inclusion. What makes the culture of learning in the field unique—the erosion of typical boundaries and the collective experience of science outdoors—can serve as crucial resources for attracting students to this type of work and thus to the discipline. However, with its history rooted in military activity and westward exploration, field culture has been and continues to align with traditional visions of masculinity, construing only those who align with those visions as real insiders. Geoscience field culture privileges norms like toughness, and then uses the expectation of toughness to justify alcohol consumption that reduces inhibitions, following which women are frequently targeted. And like other scientific fields and work settings, even when everyone is sober, women tend to play a supporting role while men dominate leadership and the "sonic space" of everyday interactions about the science.[6]

What this means is that power and voice—in leadership and everyday communication—are disproportionately in the hands of men. Of particular concern for understanding pervasive harassment and assault, I find that apparently mundane patterns of routine communication diminish women's voices and basic concerns in ways that institutionalize silence about other compromises to their inclusion. These compromises include threats to their professional voice, physical safety, and advancement. Just as the male gaze—which regards women as objects for the pleasure and empowerment of male viewers—can breed glances that sometimes turn into actions, men's dominance of sonic space can become a tool through which their power is reinforced. Such cultural conditions may lead people to disregard serious incidents like sexual harassment and assault when they occur. Geoscientists' own mantra "What happens in the field stays in the field" presumes both that inappropriate behavior will occur and that it will stay secret.[7]

In this chapter, I first sketch a portrait of geology's field culture through data from the undergraduate and graduate field courses that Núñez and I observed. Then I go more deeply into the culture of the graduate course—which included not only field but also both classroom and seminar dynamics—with an examination of gendered communication patterns and how they institutionalize women's silence.

Portraits of Field Culture

As in most field courses, students each day in the field-based courses that Núñez and I spent the summer observing would leave their common accommodations (a set of dorms and apartments) early in the morning to venture into the wilderness for formal skill-building or research exercises.[8] Exercises usually were carried out in small groups, and in the undergraduate field camp they centered on mapping landscapes (to understand their formation and histories), and in the graduate field course on collecting and analyzing rock, biological, and other samples (to understand geoscience systems). The days were long, and there was always more work to do once returning from the field in the afternoon: writing up exercises, conducting literature reviews for background knowledge, organizing or analyzing samples with additional tools, preparing presentations for the group, and more. As our participants discussed it, being "out in the field" could have one of two meanings: simply being away from campus with the group, or being in the wild for exercises with only one another and what could be carried in their backpacks.

We found that the very cultural qualities that make geoscience fieldwork potentially transformative as a means of drawing students into the discipline are also used to legitimate and normalize forms of exclusion and mistreatment that drive people away from the geosciences. The culture therefore operates as a double-edged sword, one that can be leveraged to encourage powerful learning and passion for the discipline but one that also can pose threats to inclusion, belonging, and personal safety.

Three themes—the erosion of typical boundaries, challenging physical conditions, and the legitimation of alcohol—are central cultural dynamics through which norms of togetherness, toughness, and informality are reinforced respectively and interactively. These norms also carry consequences for gender relations in the field. Messages sent to students on a daily basis (e.g., "Keep up!," "No complaining!," and "Roll with it!") epitomize these norms and contribute to the gendered communication patterns, which ultimately translate to the classroom.

Eroded Boundaries Encourage Togetherness and Informality

The field's distance and difference from everyday campus life signal the necessity and logic of new ways of interacting. We found that field culture—both by necessity and by design—erodes the usual temporal, spatial, and intergroup boundaries that characterize learning environments. Eroded boundaries create the potential for new types of interactions that, for a broad view of gender equity, can be interpreted as both negative (e.g., unprofessional interactions across gender) and positive (e.g., peer mentoring among women).

Temporally, the schedule is by necessity fluid and by design demanding: We observed that all time effectively becomes class time, as students shared not only their lectures and lab activities but also time in their residence, meals, transportation, and relaxation at the end of the day. On a typical day of the graduate course, students would be up by about 6 a.m. with organized activities extending to 9 p.m. each evening and informal activities often lasting late into the night. On days that we conducted field experiments, the class would gather by the vans outside our lodging at 6:30 a.m. or 7 a.m., travel for thirty to sixty minutes, then hike and conduct experiments and exercises in the field for five to seven hours, before returning to the lodging area for group work, dinner, and a 7:30 p.m. seminar.

Conversations about science, work, and life thus became possible at any hour of the day. The combination of separation from the usual campus environment, remote locations of the field sites, and the norm of working through the weekends meant that it became very easy to lose track of what day and time it was. I personally found myself checking the sun angle to gauge a sense of time. In spite of this fluidity, "Don't be late" was one of the rules the lead instructor handed down to students on the first day, in relation to morning meeting at the vans and evening lecture, two times that the group's collective activity depended on everyone's presence.

Spatial boundaries and the associated purposes for specific spaces and items were also relaxed in field culture. You roomed with one another, packed yourselves into fifteen passenger vans, and conducted your science without walls, chairs, tables, or much of the usual equipment. This required creativity, resourcefulness, and flexibility: I heard every instructor quip, "Roll with it!" at least once. On the first day in the field, the absence of a desired tool led a TA to repurpose for scientific use a plastic spoon brought for eating lunch (that is, until water from a hot spring melted it). Instructors unofficially condoned a group of male students running extracurricular experiments from their kitchen table. Among the several apartments we rented in the mountains, the kitchen and living areas of the course coordinators' apartment were repurposed as the "food condo" for the group. Students and instructors would trickle into it very early together to get a bite for breakfast and to prepare their lunches for the day in the field. Then, they would return late afternoons for drinks and dinner. Another instructor's apartment—the site for evening lectures and leisure—was designated the "lecture condo," and a third whose counters and kitchen table held microscopes, was designated the "lab condo." The combination, though particular to this field course, represents a broader pattern across field experiences: that spaces are still needed for specific activities of work and life, but being in the field may not permit their typical forms.

Due to the eroded temporal and spatial boundaries, members of the class no longer interacted only during certain hours in certain rooms. What is more, their science was truly collective—carried out in either small-group or whole-class activities. They learned to engage in a continuous, informal stream of science-centered life together. Some loved this. As one put it, "The longer the field season, the better, as far as I'm concerned because . . . your brain gets in that mode." For others, the loss of familiar structure to time and space—fluidity of time, work in unfamiliar wilderness settings (where they may or may not have a detailed map or compass)—lent a sense of disorientation that took time to settle into and adapt to as a new normal.

For all, norms of informality and togetherness took hold in this mode of life together, and increasingly so over the course of the summer. Students had very little time to themselves. Keeping up with the group while hiking in the field to and through your sites; contributing your fair share to the experiments, their write-up, and communication; sharing resources; and keeping common space and samples organized and tidy for peers lent order and shared purpose while operating in an atypical, potentially disordered mode.

Under the norms of informality and togetherness, boundaries defining typical personal space and interaction types also eroded. In the field, a small group working together might yell measurements back and forth from a hundred meters across a hillside, or they might huddle shoulder to shoulder and joke about body odor while examining a small sample together. In the graduate course, there were interactions like the vignette that started this chapter and much whispering about the time that a male international student smacked the butt of a woman student in the class.

Back at the apartments and field station, interpersonal boundaries eroded, too. There was ample time and opportunity for informal peer mentoring, and we observed this especially among women. Three weeks into the graduate class, students spread out on the deck during a boat ride, standing with typical personal space separating them. On a similar ride the last day of class— same boat and same deck—about eight students and a TA laid in a pile on one another, one of them strumming the ukulele while the others sang along. Instructors also contributed to the emergent culture of informality and togetherness. For example, they designated which students should sleep where for the first few weeks, establishing separate quarters for men and women; however, upon moving to a field station for the last leg of the course, they allowed students to self-organize themselves for lodging. Amid the intimacy facilitated by both the erosion of usual boundaries and the elevation of informality and togetherness as community values, it was not hard at all to see how interactions would occur that cross professional boundaries.

In sum, field culture is characterized by eroded temporal, spatial, and interactional boundaries, and that erosion both reflects and embeds collective norms of informality and togetherness. Many enjoy this way of life, but others miss the clarity, structure, and personal time and space. As scientists create a world of their own centered on science and life together, new types of interactions occur. The relaxed boundaries and pressure to "roll with it" muddle and complicate what count as shared expectations. Those who are more experienced—the TAs and professors especially—with what is not just normal behavior for scientists but normal for the field in particular set the key to which others are expected to tune their behavior. Now, let's consider how the physical conditions under which this work occurs and how the role of alcohol further engages students and poses risks.

Challenging Conditions Reinforce Toughness

Although scholars commonly discuss academia in reference to the life of the mind, demanding physical requirements marked both geoscience field courses as well. In the heat of summer, students hiked miles into the wilderness, up and down mountains and river valleys, across rugged and rocky terrain offering little to no shade. The students and instructors alike engaged cognitively with the science that surrounded them and strove to immerse themselves fully in the natural system. I learned firsthand how becoming part of the system you study—feeling the same wind that has desiccated plant life around you, tearing your shoe on the rocks you are studying, or burning your fingers as you measured the temperature of hot water springing from the ground—created a powerfully engaging and sharply human experience of science. The physicality of the work under difficult conditions is a challenge that most students took up willingly. Yet it also reinforced the value of a masculine vision of toughness as essential to the prototype of a good geoscientist, so that physical (dis)abilities and varied degrees of physical fitness and prior outdoor experience shaped students' sense of belonging. Those without strengths in those areas were either explicitly or implicitly marginalized in the field and the courses as they struggled to keep up with the group and uphold the image of toughness. Those unfazed by the expectation to be tough wore it as a badge of honor.[9]

The graduate field course happened to coincide with a major heat wave, making the high-desert settings for our field excursions all the more intense. Riding back in the van from a field experiment the first week, I thought to myself that, even though I had been active in outdoor activities for much of my life, never before had I been covered in as many layers of sunscreen, dirt, and sweat as at that moment. In this environment, forms of sun protection—both bottles of sunscreen and hats—were universal necessities, artifacts of field culture, and expressions of individuality.[10] Consistent with a view of norms as cultural tools that can be used to legitimate difficult decisions, instructors used the shared expectation that time would be more fluid in the field to adapt their daily schedules to the heat. For example, they moved up departure times to minimize time spent hiking in the hottest hours of the day. Still, field activities took longer to complete because of the heat, and we ended up returning around the same time as usual.

Alcohol Enables Togetherness and Is a Reward for Toughness
When I started the class, I knew that the geosciences had a reputation for beer drinking. As one student commented of geologists: "If you like flannels and hiking boots, that's great and it feels lovely. And everyone knows we are all proud of our beer drinking." According to the course coordinator, Bonnie, "this course has historically been a huge drinking fest," but the group I observed was "quite moderate" in her estimation. Still, almost every day's field notes in my records included some remarks about beer. Beer bottles were as much an artifact of this particular field culture as bottles of sunscreen, hats, rock hammers, and backpacks. When they drank (i.e., as soon as possible after returning from the field, then through dinner and into the night), where (i.e., in the designated food condo, but also throughout evening seminars, at the microscope or laptop in the evening, at a beach excursion, and in the parking lot between apartments), what (i.e., often local brews from bottles, with other types available), how much (i.e., variable by person, with TAs proud to consume more than average)—all these details combined to shape the prominent role of alcohol in the group.[11]

In my interviews with members of the course, I asked each person to help me understand the roles of beer and drinking in the discipline and the course. While often qualifying their responses with such lines as "it's not totally inclusive" or "it can be a double-edged sword," three-fourths of the instructors spoke about the social functions of drinking: to overcome their social awkwardness and to foster connections, community, and the easygoing culture for which geology is known. Others used the language "at the end of a long day" to legitimate beer drinking after returning from the field, even if the time they started drinking was not really the end of the day, even if they still had group work, dinner, and an evening seminar together before the day would really be through. In connecting beer drinking to the demanding work conditions in the field, they constructed time working outdoors as the heart of fieldwork and beer as a reward for the toughness that fieldwork demands.

At about 9:30 p.m. on the second-to-last night of the course, I scanned the room where the seminar had concluded earlier. At that moment, it looked neither like a living room nor like a seminar room. A TA with a glass of whiskey sat with two international graduate students, their three laptops set on the small table in front of them as they talked about new technologies in genetics. Two women were cuddled in an easy chair a few feet away, talking softly. Three more students—one with a beer, another with a laptop, and a third strumming a guitar—talked about the details of a mystery in their data. The scene exemplified how field culture erodes the most fundamental boundary of them all for academics: work and life.

Gender: Communication and Community

Gender—like race, religion, and other identities—is a system we produce. Sociologist Cecilia Ridgeway argues that we produce it through three mechanisms: shared cultural beliefs (e.g., about what constitutes appropriate gender presentations), interactions, and structures.[12] My interest in this chapter lies in the second of these, extending findings about the culture of the field to analyze interactions in the graduate field course across and within gender. Interaction as an analytic focus was a natural extension of the research process, in which communication quickly emerged as a central theme in the data from the graduate course that I had coded to gender.[13] Although emerging from a fairly specific setting, the types of interactions I observed will be familiar throughout STEM. I hope to bring them to life and help scientists see their own routine interactions in a fresh way.

I found that formal and informal communication within this disciplinary culture privileged the voices of men and institutionalized silence and a supporting role for women. The interactional style I observed—and the one that participating graduate students would, themselves, learn to think of as normal—was one in which men dominated the sonic space and airtime for daily activities, whereas women were more likely to be ignored, dismissed, or receive minimal response. In the study of sound, sonic space refers to the range of frequencies that an instrument or voice occupies when played. Were one to listen only to a recording of all the activities that I was present for, the frequencies of men's voices would occupy a much larger fraction of the recording. I propose there is much we can learn about gender dynamics in geology from the ways men and women use and abuse airtime, and by how and when people opt for or against airing their questions and concerns—about themselves, their experiences, scientific content, or scientific culture.

Macro- and Micro-Level Communication

As was introduced in Chapter 2, apparently mundane incidents can have unexpected and wide-ranging ripple effects, and perhaps nowhere is this more apparent than the power of communications. Communication dynamics were a recurrent theme in the data about women in the course—both with respect to messages they and the public received about the geosciences broadly (i.e., at the macro level) and with respect to their interactions within the field course specifically (i.e., micro-level). In studies of organizational culture, macro-level communication patterns may include the official and unofficial stories about the organization that are conveyed, whereas micro-level communication consists of how people interact (or do not). As such, language and communication, like the other facets of the culture described in the first half of this chapter, can be a double-edged sword. They can on the one hand introduce and strengthen connections, improving the quality of collaborative work outputs and enriching understanding, security, and self-determination. On the other hand, the harm that can come with negative messages and interactions is a fundamental means by which those same outcomes can be undermined.

In the field course, it was exclusively women who emphasized the importance of improving communications for the success of science—both macrolevel messages and micro-level interactions. They felt it important to elevate the status and craft of scientists' outward-facing engagement with the public, policy makers, and other external stakeholders. They understood macro-level science communication in terms of its potential to accomplish three interrelated goals: undermining distrust in scientific findings, protecting the sustainability of the enterprise, and educating stakeholders about the relevance of science to broader social concerns.

These themes recurred through the course in discussions, and they are nicely highlighted in a dinner discussion among a group of women graduate students and postdoctoral fellows. While we waited for tacos and margaritas, Maria, a second-year PhD student who had not yet told her advisor that she intended to use her PhD for a career in science policy, noted a distinction within the macro-oriented communication efforts of education. There is a "here's what we know" approach, she observed, while other efforts take descriptive knowledge and turn it into advocacy. Such efforts at persuasion emphasize "here's what we think, and what you should do." These communication patterns too often frame communication as a matter of expression rather than real back-and-forth, she felt. When someone asked the table what the biggest barrier to increasing public appreciation of science was, Maria drew a connection to micro-level communications, lamenting of scientists, "We don't listen very well." The drawbacks of being "poor listeners," as Maria and her peers believed, include failure to connect meaningfully both with those outside the community and among themselves.

The women I spoke to understood communication among class members as well as among their colleagues outside the course to be determinative of work quality, relationships, and their own sense of belonging and inclusion. And indeed, there is growing recognition throughout science that communication is a foundation in establishing or compromising a culture of collaboration and community. For this reason, instructors, principal investigators, and others across science disciplines are beginning to establish guidelines for communication at the beginnings of their courses. Meeting organizers, similarly, are beginning to establish codes of conduct to make clear what forms of interaction are desired and unacceptable.[14] All evidence suggests these are positive moves for creating more inclusive cultures and climates, for as anthropologists have found for decades, cultures are transmitted both in everyday activity and in the rules officially laid forth as individuals are socialized into new environments. When scientists gather for the first time—either ever or in a while—clarity about communication expectations will almost certainly result in better work.

On the first day of this course, the professor presented communication expectations. He introduced "ideas, methods, and people" as anchors for the ways he wanted students to think about the course. With the other instructors, he went to some lengths to highlight the importance of "the people part" and "the value of community." He pointed out that how students and instructors choose to connect in the first few days in sets the tone for the entire class, and he listed nine rules for the course, several of which centered on togetherness and the role of communication in encouraging it. The list included "Strive for good communication," "Be sensitive to the need for all kinds of questions," and "Attend to group dynamics." Although he did not comment on the specifics of "good communication," he made group dynamics more concrete by saying he wanted people to "be on time. Have a positive attitude. Be neat. Be patient, just be kind to each other. . . . Really, this is the most important one." He continued, "Group dynamics may seem to be this thing on the side, but it turns out to be really important . . . especially in about week 4.5. A surprising amount of effort goes into the class, but it's up to you to make it great." These comments highlighted a thoughtful use of his platform on the first day, but without acknowledgment that people in the group may have different assumptions about what constitutes "good communication" or what it means to "be kind,"[15] it was no surprise to see that gendered communication patterns in the course emerged.

As a cultural foundation of institutionalized inequities, as a common challenge across STEM disciplines, and as a practical domain of activity that scientists and students could work to improve, the next sections analyze three gendered, micro-level communication patterns in the class: women's expressed concerns being inadequately addressed, gender disparities in question asking and answering, and gendered challenges to instructor authority. There were other patterns, to be sure, but I emphasize these because I observed them across two of the three settings in which the course took place: the field, the classroom, and the evening seminars.

Women's Concerns Expressed Are Inadequately Addressed

Growing attention to the difficulty of reporting sexual harassment and assault compels a need to understand barriers within academia to speaking up about difficult matters generally. One instructor, Rose, had personally opted not to report "a major incident in [her] past with a professor," and she spoke to me at length about the decision not to report.[16] "I just sort of sat on it," she said, "but he was a serial predator. . . . He has not suffered any repercussions for his behavior. Thankfully that didn't chase me out of the field, but I think a lot of people it would have." I invited her to explain more about the decision not to report. She responded:

> It's hard to deal with. I mean it's the same thing as not reporting sexual assault in the greater population, right? Like if you report a rape or something,

you have to, one, report that to someone who's probably a superior—or like your superior in terms of rank. Two, you have to prove it and therefore have to, like, deal with that and probably admit things like probably being under-age and drinking and that kind of thing. So it's just not worth it. [*Long pause*] But I just wish the dirty old men would keep their hands to themselves.

I propose that one gendered aspect to the hidden curriculum of graduate school is women (and no doubt other people with minoritized identities) learning to see speaking up about negative experiences as "just not worth it." Women pick up these messages by learning that when they do speak up about such matters, little positive for them comes of it. When the institutionalized rules on reporting require speaking to superiors and risking negative judgments for doing so, women may learn that it is easier to self-silence or opt out than to speak up.

The field course offered vivid examples of women grappling with this. The intense physical, social, and environmental demands of the course created pressure in both individuals and the group. It appeared to be akin to what other social scientists have called a toothpaste-tube effect: pressures from the outside forcing the release of latent internal pressures.[17] Women in the class wanted opportunities to discuss mental health difficulties that the intense hours and demands of the class made salient for them—and in some cases they initiated interactions with instructors about them—but they also felt that the concerns they expressed were inadequately addressed. Concerns about the intensity of the course were universal, but only women came to feel it was useless for them to share these concerns with instructors.

Maria, introduced just earlier, shared one such example of this with me. After five hours into an especially hot day's work, with the group spread out over a broad hillside that provided no relief from the sun and temperatures over 105 degrees, she pulled me aside and asked if we could talk. Within moments of stepping away from the group, she broke down. She admitted that the structure of the class was tough on her anxiety (for which she was presently taking a prescription), that she was exhausted and dizzy from the heat, on the verge of a panic attack, and feeling frustrated because the instructor she approached had dismissed her concerns. We sat together and talked for about ten minutes about the extenuating personal factors she was dealing with, not least of which was the physical exertion required for fieldwork—the likes of which she had never experienced.

A few weeks later, while formally interviewing her, we discussed that day. She said: "You might remember I was complaining of dizziness and it felt like no one was responding. I told Caleb [the TA] this, saying, 'I feel really dizzy. I drank *five liters* of water, I still don't feel good.' And he was like, 'Well, you should, you know, just drink more water and you should put some water on your head.' I was like, 'Okay, but?!'" She threw up her hands in the air.

I asked, "You weren't happy with his response to your concern?"

"Yeah," she said, "and I don't feel like this is going to go away. Other people were also experiencing issues that were just being ignored."

Indeed, Maria was hardly the only one who shared frustrations that concerns they raised about their needs or well-being in the field were insufficiently addressed. Notably, all those who shared this feeling with me were women. It was also exclusively women who disclosed to me that the daily schedule and environmental conditions, combined with expectations of toughness and "rolling with it," exacerbated preexisting anxiety. Indeed, this is consistent with surveys that find women in higher education have both higher risks of depression and anxiety and also report higher academic stress.[18] It appears that, at least in this particular class, it was both a general problem, and more specifically that physical and mental health issues aggravated by the intensity of the course went insufficiently addressed.

Another student who struggled with this was Amy, a tall, athletic second-year PhD student who passed her qualifying exams just before the course started. Her mother's successful career in medicine led her to take for granted that women could pursue whatever path in life they set their minds to, but her own PhD qualifying exam experience sensitized her to engrained sexism in the culture of the geosciences. Most acutely, she was annoyed by the formal performance report from the department following the exam, which said that her academic performance was excellent, but that she should reconsider the running shorts she wore on campus. These comments offended her, as a geoscientist whose work took her outdoors to hot climates and as she looked around at her peers, who dressed equally as casually. The feedback also bothered her as an athlete and person for whom daily exercise was an important guard against a generalized anxiety disorder.

Like Maria, Amy interpreted instructor inattention to her concerns as a sign she had no recourse but to perform "strength with ease" and to "play along with" togetherness. Yet she and others grew increasingly frustrated with instructors' lack of responsiveness and the absence of channels for requesting accommodations in an unusually demanding course. In both our everyday conversations and our formal interview, she told me about repeatedly asking the lead instructor, whom I call Brian, to build a little personal time into the day, so that introverted peers could have some down time and she could get the exercise she felt she needed. However, the instructors' explicit expectation that students ought to "roll with it," combined with the informal style of interactions, their long hours, and everyone's isolation from campus resources dedicated to accessibility and disabilities left no recourse for posing formal requests for accommodations. "I'm not going to sit down and explain it [to him], you know, 'cause that would be awkward," she lamented.

Norms for field research, I learned that summer, include keeping up with the group, working hard and not complaining under difficult physical conditions, and maximizing every minute of the research opportunity in that space. These norms, however, intersect problematically with health issues in which one might need a little time or space from the group—such as for personal time, exercise, or rest. Although informality served a purpose in facilitating research without usual boundaries, it also made it "awkward" for Amy and other students to formally request support or to escalate concerns they felt had been insufficiently addressed following informal discussion.

Indeed, formal policy can bring balance to power asymmetries that exist where men greatly outnumber women.[19] Women in male-dominated fields, for example, benefit from having formal policies for reporting dissatisfaction and grievances of all sorts—although having such policy does not ensure people use it, given widespread fear of reprisal, retaliation, and a continued insufficient response from authorities.[20] Similarly, although togetherness supported the field culture's collectivist approach to knowledge production and enabled appreciation of an environment without the usual structures that bound time, space, and interactions, instructors also deployed the norm of togetherness to rationalize extremely long hours and, in some cases, to trump the need for privacy or personal time in instances where students felt they needed it. And finally, although designing and implementing the course to align with the norm of toughness enabled participants in the class to take pride in themselves for managing its challenging expectations, it also presented safety risks. I saw no evidence personally that it demonstrably improved the quality of science, but I did see evidence that it compromised a sense of belonging of those who struggled with the intensity—for any reason. An important note here is that the concerns students raised in this course were largely about the gendered intersection of field norms (e.g., toughness, togetherness, and informality) with communication about mental and physical health needs; however, the same organizational norms may also implicitly or explicitly discourage workplace sexual harassment and the reporting thereof. The course also highlights how the costs of engrained expectations about "intensity" and "toughness" in graduate school come with unique costs for students with mental health struggles. Graduate school does not have to be that way, but rarely are professors encouraged to think critically about the hidden curriculum they picked up in graduate school themselves, about appropriate workloads and challenges relative to outputs and student well-being.

Amy eventually began to take personal time for exercise each day after returning from the field, regardless of whatever activity was to come next. This meant she occasionally missed course activities, but she did not try to conceal it from the group: I saw her jump roping in a parking lot, stretching on a yoga mat outside her shared apartment, and heading to or from a swim. She decided, she told me, that if the instructors were not going to address her needs, she would have to address them herself and accept the consequences for breaking with the field norm of rolling with the group.

Other students saw Amy taking free time, and this catalyzed more open discussions about how many others were also struggling with the sixteen-hour days. By this point, one instructor commented that the students were "bordering on mutiny." Entering into the second half of the course, I overheard Amy venting in the dinner line to another student, Tess. Amy had once again had spoken to the lead instructor Brian about how she and several other students were struggling with the hours they were expected to keep. As Amy recounted it, "Brian said to me, 'Well, Nathan was in the military and is able to work sixteen hours per day without complaining. I guess he'll just be more productive.' And I thought to myself, 'Well, he was in the military! He's used to it!" Respecting that this was a reconstruction of an emotionally charged situation, I nevertheless thought it intriguing that, unsolicited, Brian made the military link in legitimating a grueling workday. It was an implicit acknowledgment that field culture, which has roots in military history, still carries expectations for toughness—mentally and physically—for which people with a military background may be adapted.

Brian was well aware of the tension between the need for personal time and the design of the course. In our interview, he said:

People like the alone time. I mean we kind of joke about the fact that we're—
this class is always 98 percent introverts—right, who just, like, wanted some
quiet time alone. And [the class] is exactly the opposite. It's sixteen hours a
day of intense group activity, and people talking, and by the end, we're all
like, "I just want to go to a quiet place and sit alone." . . . I think it's that
that's so exhausting to people, more than having to think about things for
twelve hours a day. I think it's the social part.

In the last ten days or so of the course, instructors took steps to squeeze about
twenty minutes of free time in per day, and the course coordinators helped
create optional, informal outings outside the regular course activity time that
played on the desire of many in the group for additional exercise and learning.
There was a late afternoon visit to a hike-in beach, an early morning kayaking trip to sea caves, and a late-night swim in bioluminescent waters. As I
describe below, these experiences set the stage for some of the most profound
learning experiences of the class.

Although the norm was for students to "roll with" the experiences that
professors set out, it seemed natural and appropriate that in a course that
privileged togetherness and informality that instructors, themselves, learned
to "roll with" students' needs. And indeed, faculty responsiveness to the needs
of graduate students from historically marginalized groups is a theme that
will come up in almost every chapter of this book, and thus is one dimension of the holistic support model in its conclusion. Responsiveness to women
students' needs was particularly salient in this course, but listening and responsiveness may be a general strategy for full participation of other groups as
well. The need to improve listening and responsiveness to academic questions
is the theme I turn to next.

Who Is Centered in the Sonic Space of Discussions?

In addition to feeling that health concerns were inadequately addressed, most
women in the class felt that their academic questions in classroom activities
and evening seminars were not taken seriously—and in some cases simply
ignored. On the first day, Brian included sensitivity to all types of questions
among the course guidelines, and he specifically said that asking questions is
"very important because it's how people learn." He exhorted students not to
"roll your eyes" because "people will not stop asking questions." In a course
where students and instructors spend so many of their waking hours together,

discussion of science was not limited to the formal activities. However, given widespread concerns among the women in the class about the climate of course sessions involving didactic instruction (e.g., seminars, formal lessons), and given other recent studies that reveal gendered and racialized patterns of interactions in academic seminars and conferences, I focused a subset of my analyses on academic questioning and answering in the seminars that took place each night after dinner.

In addition to an official question-and-answer period at the end of each seminar, it was typical for participants to raise hands to ask questions throughout the talks. I consistently sat near the back to gauge group seating patterns and engagement. With a few regular exceptions, women sat near the sides and back of the physical space—literally occupying the margins—while men were concentrated near the front and middle. With a couple of exceptions, men in the audience (including students, professors, TAs, and guest instructors) asked most of the questions. Early in the course, I observed several instances in which both men and women instructors answered questions of men who had their hands up but ignored women with their hands up. And just as Brian had predicted, some women eventually shut down into silence in evening seminars altogether.

After several evenings of observing this pattern, I started formally tracking who asked questions, both by gender and by student or instructor role. The proportion of questions asked by men and instructors increased over the course of the class, suggesting that women may have eventually started opting out of asking questions. Put another way, men were increasingly central in both the physical and the sonic space of the seminars and lectures.

This gendered pattern became most evident during a few days at the field station in which several guest instructors all attended the lectures. Although they were present for only a small portion of the overall class, their attendance increased the total number of instructors to nearly that of the number of students, and it also increased the total proportion of men in the group relative to women. In one such lecture, given by a midcareer white woman about her research and the sorts of geoscience scholarship that PhDs could pursue from within industry, the percentage of questions that students (52.4 percent) and instructors (47.6 percent) asked split fairly evenly. But while women comprised about 40 percent of the total attendees, men asked 91 percent of the total questions.

In addition to these observations, several students—all women—organically raised during my interviews with them their experience of the gendered pattern of question asking and answering. Tess, who had just finished her PhD in geology from a top-ranked program and was on her way to a postdoctoral fellowship, said:

> I don't know if discrimination really covers this, but there were a couple times in this course where I asked a question and it was just completely ignored—and it was very unclear to me why that happened. And I thought it was just like—in the beginning I thought it was just me. Maybe . . . the question wasn't relevant enough for the time, which still like merits acknowledgment. But then I heard other people . . . saying that they felt the same thing was happening. So I still don't know why that was happening, where we would ask a question and either get a one word answer that effectively shut it down or no answer at all.

She noted how it was not only the absence of an answer but also a cursory or "one-word answer" that could shut down women. Mirya, an international PhD student with years of field experience, also expressed concern about this. She had a confident, assertive, almost unrelenting persona, but privately she had been dealing with discrimination in her research group. The evening lectures in our field course helped her understand her experience a better. I quote our interview at length:

> MIRYA: Women still have a massive glass ceiling, massive, even in earth sciences where everyone is a hippy and is chill and whatever. Even here [in this course], I see this older generation of professors that were invited to be guest instructors, I was like—what is this? An old boy's club? You know, some of these evening lectures . . . there are like five old men in the front, giving lectures just to each other. And there are five girls raising their hands in hope from their seats somewhere in the back, in the corner. It burns my eyes just to see these men talking basically to each other, you know, joking just with each other, talking only to each other. Old boy's club. And then you want to go ask him a question and he lets you stand there for ten minutes while he chats with his old colleague, you know? Who is next to him in the office every day and they can talk [*she pauses, clearly upset*]. . . .
> JULIE: They can talk anytime. That's gotta be really frustrating.
> MIRYA: So I blame myself a lot because I am very self-critical. I am constantly thinking like everything is wrong with me. But now I'm seeing that it might be different.

As one of the "five girls raising their hands in hope from their seats some-where in the back," participating in this course helped her appreciate that the inattention to her on her own campus was not a function of something being "wrong with" her. Rather, it was a vestige of science as an "old boy's club" that is present elsewhere too, in which men are more likely to talk to one another than to include women in the conversation. Later in the interview, Mirya re-visited her experience, speaking candidly:

> I have to say in this course I have been made very aware what it means to be woman in science—not necessarily by the lead professors here, but all the invited guests and instructors. And it made me reflect back on what I am going through back at my own university. It made me see that perhaps, some of the things that I have been experiencing from all of these male as-trobiology professors and from these male teams are not because I am stu-pid or because I am bad or because I don't whatever enough . . . but maybe because you are just being bluntly disrespectful.

Marginalization during seminars in the field course inspired reflection that helped her reframe her own self-doubts of being "stupid" or "bad" or not "enough"; she came to see the problem was her male professors and research colleagues being "bluntly disrespectful."

My observations made it easy to see how extended time in a learning en-vironment where one feels actively excluded from the scientific conversation and where your curiosity is left unsatisfied would ultimately weaken engage-ment with the material—and maybe desire for a career in that field. What I could not have seen from my observations alone was that Mirya was so "self-critical" or that she felt "everything is wrong with me." Indeed, in the every-day work of field exercises, she was the only woman in the class who stood up to a combative student in the class, a European PhD student and geophysicist. Philip asked questions in the evening seminars frequently—at least daily—that almost always took the content to deeper levels of process and nuance. He genuinely wanted to understand the science and on at least one occasion thanked the lecturer for the discussion. But he also seemed to lack any self-awareness, self-monitoring, or concern for the airtime that he occupied in indulging his curiosity. Philip's behavior is not abnormal in science. Other scholars have also found men tend to interject with questions more often than women in scientific settings and that this confers them both additional so-cial capital and legitimacy.[21] If disparate attention to men who ask questions at the expense of women is a problem, then it will take both instructors becoming more mindful of how they interact with students as well as better self-monitoring from students like Philip, to engage in discussion not just for one's own, but for the whole learning community's, benefit.

Amy, introduced earlier, also felt that her early questions in seminar went unanswered. But just as she had created a work-around for insufficient instructor attention to her personal needs, she also implemented a midcourse strategy to address feeling ignored in seminars; in both contexts, her agentic behavior thus differed markedly from the opting-out behavior of many of her female peers. Most evenings, she approached the lecturer individually after the seminar concluded. Perhaps these conversations emboldened her, for on the second-to-last night of the course, when student groups shared their final research projects, Amy was the audience member who dared to persistently question Philip about his contributions to his group's project. "It seems like your explanation is really complicated," she observed. "Have you thought about the role of mixing mechanisms?" A long back-and-forth ensued between the two of them. She pushed back Socratically, asking thoughtful questions that challenged Philip's assumptions and clearly had him on his toes: "What's the advantage of the complicated explanation?" she asked at one point. "It can make predictions," he replied. "But can you actually test this model?" He said nothing in response, and the exchange ended. Amy's questioning that night represented one of the only examples that I observed of a woman in the class actively challenging another student. The much more predominant pattern I observed was of men challenging instructors' authority.

Challenging Instructor Authority

I observed two forms of direct challenges to instructor authority, both gendered: men (who were students) publicly challenging instructors' pedagogical decisions and men (who were both students and instructors) interrupting female lecturers in the evening seminars. As just one example of the former, Philip grew exasperated with what he perceived to be a slow pace of a computer modeling activity built into a lab exercise. He challenged the TA's choice to require students to write their own code. "You could just give us the code," he said. The TA, who was also a white man from Europe, patiently replied: "Well, I kind of dislike copy-paste teaching." Philip pressed further, "But it would be more efficient," to which the TA quickly retorted, with a smile and tilt of the head: "But this forces you to learn." It was one of several examples in which a student actively challenged an instructor's considered decisions and authority by proposing alternative approaches in the middle of class.

Of the evening lectures I observed, the only instructors to be openly challenged or interrupted were also women. This pattern is consistent with research that has found a tendency for implicit biases and power asymmetries to manifest in the treatment of instructors with less positional authority. I could not ignore the tenor of interruption and challenge during the onslaught of questions the night that a woman guest speaker gave the seminar. Perhaps not coincidentally, that was also the night that men asked 91 percent of questions. It may have been the case that being both a woman and a guest speaker opened her to both gender and out-group biases.

Another evening where this happened was the first seminar of the class. Heidi, the one woman professor among the three lead instructors, was responsible for teaching that night. The setting exemplified field informality: a living and dining area of one apartment had been transformed into lecture space with a projector balanced on a bar stool, a laptop on the dining room table, and a collapsible screen set up behind it with the PowerPoint presentation. Wearing socks, cutoff jean shorts, and a T-shirt, Heidi, too, was casual and relaxed. Students and other instructors took whatever seats and floor space they could find and passed bowls of snacks. Most drank beer, but a few sipped wine or drank from their personal water bottles. The lecture that followed combined this informality (e.g., "Microbes are yummy food for other organisms")[22] with technical content that was well beyond my and some students' understanding. One might have interpreted a woman giving the first lecture as a cue for gender equity—indeed, that was my initial expectation. As her talk went on, though, other instructors—all men—repeatedly interrupted her so that she had to re-explain things multiple times. I counted five times in a seventy-five-minute talk that male instructors talked over her.[23] Thus, even when a woman held both the authority of positional status (i.e., as an instructor) and rights to the floor (i.e., as the lecturer), she was subject to being challenged.

The posturing and performativity that underlies such challenging in classrooms and seminars reflects same norm of toughness that many geoscientists rationalized as necessary for managing difficult physical field conditions. However, an environment in which no one sanctions men for unnecessarily aggressive or otherwise disrespectful communication runs the risk of becoming more confrontational for everyone.

There are several ways that women in historically male-dominated disciplines may respond to inattention to their questions and needs, and to the tendencies to interrupt, overtalk, challenge, and escalate. One may be learning and adopting "tough" interactional styles that are not their own; indeed, learning to adapt, fit in, and survive on the community's terms is often part of the hidden curriculum of graduate school. Those unwilling to do so may opt out of the sonic space through self-silencing but remain physically present by playing along with other cultural rules of the community. Others may opt out of the community entirely or choose nonacademic careers in science.

The formation of whisper networks is another strategy some women use—an outcome of women's distrust that institutionalized rules for communication and behavior will serve their interests. When informal community rules for who can speak about what preclude discussion of topics that disproportionately affect women's belonging and safety, women may turn not to the official representatives but to one another. Indeed, the only time that I heard the challenges to women instructors' authority that I had observed, actually discussed aloud was through a whisper in my ear from Eliana, a second-year graduate student who had attended an all-women's college as an undergraduate and held strong feminist commitments. These outcomes—collective adoption of conventionally masculine interactional styles, as well as women's self-silencing, forming of whisper networks, or opting out of the careers in this discipline altogether—share in common the preservation of men's voice, interests, and ultimately power above those of women. Though common coping mechanisms, they are hardly acceptable long-term strategies toward equity.

Care for Disciplines as Inhabited Institutions

Of all the scientific settings I studied, the geoscience field course most directly manifested a posthumanist view and the quantum insight that scientists are part of the reality they study. I learned through my summer of fieldwork about the possibilities for engagement that come with field science, which one TA thoughtfully described as "knowledge with inspiration." Inhabiting the scientific landscape offers an immersive experience that can serve as a powerful resource for drawing students in and creating memories that develop an attachment with the field. It benefits from the norm of informality by lowering barriers to engagement. It similarly benefits from the norm of togetherness by encouraging science as a communal experience. In these highly unstructured learning environments, informality and togetherness fueled enthusiasm about learning.

Nevertheless, the field experience also requires careful design and management to minimize risks of harm and to facilitate inclusion and a shared sense of belonging. Conventionally enacted norms of informality and togetherness—especially intersected with men's power in the group—appeared insufficient to facilitate the equitable communication that is a foundation of healthy one-on-one interactions and group dynamics. As women "roll with" norms and communication patterns that minimize their involvement, in this discipline or in others, it reinforces the academic discipline as an institution whose rules diminish women's voice and their engagement. Fieldwork in geoscience offers a case of these phenomena, but it is hardly a problem for geoscience disciplines alone. Every discipline has cultural norms and entrenched communication patterns that merit consideration.

I introduced in Chapter 2 how a posthumanist perspective compels us to attend to science as an inhabited institution, even as we recognize that policies and systems represent nonhuman influences and realities as well.[24] I hope in this chapter to have demonstrated how institutions are inhabited and animated through routine interactions—through the qualities of listening and the frequency of interrupting, through the asking and answering of questions, and through shared preferences for how to respond when a learning experience seems too much to handle. Such micro-level dynamics as these are present in their own ways throughout the disciplines, and they compel our attention because, through them, human connections are created, sustained, or broken. Without these human connections, scientific work simply cannot happen.

Some types of interactions more obviously contribute than others to the formation, maintenance, and interruption of institutions. If we pay attention to the interactions that we are involved in and that take place all around us, we will notice how people manage impressions to earn favor, give respect, and respond to the impressions they receive of others.[25] We will see people assert rights of inclusion and belonging, within the time and space of the organization. Through interactions, we will also see powerful parties transgress cultural norms befitting ostensibly democratic, egalitarian organizations. People use language, their bodies, shared space and other commonly or individually held resources as tools—to withhold, demand, or take what rightfully belongs to others or to the collective.

Findings from the study of geosciences here suggest that disciplines establish normative cultural boundaries on interactions, whereas the temporal and spatial context of work within a given discipline establishes the practical boundaries for interactions. Interactions help create gender, and interactions take place in organizational contexts marked by cultures, by structures like policy and reward systems, and by commonly held individual identities. Sargent's study of gendered interactions and masculinities in music stores notes that even within the same organizational type, demographically different music stores create "different styles of masculinity. . . . These styles, found in interaction, are not produced ad hoc in the moment, but in relation to the overall gendered culture of rock music and the stores as work environments." Sargent also notes that "gender can become a currency within organizations." By either enacting or being regarded as enacting accepted models of masculinity or femininity, one may be better able to advance within reward systems, to get along with other members, or simply to accomplish more functionally. Those whose gender identities and performances seem to "fit" the environment are more likely to advance—a crucial social fact for those concerned with opportunity and inclusion in disciplines dominated by narrow conceptions of masculinity.

In the scientific context discussed in this chapter, the institutionalization of women's silence was a mechanism for reinforcing men's dominance, despite men's and women's relatively equal representation in the group. Silence and dominance were two sides of the same coin in an environment where toughness, togetherness, and informality ruled. Institutionalizing women's silence happened both through patterns of dismissals and inattention when women did speak up or asked questions, and through informal penalties and sanctions exacted for speaking up in ways that made men "uncomfortable."

Why do silence and voice matter? From a sociocultural perspective, they reflect presence, belonging, authority, and hierarchical positioning. To diminish voice is therefore to diminish presence and power in a given space, both objectively and subjectively. There should therefore hardly be a question about why women—as individuals and as a group—do not stay in environments in which they are ignored, shut down, or talked over. The bigger questions, perhaps for future research, are why and when they do stay, how they persist, and what enables them to thrive.

Today, powerful organizations in science are leveraging their influence to reduce the frequency of two specific types of interactions that depend on institutionalized silence: sexual harassment and assault. An update to the American Geophysical Union's policy on scientific integrity and professional ethics has put harassment "on equal footing with fabrication, falsification and plagiarism in a research environment."[26] Shortly thereafter, the National Science Foundation announced a proposal to suspend or rescind grants, and in 2018, NASEM issued a major report on sexual harassment—the result of two years of research. These policy changes are intended both as immediate sanctions and to stimulate a broader discussion of gender equity in the sciences. And indeed, the latter is needed, for as Glinskis writes, "Harassment in the sciences doesn't only come in the form of neatly packaged Title IX reports of sexual abuse."[27] Routine violations of bodies and personal space; comments that diminish people as professionals; and occupations of sonic space suppress voice, authority, and opportunities to learn—these everyday behaviors help constitute the cultural repertoire of sexism in the scientific disciplines. We will understand incidents that break laws as typical or normal only by mapping the full landscape of typical gender interactions. By making headway with the small wins of everyday interactions, we can reshape the power dynamics through which scientific institutions are inhabited. Barring the requirement of undue social capital, actors can be nimble and agentic with everyday practice to achieve small wins.

Reconsidering the Hidden Curriculum

To more thoughtfully train the next generation of scientists, we need to bring into the light of day, and in some cases reconsider, more of the hidden curriculum of science: its institutionalized norms, styles of interactions, and standard research practices. Graduate training is the most important time for aspiring scientists to learn what counts as bad, acceptable, and ideal behavior within their disciplinary and departmental communities. That norms and other informal rules are socially constructed means that they are often invisible to insiders, and therefore difficult to recognize as problematic. Once made explicit and exposed as socially defined, however, they are potentially easier to interrupt than structures like bylaws and formal policy. Individual members may simply stop adhering to such norms, either for their own sake or for that of the group. And leaders can quickly intervene in everyday practices, making the call that they want the group to play by different rules.

With this in mind, let's close this chapter by revisiting specific practices discussed in this chapter that need intervention. In addition to sanctioning harassment and assault directly, we need to change the conditions and root causes that enable it. If a root cause is silence by women that becomes taken for granted as normal (i.e., institutionalized) via routine communication patterns that privilege men, then we need to interrupt some styles of interacting that lead women to self-silence and norms that privilege men. Educators must break with the pattern of neglect represented in ignoring women's questions, dismissing their concerns, and interrupting and talking over them. Unlearning these behaviors may require intervention at multiple levels: individual professional development for bystander intervention, reduced barriers to speaking up (e.g., adoption of structural mechanisms for independent reporting and enforcement of grievances and problematic behavior), and advocacy from leaders.

Professional Development and Bystander Intervention

Faculty and other field scientists hold primary responsibility for shaping the climate of learning and research environments. However, while scientists are prepared for a variety of activities in the field, they "are rarely trained in the interpersonal skills of conflict management, negotiation, and resolution that would allow them to informally and formally confront personnel issues as they arise and before they can escalate."[28] Professional development opportunities and bystander intervention training such as that offered by the NSF-funded FIELD project can build capacity for these important skills.[29] By bringing together leaders from diverse field research settings, FIELD raises awareness of disrespectful, hostile, and discriminatory behaviors that come up in the field; clarifies and provides the chance to practice more inclusive behavior; and provides opportunities to reflect upon the current design and practices in one's own field experiences.

Reducing Barriers to Speaking Up

We should also create policy and practice that enables people to speak up when concerns arise and that empowers people with safe means of doing so. Much has been made about the overt behaviors of harassment and assault that traumatize people, but I hope to have shown here how the seeds for such behavior are sown in mundane, routine interactions. Indeed, dismissing women's concerns, ignoring their questions, and interrupting them set a tone that institutionalizes silence about things that matter. As a result of men's behavior in this course, women asked not only fewer questions about scientific subject matter. Many also came to ask what the point was of speaking up with questions if they were going to be shut down or ignored. The directives on the first night of class may have been for students to respect one another's questions, be kind, and communicate well, and such expectation setting was a positive first step. However, women students felt that instructors ignored or insufficiently addressed the concerns they expressed, leading most to eventually stop raising their hand or asking questions at all.

An environment in which women learn it is not worth speaking up to the powers that be about either the content of science or their well-being is an environment in which women are much less likely to speak up to their instructors, advisors, or other superiors about sexual harassment and assault. Recall the example of the guest instructor, Rose, who linked underreporting of sexual assault in the field to women's learned silence and the "blind eye" that instructors often turn toward men's dominance in the everyday work of science. Similar forces to those associated with reporting sexual harassment and assault—the difficulty of reporting to superiors, the pain of documentation, and avoidance of admitting personal vulnerabilities—made it difficult for Amy and Maria to raise their concerns about their mental health and need for accommodations.

Several women similarly discussed the futility of speaking up in evening seminars—first with their questions, then with their frustration that those questions were being ignored. Amy demonstrated agency in both situations by creating work-arounds (e.g., taking personal time for daily exercise regardless of the repercussions, directly approaching instructors after seminars rather than during the question-and-answer period), but she was an exception. Most other women shut down. Educational organizations of all sorts—classrooms, departments, universities, disciplines—need systems that lower the bar for conversation and reporting when needs are not being met and problematic behaviors occur. We need to empower people who feel silenced and create mechanisms for raising concerns, reporting abuses, and protecting those who do. Grievance policies and the ombudsperson role are obvious places to start, for those organizations that do not yet have them in place, so that students and other employees need not report problems solely to individuals who hold supervisory power over them.

Leaders Must Advocate

Finally, deciding that it is worth it or safe and easy enough to speak up about what happens in learning environments and workplaces cannot fall only on those in our communities with the least power, who are poorly represented, or who have been victimized.[30] Silence is also institutionalized—and implicitly rationalized—when those with power stay silent about problematic patterns. As Tierney and Bensimon put it with respect gendered barriers to academic socialization, "The problem is not one of overt sexism or discrimination but rather that unwelcoming climates are created by unconscious actions that take on gendered meanings."[31] People in positions of power must therefore both become more conscious and vocal about the overt and subtle ways gender shapes learning climates. Doing so will require attention to seemingly small slights and signals of disrespect that, cumulatively, shape what we recognize as broader patterns of power and human rights. As Eleanor Roosevelt wrote:

> Where, after all, do universal human rights begin? In small places, close to home—so close and so small that they cannot be seen on any maps of the world. Yet they are the world of the individual person; the neighborhood he lives in; the school or college he attends; the factory, farm, or office where he works. Such are the places where every man, woman, and child seeks equal justice, equal opportunity, equal dignity without discrimination. Unless these rights have meaning there, they have little meaning anywhere. Without concerted citizen action to uphold them close to home, we shall look in vain for progress in the larger world.

The rest of this book focuses largely on organizational equity and inclusion efforts in larger worlds of science: academic departments and the PhD programs within them; then, disciplines; and finally, the institutions that fund the scientific enterprise. These all require our attention, but they will always be limited in effectiveness without consistent and concerted attention to the qualities of everyday interactions in the relationships and social contexts that form graduate worlds, particularly the student-advisor relationship and that of the research lab or team. It is in these relationships that students receive their strongest messages about performance, potential, and belonging.

4 Impression Management and Organizational Learning in Psychology and Chemistry

University of Wisconsin–Madison student Diallo Shabazz was walking through campus one day when an admissions counselor stopped him to mention having seen him in a photo on the front of the university's new application for admission. The photo depicted a crowd at what appeared to be an outdoor sporting event. Although as one of relatively few African American students Shabazz was used to seeing his image used for university marketing purposes, this image troubled him. He had attended no such sporting event as a student. It turned out that the university, deciding it wanted to convey on the application for admission a portrait of a diverse crowd at a football game, pored through thousands of photos in their archives looking for such an image—to no avail. They found many photos of crowds at football games, but none with smiling people of color. So they Photoshopped Shabazz into an otherwise white crowd. Shabazz sued the university for $10 million, won the lawsuit, and had funds directed back to the university for the Office of Multicultural Affairs.[1]

THE STORY OF DIALLO SHABAZZ HIGHLIGHTS A FUNDAMENTAL TRUTH of twenty-first-century higher education: it is serious business for universities to manage public impressions of how they secure, maintain, and promote diversity.[2] Sociologists have been writing for nearly one hundred years about the dynamics and importance of managing impressions. The Thomas theorem, articulated by Dorothy and William Thomas in 1928, espouses the importance of managing not only objective reality but also appearances, because people feel and act on what they perceive, not only on what "is." Comparing social life to theater in the 1950s, sociologist Erving Goffman's dramaturgical theory argued that much of human behavior involves managing others' impressions of us.[3] In higher education, specifically, whether it is a department's attention to its reputation for promoting women or an enrollment management office's attending to the composition of the university student body, diversity management is a widely acknowledged dimension of institutional legitimacy and status.[4] Thus, apart from normative commitments, even many white and male administrators, professors, and students in higher education have come to espouse diversity and to invest resources in order to achieve a plausible appearance of "commitment."

Indeed, the need to "change the face" of STEM by changing the composition of departments and disciplines is largely accepted as legitimate and even admirable given changing social demographics and labor-force participation.[5] Within STEM and throughout higher education, there is widespread support for the idiomatic goal of "moving the needle" on representation in order to more closely resemble the population, albeit with vagueness about how much and for whom. The focus on optics and vagueness about progress implied in engrained phrases like "changing the face" and "moving the needle" upholds the equally vague goal of diversity. Initiatives for diversity are so diffuse that they have come to serve as a selling point for recruiting white students and students of color alike.[6] A major outcome of this emergent common sense is that diversity work is practically ubiquitous in colleges and universities today—related to and yet decoupled from efforts to achieve equitable outcomes or an inclusive climate.

How does it work in practice? Universities are large, decentralized organizations, and faculty members hold autonomy that allows for their individual behavior to diverge considerably from a department's or university's official messaging.[7] They, with many administrators, face ambiguity and anxiety about what the law allows with respect to pursuing diversity through admissions.[8] A PhD program may also struggle to recruit students who will diversify the student body, whether it is because the program is inexperienced in doing so, because the program has developed a negative reputation in networks, or because professors hold false assumptions about what students of color are looking for in a graduate program. Sometimes it is all three of these. A methodologically rigorous study by Samuel Bersola and colleagues compared what department leaders at a large research institution they call Western University thought was important to prospective graduate students with the self-reported views of admitted students of color who opted to go elsewhere. They call these students nonmatriculants. Faculty believed the most important factor to recruits was financial aid, for example, but 77 percent of nonmatriculants said they still would have enrolled at their current university if Western had matched the financial aid at the place they ultimately enrolled. Other findings from this study support the broader claim that faculty often operate from inaccurate knowledge, insufficient skill, or counterproductive attitudes in advancing diversity or its related goals of equity and inclusion.

Another challenge that academic organizations face is balancing institutional mandates for diversity with varying levels of commitment and engagement among their own members. In prestige-seeking PhD programs, faculty often feel ambivalent about pursuing diversity- and equity-related reforms that might require members to face their complicity in systems of power and privilege.[9] This ambivalence manifests in a certain conservatism in the discourse and activities that fall under the diversity umbrella. This conservatism is reflected, for example, in the limited focus on statistics about presence or absence of certain students versus a dialogue about power imbalances within the department and what to do about them.[10] Recent studies have found that when reviewing applications with diversity in mind, decision makers preferred applicants from underrepresented backgrounds who did not have histories of activism.[11] My own research of graduate admissions committees found the same, revealing cases in which faculty compared women applicants with one another and spoke negatively about those whom they thought might "rock the boat" or come "with a chip on their shoulder." Such coded language reflects indeed a primary interest in changing the image and optics of academic communities more than the priorities, rules, and practices by which power and resources are distributed. As such, "diversity work" can become institutionalized as normal, yet remain a domain of activity that preserves the status quo.

In assessing diversity efforts, therefore, numbers about who is present and absent are but a starting point in tracking what counts as progress toward equity; looking beyond the numbers to the quality of interactions and presence or absence of across lines of social difference (as discussed in Chapter 3), who is doing the work of diversity work, the trajectories of organizations over time, and the details of everyday life within them provides a fuller picture. Diversity efforts vary in type, focus, sources, and extent of funding, as well as efficacy, and they are an emerging area of study in themselves. Scholars have studied assessments and interventions on implicit biases, institutional programs to develop positive intergroup relations and social justice, institutional policies or interventions to reduce structural inequalities, and coordinated processes of organizational learning through self-study and practitioner inquiry.[12] Disciplinary-based scholars in STEM fields have also written about their own programmatic and intervention efforts, which often fall into the types just listed.[13] So extensive is the research and writing in this area that whole journals now dedicate themselves to publishing it, such as *Journal of Diversity in Higher Education* and *Journal of Women and Minorities in Science and Engineering*. Few studies, however, have examined the trajectories of colleges, universities, and departments within them to understand how changes to who is enrolling and completing degrees may be embedded in more textured stories of organizational change.

Trajectories Toward Diversity in STEM PhD Programs

In this chapter and the next, I present comparative case study research carried out with student research assistants at the University of Michigan.[14] Three prominent PhD programs in the United States—in chemistry, psychology, and an applied physics—have recently increased their enrollment of women and students of color to rates significantly higher than that of their fields as a whole. My team identified the chemistry department for having reached gender parity in PhD student enrollment and degree attainment; the psychology department for enrolling over the last three years Black, Latinx, and other groups classified by the university as underrepresented minority at rates double that of psychology nationally; and the applied physics program for extremely high rates for more than a decade of Black and Latinx PhD student enrollment and degree completion. The project took place at two well-known flagship research universities (one on the West Coast, and one in the Midwest) both in states with state-level bans on affirmative action.

Our goal was to learn from outliers: PhD programs who, despite a policy context that precludes them from using a go-to strategy for increasing access and whose institutional context compels attention to prestige, have performed significantly better than their fields in percentages of underrepresented populations who enroll and graduate. We wanted to understand attributions for their success from departmental insiders of various roles, looking for patterns in their organizational conditions and practices as well as tracking each program's trajectory over time. Our data include administrative data from the graduate schools, information from their websites, and most importantly verbatim transcripts from seventy-two interviews with faculty, staff, and other administrators, as well as current students and recent alumni. In addition, we conducted focus groups with students in the departments.

This chapter compares the chemistry and psychology programs as examples of two programs that each tried to increase the diversity among their admitted students by changing the public image of the program and their admissions and recruitment practices. One was successful in learning its way into a virtuous cycle through which change itself became normative. The other fell into a vicious cycle in which failure to bring about substantive change prevented students of color who did enroll to deny a positive report to prospective students. Differences between the two programs' trajectories that help account for their different outcomes include the time they dedicated to creating change, prior momentum on the type of diversity they sought, engagement versus ambivalence on the part of leading faculty, and most fundamentally, leaders' expectations that organizational change constitutes an area of learning and collective effort versus the expectation that it would work as the mission of a few "champions."

What we learned from these departments offers new insights about the organization of graduate programs as well as about the networks of strategies that they deploy to change who enrolls and completes degrees. A major finding is that, even without the ability to consider race or gender as a factor in admissions, there is much that departments and PhD programs can do to diversify their graduate student population. In addition, the position of graduate programs between undergraduate education and the professoriate also presents a strategic opportunity. Doctoral programs changed who enrolled by leveraging their structural position in one of two ways: Some took a bottom-up approach, changing admissions policy, cultivating undergraduates at their institution or partner institutions and then recruiting students from there. One program, taking a top-down approach, diversified its department faculty and individuals who were skilled in and committed to mentoring; this attracted a more diverse group students to the PhD programs. Of course, the more closely we look at anyone or anything—including organizations—the more likely we are to see and learn its imperfections. Our case-study approach permitted insights into both positive and negative lessons about diversity work as a matter of organizational learning and impression management for departments and PhD programs.

Chemistry: Lessons in Organizational Learning

When the chemistry department members of what we call High Tower University recounted their stories of working toward gender equity in graduate education, those stories were inextricably connected to the department's journey toward recruiting and retaining well-respected faculty who were women. A groundswell for change developed in the late 1990s from recognition that the department's national reputation was suffering as the result of a number of failed tenure cases among women. The current department chair recounted:

> When I arrived in 1999, I was the second full professor female ever in the department. There was one associate professor and the first full professor retired the year after I got here. They had hired a number of female assistant professors who didn't get tenure. A year before I came there was a legal challenge over one of those. So when I went back and looked, you know, thirteen of sixteen male faculty members had gotten tenure and one of seven females had.

Around this same time, the PhD program dropped precipitously in rankings, well below that of the university. A professor discussed the impact on faculty morale:

> As an academic department at High Tower University it is very difficult to understand what it is like to be ranked 45. It is a head hanging embarrassment in your professional community. . . . It is the faded movie-star [laughs] kind of thing, to the degree that people say, "You are High Tower, how can you be 45? You're High Tower, you're better than that." The place was devastated.

It was largely as a response to the "head hanging embarrassment" of the lawsuit and drop in the rankings that leaders began examining data about their hiring, tenure, and promotion history. They did so in partnership with other offices on campus (e.g., institutional research, office of gender equity), and with the support of an NSF ADVANCE grant that was oriented around answering the question, "Why have so many women been denied tenure in this department?"[15] Their review concluded that a root cause concerned the department's mindset about hiring: It had been a mistake to think about hiring women as a matter of diversity. As one female professor put it, that mentality led them to "hire women that were not at the center of what the department was working on, so they had no natural mentors or allies or even collaborators. They were pretty isolated." In response, they proposed a new strategy for recruiting women, one that would seek to hire women "at the center of the department's intellectual interests."

The executive committee supported this shift in strategy and began making systematic policy changes: "We went through all of our policies, all of our procedures, and worked on trying to make them more inclusive." Their efforts to do so earned positive attention throughout the field that contributed to successful hires of several widely respected women faculty, including one recognized as "the top candidate in the country her year of any chemist, any gender." Reflecting on that win, a male faculty member said:

> That was a big watershed moment for the department because we went ahead and made her an offer even though it almost seemed hopeless. . . . She accepted our offer, which we were obviously really happy about. . . . She came because she perceived—this is what she's told me—she perceived this changing culture, and a culture that was going to allow her to do her science and live her life and be happiest in her career.

The "watershed moment" of attracting a star recruit to the faculty enabled the hiring and recruitment of several more women, all white, including multiple participants in our research study. Each of them cited the emerging critical mass of women faculty as a major factor in their own decisions to take positions there. One explained:

> For my PhD, there were two women faculty I think in my department. . . . And then you come here and there are ten or twelve. It is just like a ridiculously large number compared to everywhere else. And that changes the atmosphere a lot for a women working in the sciences, like you're not the one or the two women viewpoints on everything. You're no longer. . . . I feel like we're not a minority in the department here at all in faculty meetings and everything. And our chair is a woman.

As reformed hiring practices became the new normal and others scholars in the discipline recognized that the department had developed a critical mass of women who were thriving, the department's reputation also shifted. Critical mass signaled cultural change. A university administrator who advised the ADVANCE grant recalled: "It became a place that was really well known to be good. . . . They literally turned around a negative reputation as a place to be as a woman to a positive one." The community especially took note that the department was even "friendlier to women, particularly in certain areas like organic synthesis which is typically really macho." In the years that followed, the critical mass of women faculty would have ripple effects extending to the PhD program as well.

Faculty and staff we interviewed concurred that attaining a critical mass of women faculty went a long way to "organically attracting" women PhD students who were eager to study with women and/or be in an environment with a number of female role models. However, with recruitment such an important part of their efforts to improve gender equity at the faculty level, it was also natural for the department to begin engaging in more intentional PhD recruitment activity. A staff member acknowledged that for both the graduate student and the faculty community, "recruitment is extremely important to the continuation of this department."

Leaders came to recognize three ways that prospective student impressions of the department affected their interest in enrolling. First, the reputation of the department "out there" in the broader disciplinary community mattered much for who would apply in the first place and take seriously offers of admission. Second, the view of the department that students constructed through their own interactions with the department and the faculty within it (both online and in person) played a formative role in shaping engagement and matriculation decisions. Relatedly, and third, the quality of current students' experiences was a powerful force, for current students could either serve as ambassadors for the department or as recruitment killjoys.

In asking them about what the department specifically did to recruit women graduate students, a majority of professors discussed their carefully designed campus-visit weekends, which a member of our research team was fortunate to attend as an observer. Department leaders had seen what a difference a successful visit made in their faculty recruitment efforts, so they began attending to who was physically present for specific events throughout the student visit weekend. They worked to keep alive the sense of critical mass. They also orchestrated interactions, even going so far as to assign seating for dinners to ensure that prospective students would speak with key people. They also made efforts to communicate subtle cues about gender to prospective students over the course of the weekend and in the physical space of the department. Recognizing the lab as a critical context for graduate student life, for example, a lunchtime poster session allowed prospective students to walk around and mingle with current students, learning more about the various labs and their work. Each lab's station used the professor's name to identify the team, and a photo of the group conveyed the centrality of the team as well as visual evidence about gender and racial composition of each team. Other cues focused on showcasing the department as welcoming to families and as promoting a well-rounded lifestyle for faculty and students alike. Men and women professors brought their children for campus visit weekend activities so prospective students would "see kids running around." At least two participants had treadmill desks in their office and another had a yoga mat. As is the case in many places, the offices of most faculty we interviewed displayed family photos or children's artwork. Activities like these may have been be more or less intentional impression management moves on the part of individual faculty members, and they were so subtle as to be missed by some students even when they were in the minds of the faculty; however, there was collective awareness that physical space could communicate cultural values that make the program all the more attractive a place to study chemistry.

A Virtuous Cycle Emerges

It was emblematic of a larger pattern in this department's history that chemistry faculty collectively learned from improving campus visits for faculty candidates how they might improve visits made by prospective PhD students: revisiting their systems for hiring, recruiting, and promoting faculty normalized the reassessment of practices used to admit, recruit, and educate graduate students. Whereas in many academic departments faculty look on change to organizational policy and practice as a stumbling block to the "real work" of science, this department had seen firsthand its ability to make real changes to practice and to see those changes to practice result in desirable outcomes for the department. This success emboldened them with confidence with making changes as needed, and it made equity-oriented policy change a normative aspect of department leadership—so much so that "good leaders" in the department were understood as ones who would make changes that nudge them toward equity. Through repeated cycles of looking at their data, reconsidering the associated practices and their underlying assumptions (e.g., hiring women with a diversity mindset instead of hiring women whose work was at the core of the department's interests), implementing changes, and evaluating the outcomes, they learned how to do change. Thus, they grew in confidence with making change and embedded change oriented toward gender equity as a cultural norm for the department, thereby creating a virtuous cycle.

What started as a focused effort to diversify the faculty turned into a top-down process of drawing women graduate students via the presence of women faculty. Having obtained a critical mass of women in the department fuels this cycle today; indeed, its share of women PhD students was how it came to our attention. No such similar critical mass or virtuous cycle presently exists with respect to racial equity, however, although several individual faculty in the program express strong commitments to it and acknowledged to us the need to redirect change efforts toward both faculty and PhD student participation.

Racial Equity and Graduate Admissions

Graduate admissions is one way in which the PhD program is beginning to work on racial equity. In recent years, the program has made comprehensive changes to their admissions practices in the hopes of both approaching gender parity and increasing the number of domestic students of color admitted. Several factors—each related to a context in which the department is situated—motivated these changes: the state ban on gender and race-based affirmative action in public institutions forced a reevaluation of the admissions process; a national conversation about the need to reduce reliance on the GRE; and university efforts to translate professional development for faculty searches to the graduate admissions context.

One of our participants was a recent admissions chair who explained that attending a campus-wide professional development event on graduate admissions had convinced her that GRE scores were insufficiently correlated with desired academic outcomes to justify the inequities that reliance on them introduced. In her first year as admissions chair, she dissuaded committee members from looking at scores on the GRE general test (verbal, quantitative, and analytic writing). The next winter, she made a formal proposal to the department to stop collecting scores altogether. One faculty member felt strongly that scores added information, but he could not marshal evidence for his position and vocally resisted the proposal. In response, the department chair allowed a study of ten years of data from the department, which to the surprise of some found a negative correlation between GRE scores and academic performance. That is, enrolled PhD students who had scored well on the GRE general test performed more poorly as PhD students. The admissions chair presented this data to the department faculty and voted once again on whether to collect scores for that year and going forward. The vote to stop collecting scores was unanimous, and she said, "There has been no looking back."

At the same time as the GRE policy change, the admissions chair wisely created a new system for conducting systematic holistic review of every applicant by faculty members who hold expertise relevant to applicant research interests. They have begun to privilege applicant research experience because they feel that it is less likely to be racialized or gendered and more likely to align with the type of work that graduate students will be doing. Whereas many PhD programs limit formal file review to a committee of delegates who serve on behalf of the collective faculty, they distribute to each faculty member the files of all students who express an interest in studying with that individual. The chemistry program's actions have inspired other PhD programs on campus to revisit their GRE policy and to implement holistic review. "We're not alone in doing this," the current admissions chair noted, and she anticipates that other departments will soon follow.

Psychology: Bait and Switch

Comprising nine program areas ranging from social psychology to neuroscience, the psychology department has long held a prestigious reputation in the field, and for the last several years it has been successful enrolling students from groups classified by the university as underrepresented minorities. The faculty participants in our study, however, were divided about the extent and continuity of a department-wide commitment to these goals. The most senior faculty among those we spoke with could point to recruitment and retention activity as far back as the 1960s but described serious departmental engagement with race as an "ebb and flow." Another commented, "There have been times where there has been a greater departmental emphasis placed on admitting minorities or diverse students."

Faculty agreed, however, that a pivotal moment for the department occurred about eight years earlier when, upon checking the demographics of their list of admitted PhD students before sending the data to the graduate school, admissions leaders realized that of the twenty-five students they had admitted, all were white. This realization had "a certain shock value that got people's attention." A professor of health psychology described the response:

> We sort of quickly recognized there was an issue and had a faculty meeting around that and talked about it. That was, I think, telling about how much we're trying to keep an eye on things, and wanting to sort of self-examine.

This self-examination sparked a conversation about the ways admissions should change, as well as a broader "policy shift towards seeking out underrepresented groups," with one apparently "unrelenting" faculty advocate spearheading several of its efforts. Their multifaceted approach quickly yielded enrollment gains from desired groups, which is how the department came to our attention. Yet as I will discuss, their approach was not sufficiently balanced or distributed within the department to ensure that the students whom they attracted would thrive or support future recruitment.

To ensure distributed leadership across the concentrations, the department reinvented and convened its diversity committee. It had been formed under the banner of minority affairs in the late 1960s "to attract both Black graduate students and Black faculty" but had been flagging for some time. At the time of our data collection, the diversity committee comprised at least one faculty member from each concentration who were anointed "diversity officers" and served on the admissions committee. With this infrastructure in place, they set about developing a network of recruitment strategies and reconsidering their admissions practices.

Department leaders rationalized a major website overhaul as necessary to attracting both faculty and graduate students from more diverse backgrounds. Noting that they already had "a lot of faculty who were studying underrepresented populations," the department chair explained that the revamped website and admissions materials "should feature what we're doing." The website also prominently advertised another recruitment effort: the creation of a curriculum initiative focused on theory and research about communities of color, drawing from a variety of standpoints and topical areas within psychology. The former chair recounted this as a "major priority":

> So the first step really was to add [the curriculum initiative] to the website. . . . And then we started getting inquiries from prospective students saying, "I'm really interested in your new [curriculum initiative]. What are the courses? What's the nature of your program?"

As they hoped, the initiative provided "something tangible" for the department to discuss with prospective students. Meanwhile, a student organization created by and for underrepresented students within the department began leading outreach efforts to prospective applicants of color. That group has since become "a coalition of support" and activism within the department.

With respect to admissions, another "upshot from the faculty meeting" where the department recognized how far short it had fallen of desired admissions outcomes was recognition that its usual selection processes—and in particular reliance on GRE scores—undermined admission of Black and Latinx students. In a long-standing admissions practice that, as one professor put it, "kind of flies in the face of most research evidence, and the [Educational Testing Service, or ETS] guidelines for how you're supposed to use GRE scores," they had been making their first cut by calculating and ranking applicants on an index score created from their college grade point averages and GRE scores. A conclusion of that faculty meeting was the need for a more holistic review from the start of the process and that they should take GRE scores "with a grain of salt and read more of their stories, go into their grades, and go into their practical experiences." However, in this large and distributed department, possibilities for deep change of the sort observed in the chemistry department seemed to be limited. Senior professors' mindset about what constitutes merit, combined with their influence, was a powerful combination. I quote at length a member of the admissions committee:

> You know there are still some faculty who are definitely "pure merit" faculty where it is like "let me look at the scores" and, I mean, to a lesser degree the CV. . . . And then there are the other folks who are more, "The numbers have their limitations. Let's go and really think about the overall picture of this candidate." And so I think there is still that divide. Some of it seems to be—at least what I've seen it seems to be—seniority based, the more senior folks who obviously were in a more homogenous environment when they were coming through graduate school where the only awards were only for merit. There was less attention paid to you know sort of overall life experience. Granted, there wasn't a lot of heterogeneity in that when they were coming up so you've got folks who are still in that mindset I think. And so some of us are having to work with that to some degree.

He described what others also discussed: the difficulty of managing diverse views on merit, and the formative role that norms to which students are exposed in graduate school play in their later mindsets as professors.

Others whom we interviewed concurred that single-mindedness about the GRE and its role in the index score—especially among senior faculty—posed a real barrier to increasing enrollment from students of color. The diversity officer for the developmental psychology concentration explained her discomfort with the use of index scores to sort the pool:

> For a student who happens to have a low index score, whether they're a minority or not, we have to argue for the student's admission. And that doesn't feel so well sometimes when you constantly are arguing for a particular type of student.

Still, when the main thrust of data were collected for this study in 2015, some felt that change was afoot. A Latina assistant professor who served on the admissions committee said, for example, "I feel like we have a lot of sympathetic voices in the cause of this more holistic approach to admissions."

In 2019, I followed up with the chair of the admissions committee to see what, if anything, had changed. She indicated, "Marginal changes have been made to the computation of the index score," so that it was now two-thirds based on GRE and one-third based on undergraduate grade point average. Some areas had stopped using the index score for triage purposes and were involving live readers in the first read through every application, but others with especially large pools (e.g., clinical psychology) continued to sort using the index score alone. Just as detrimental to change as reliance on index scores in her mind, however, were three key structural problems with their admissions process: a failure to coordinate change, anchoring bias introduced by the admissions software, and absence of collective engagement.

First, there has been no common committee to provide oversight for, track, or coordinate change in admissions practices. There is a fellowship committee, but admissions slots for each of the nine areas are filled by faculty within those areas, with varying degrees of fidelity to ostensibly department-wide principles. Therefore, "Whomever chairs the area admissions matters so much." Second, GRE scores and index scores are "salient in the interface" of the software that faculty use to evaluate applicants, so reviewers' judgment tends to anchor on metrics, even where the index score is no longer used as the sole means of "triage." In these two examples, we have excellent evidence of the need for a posthumanist view of change that was introduced in Chapter 2—that is, one that focuses not only on individual or collective hearts and minds but also on the organizational infrastructure and technological apparatus by which we conduct activity in science. Finally, although it is possible for any faculty member to advocate for a given student's admission, in practice faculty reported that it was mostly members of the diversity committee who also served on admissions who pressed their colleagues to ensure all "applicants get a fair look." Despite "tacit encouragement" for everyone to use holistic review as part of the department's support broader equity and diversity efforts, it was not yet a matter of collective responsibility, but rather the purview of select "diversity champions." The implications of leaving encouragement for diversity and equity a tacit matter, rather than one that is explicit, become clear as we see how psychology students of color who did enroll experienced life within the department during these years.

Bait and Switch

Most staff and students in our sample and about half of the faculty reported a bait-and-switch experience for PhD students; that is, the day-to-day climate for diversity did not live up to the rosy image portrayed on the website and by faculty for the purposes of recruitment.[16] Aggressive recruitment paired with uneven support, neglect, and/or harassment once students enrolled gave at least half the students of color in our sample experiences of being "terribly mismatched." There were three common elements of this mismatch: poor or uneven mentoring quality relative to the messages of commitment and support that faculty conveyed; discussions of race being shallow or absent despite the department website communicating them as central; and racial stigma associated with admission and fellowship opportunities despite formal commitments to diversity. I explicate each of these.

As a primary force in the graduate students' development, mentoring can make or break a student's learning experience. When I asked, "What happens after students enroll?" of a Latinx professor who commented on the growth of "sympathetic voices" for holistic review, she sighed and admitted:

> That's a very good question. I think there is something missing there. In fact, you hear from some of the underrepresented minority students . . . about having been recruited here aggressively and then [pause] kind of left to their own devices.

Students indeed shared with us such stories. In fact, some of the most difficult interviews I have conducted in almost twenty years of qualitative research emerged as students disclosed their experiences.

When I saw Lydia from across the courtyard for our second interview, for example, I didn't even recognize her. In our first interview, a year earlier, she was polished and put together, her height and posture the perfect embodiment of the strength and confidence she exuded. The program had been proud to attract her from an Ivy League university after she had been accepted by a dizzying array of PhD programs. She enrolled here specifically to study with a famous scholar, drawn by his expertise in her research specialization and reputation for career sponsorship, as well as their shared Black identity. Shortly after our first interview, however, he began harassing her sexually and continued to do so for months. She learned through the department's whisper network that she was not the only one enduring this, and although she reported it, the only actions taken did not stop the harassment. A month or so before our second interview, she opted to change labs and advisors. The decision was a necessary course of action and that was nonetheless fraught for Lydia.

For our second interview, with her head hanging, eyes framed with huge bags, and rumpled shirt awkwardly untucked on one side, my first thought upon seeing Lydia was that it must be someone else. She told me in detail the pains of the year, taking me up to the present in confessing fear about whether she would receive from her new advisor—a white woman—the career and professional sponsoring that she had come to the university to receive. When I followed up with her once more a few months later, Lydia was relieved that her new advisor far exceeded her expectations: "She invites me to everything. She makes sure to brag about me to people and things like that. . . . Now that I'm her student, she feels invested. Now, I don't know if this is about race." Still, she was angry about how the department had handled her case—or, rather, had failed to handle it. Reflecting on why the department could get away with conveying a positive environment for studying race and psychology, she recognized a distinction between "rhetoric at the university-level or the department-level" and "action at a more individual level, faculty or administrators or both." And Lydia is right in this assessment: three recent NASEM reports—on sexual harassment, on graduate STEM education, and on mentoring—have also recognized the absence of accountability mechanisms for individual faculty mentoring and other behaviors as barriers to inclusion in STEM.

Other students discussed a pattern of "benign neglect" from their advisors, while a separate contingent discussed the barriers to mutual understanding and cultural resonance that came from being mentored by even the most socially conscious white professors. Faculty members themselves acknowledged that mentoring quality "varies widely on who the faculty member is" and that not every professor advising underrepresented students was a safe confidant or even "culturally competent."

In addition to uneven quality of individual mentoring, students of color felt that the lack of explicit discussion of race—especially in courses—came as a surprise given its centrality on the website. According to one Latina student, "When I came in it was like 'diversity-diversity-diversity' on the website, and when I came here there was nothing." In data collection with PhD students in the department, this topic yielded long, rich dialogues. With respect to course curriculum and discussion, one student described race as an apparent "thing to check off"; others indicated a "colorblind" or "postracial" tenor to most discussions. "No one brought it up, like it doesn't exist," and for Latinx students in the sample this was particularly ironic given the strong Latinx population in the surrounding community.

It bears noting that the psychology program is hardly alone in its relative silence on race. Amid subjectively held commitments and expressed desires to be viewed as committed, we see throughout higher education ambivalence in some places and resistance in others to conversations about race that surface personal pains, gradients of privilege, and systemic injustices.[17] Through interviews with staff at several universities whose jobs focused on diversity work, anthropologist Sarah Ahmed found that diversity work has come to be a substitute for honest engagement with race, for race elicits tensions and disagreement that many academics avoid under community norms of collegiality. Arguing that most diversity work is fundamentally performative and self-promoting, she proposes the value of going deeper than the surface-level "happy talk" of diversity to realities of racism and other systems of oppression:

> Diversity might be promoted because it allows the university to promote itself, creating a surface or illusion of happiness. We could call this simply the "happy diversity" model, in which "diversity talk" becomes "happy talk." . . . The smile of diversity stops a "rotten core" from surfacing. . . . If, for some practitioners the positivity of the term "diversity" makes it useful as a way of getting people to the table, then for others the positivity is a problem because it allows the reasons you might want people at your table to be obscured.[18]

Ahmed's comments clarify how a range of individual realities underlie a group's performance of diversity and how we might understand the apparent contradiction of espoused commitment to race without open discussion of it. The very need for a conversation about some groups' persistent absence from seats of influence in academe and society contradicts the vision of diversity as something to be celebrated.

Such tensions indeed arose among students and faculty arose as the department's composition shifted, further contributing to students' sense of a bait and switch. It caused some to question whether they were actually welcomed. Often tensions bubbled up in the form of what social scientists call microaggressions, "subtle insults (verbal, nonverbal, and/or visual) directed toward people of color, often automatically or unconsciously."[19] For example, as the student community caught wind of the advocacy required to admit applicants with lower GRE scores, students of color reported experiencing both subtle and overt messages from peers who assumed that they had been beneficiaries of such advocacy, which those peers considered an "unfair advantage." A similar tension emerged in a recent cohort around NSF fellowships. As one student reported, "When they were announced— almost everyone in an entire cohort got it except for three students and they all were white. And then the narrative was like, 'You only got NSF because you're Black.'"

Slights like these comments, alongside the problematic discussions of race in courses, in a context of inconsistent mentoring, drove home to students that, despite the public impression the department communicated about its commitment to racial diversity, it was hardly a universal value. Misunderstandings like these are one reason it is so important to conduct admissions in a way that evaluates everyone based on a common definition of merit – that is, according to criteria that are defined in advance and that reflect collective commitments. Transparency about the use of common processes is itself a strategy for impression management, because it may prevent perceptions that some have been through an easier review process or are present merely by making exceptions to the usual rules.

Consequences of the Bait-and-Switch Experience

What were the consequences of students' collective experience of bait and switch? At the individual student level, academic engagement and personal well-being suffered. Students of color, especially women, reported emotional exhaustion and self-doubt following racialized incidents; the toll of providing extensive peer mentoring and support to peers in the absence of reliable mentoring from faculty; and in at least two cases, unchecked sexual harassment. A theme threaded through all three of these types of struggles was the pain of uncertainty about knowing what to do—both whether and how to respond to issues as they arose and how to support peers in the same. In my second interview with her, Christina vividly expressed, while on the verge of tears, the difficulty of knowing how to respond to harassment from a lab mate:

> I thought, "How are you OK with saying those things in front of me?" . . . And I don't know whether to speak up . . . because then I'm going to be the crazy Latina that . . . reinforces some of the things that you already thought. Or like not say anything and just carry that weight that gets bigger and bigger. . . . I'm going to choose not to take action on that because I have to see this person for the next five years in my lab. And at some point that makes me guilty. But I know there are repercussions about bringing this up.

Christina and students like her "carr[ied] the weight" of recognizing that they were positioned as the diversity the department sought, and of calculating the costs and benefits of "whether to speak up." They knew, for example, that their reactions could challenge or reinforce stereotypes and that there could be untold "repercussions" that would compromise their progress or day-to-day learning experience. As we saw with most women students in the field course, students of color in this department often chose the burden of silence over the risks of speaking up.

A second, related consequence of the bait-and-switch experience was an increasingly vital role for the student organization, which I will call Students for Equity in Psychology (SEP). Every single person in the sample mentioned SEP as a force in the department's trajectory toward increased racial diversity. Although its official function was to encourage a community of support among students sharing underrepresented backgrounds, the group had additional functions that participants cited as helping advance the department. These additional functions included advocacy with the faculty diversity committee (e.g., for revisiting policy; for addressing instances of racist, sexist, and homophobic behavior that individual students might not want to personally report) and coordination of outreach and recruitment activities. The need for better clarity on faculty members' part about the struggles that graduate students of color in the department faced was driven home, in one participant's view, that the department as a whole "is not built to support the [student] struggles that [faculty] are probably unaware of." SEP worked to help translate student struggles and needs to department leaders who could take action to address them in an official capacity.

As we conducted the final round of interviews, a third consequence of bait and switch—and the insufficiency of implementing only structural reforms to re-create a department's image—became clear. A major theme of the interviews was that students of color admitted that they struggled to speak positively about the department to prospective students of color. Thus, although it had improved enrollment statistics in the short term, the department risked undermining its own progress by not attending to the quality of the climate and mentoring for students who enrolled. Several of our participants described tension during a coffee hour that was hosted by SEP during the department's campus visit weekend. Some current students wanted to "keep it real" with prospective students by sharing that life in the department did not match the image on the website. Others felt compelled to recommend PhD programs that, within whisper networks among doctoral students of color in the field, presented "better options" or "a safer space."[20]

Their comments highlighted how current students can be a PhD program's best ambassadors—or its worst. Strategies to increase diversity by changing the composition of the student body are thus necessary, but they will not on their own undo harmful patterns of racialization micro-level interactions or that reflect it. Without attention to these dimensions of the racial climate, negative student experiences may threaten a program's ability to recruit students of color in the future.

Make no mistake: improving admissions and recruitment are vital steps in facilitating student enrollment, which is a prerequisite to remediating inequalities in racial representation.[21] However, research on undergraduate education demonstrates that while critical mass and representation are necessary, they are also insufficient conditions for producing an environment in which students will thrive—one in which they feel that they belong and receive a balance of challenge and support.[22] To this end, changes that affect student interactions with faculty and others, such as accountability for the quality of mentoring, are also important to improving the system of graduate education for a more diverse population. In envisioning sustainable trajectories toward diversity and equity, this psychology department thus offers as much a cautionary tale as an exemplar of change.

Virtuous and Vicious Cycles in Organizational Learning

The chemistry and psychology departments exemplify the potential for de-partments to enter into vicious and virtuous cycles in the pursuit of greater diversity, and their stories map broadly onto what Argyris and Schon describe as single and double-loop organizational learning processes. In single-loop learning, an organization modifies its behavior to fix perceived problems or avoid mistakes, thereby bringing outcomes into alignment with those they desire. It focuses on adjustments at the operational level, which leaves root causes unaddressed. Typically, such causes involve the shared assumptions and norms that justify operating practices. Indeed, we can think of practices as symptoms or markers of the underlying cultures. Single-loop learning thus tends to be primarily structural in nature, reform oriented, and limited in both scope and sustainability. It takes the values that are espoused as given, rather than examining values, norms, and assumptions themselves as unspo-ken theories (i.e., "theories in use") that drive behavior and structure.[23]

Double-loop learning, in contrast, involves engagement with both behav-iors and the underlying theories in use that reinforce behavior. Engaging at the level of both an observed problem and its root causes encourages deeper reflection, more holistic solutions, and cycles of continuous improvement. What does the distinction mean in a practical sense? As is the case in single-loop learning, reforms will be made under double-loop learning. However, with the effort that double-loop-learning makes to recognize underlying as-sumptions and root causes also comes a recognition that easily observable behaviors represent a partial portrait of the complex system. Predicated on a group's capacity for self-awareness and critique of its implicit or taken-for-granted assumptions, this also involves candid discussion and collective re-sponsibility. For faculty, who so prize their competence and problem-solving capacities, such recognition and discussion can be uncomfortable work. Ar-gyris's empirical work suggested that it is most likely to occur when the single loop is in crisis—that is, when it becomes clear that reform alone has been insufficient, and a deeper conversation about values is needed.[24]

The admission of an all-white cohort in the psychology department, for example, provided a wake-up call to faculty about the existence of a "diversity problem" that needed to be fixed. Improvements in student compositional diversity that followed from the immediate actions they took reinforced these actions as positive steps: changing their public image to draw more students of color, creating a loophole in the admissions process for applicants of color who applied with low GRE scores, and more aggressively recruiting the students of color whom they did admit. But the program did not make diversity work a collective responsibility, which might have forced the sort of dialogue about underlying norms that double-loop learning entails. Instead, after one full-faculty meeting about the topic, the department effectively bureaucratized diversity work; it was an agenda with activities carried out by advocates. The department recognized a small handful of leaders who played the role of "diversity champions." The department also delegated leadership to a committee, and it outsourced the student support role to preselected faculty and the student organization.

I found that while bureaucratizing diversity in psychology improved recruitment, and therefore enrollment, it did not touch the quality of everyday life and learning in the department for students who enrolled: mentoring relationships, the place of race in discussions, and other aspects of departmental culture and climate. Students of color reported a bait-and-switch experience, in which impressions of the department's commitment to diversity conveyed for the purposes of recruitment fell far short of students' everyday experiences. This threatened the sustainability of their impressive enrollment gains because enrolled students of color—at least those whom we spoke with—struggled deeply with the mismatch between the department's public impression and their own lived realities. They considered or took leaves of absence and were unable to offer a positive report about their experience to prospective students of color. This contributed to some prospective students enrolling elsewhere, thus restarting the cycle in which students of color would be underrepresented. Thus, a single-loop learning approach centered on reforming the image of the department may be a vicious cycle—one that I have seen to be all too common in my work around the country with graduate schools and PhD programs.

The chemistry department admitted it had a long way to go with respect to racial equity, but it provides an excellent example of double-loop organizational learning on gender equity. In contrast to single-loop learning that changes the policy and practice landscape through top-down "fiat or finger waving,"[25] the faculty in this department engaged in systematic examination of the theories in use that had been driving their policies and practices.[26] Recall, for example, the recognition that they needed to rethink their mindset about hiring women. Instead of thinking about hiring women as women, they acknowledged the potential of hiring women who conducted research at the center of the department's intellectual interests, so as to position women at the center of its work and its future instead of at the margins. They learned their way into a virtuous cycle of implementing data-driven structural reforms and cultural course corrections that shifted the faculty composition (attracting some students), improved the quality of the culture for everyone, and emboldened leaders to pursue new forms of organizational change. By successfully achieving a critical mass and near parity with respect to gender on the faculty, they had confidence and comfort with pursuing changes in the PhD program that would bring the student composition closer to parity as well. Now, the chemistry department is in a process of intentional change with respect to race. Making change normative also normalized discussions of potentially controversial issues and normalized equity-related change as intrinsic to good leadership. Indeed, it came to be expected that "good leaders" in this department would seek systematic improvements in the domains for which they hold responsibility.

Diversity Work as Impression Management

Both departments worked hard to change their image—chemistry with respect to gender and psychology with respect to race. However, the means by which they did so differed markedly. Chemistry's reputation changed slowly, one professor at a time, as it turned around its approach and ability to recruit, retain, and promote women faculty. Psychology's intense and immediate focus on transforming the public image via the website exemplifies how diversity work can easily become a matter of impression management and performance on the front stage of organizational life.[27] With carefully curated photos of optically diverse members and strategically placed headlines and font sizes for select activities, the website redesign intended to draw attention to the good that was "already going on" in the department, so as to attract others who would contribute to diversity. The psychology department is hardly alone in making such an effort, for the appearance that a department is steadily working on diversity sends one signal of institutional commitment to prospective students and faculty, regardless of how that image aligns with individual lived experiences.[28] Meanwhile, however, unresolved cultural debates and avoidance of the thorniest issues marked the backstage life of the department during these years. Within faculty meetings, they struggled for consensus about whether, how, and to what degree they should redefine what counts as merit for admission. At least according to our data, there were at least two cases of sexual harassment—both unsatisfactorily resolved from the standpoints of the students involved.

It is all too common for the self-generated public image of organizational reality that a group asserts to contradict what individual members experience. Indeed, we can think of the public image as a collective performance, one representing a compromise about "what is," which is achieved by negotiating many perceived realities and then translating it to maximize the likelihood of a positive impression. The performance involves orchestrating optical tactics, rhetoric, and publicity.[29] Similarly, Goffman's theory suggests that we might interpret the face of diversity constructed for a department website as a "veneer of consensus" around "the view of the situation which he feels others will be able to find at least temporarily acceptable."[30] The working consensus requires subordinating some perceptions and claims to others. Thus, the "overall definition of the situation" that a person is likely to make based on his or her own observations "involves not so much a real agreement as to what exists but rather a real agreement as to whose claims concerning what issues will be temporarily honored."[31] All of this means that we are likely to see through deep case-study research a more complicated picture than the intentionally attractive and clean image that a department presents of itself on a website. The more complicated picture of the department's diversity efforts emerged by soliciting perspectives on it from people who hold different social identities and professional positions. Certainly, the image will be more complex than any inference that might be made from participation numbers alone.

Top Down, Bottom Up, and Inside Out

The positioning of graduate education between undergraduate education and the professoriate means that both top-down changes in the faculty and bottom-up changes in who is recruited can effect overall changes in who enrolls within a given PhD program. For example, an unintended ripple effect of changing the gender composition of faculty in the chemistry department was to catalyze an uptick in women PhD students who were attracted to the department's critical mass of women role models—a case of top-down change.

In psychology, focused efforts to increase the number of applicants of color and recruit those with either conventional credentials or significant research experience represented bottom-up efforts that, along the way, developed a new sense of how large the plausible pool of students of color was.

In addition to working top down and bottom up, the trajectory in chemistry has been characterized by work that is systemic and inside out. Chemistry recognized interdependencies between faculty and student diversity and between goals of student access and success. It also came to see domains of institutional practices (e.g., recruitment, admission, mentoring, creating an inclusive climate) as a system whose performance would affect its progress toward equitable access and success. Finally, we see in chemistry an important role for not only change that affects the outward appearance of a department but also work that is inside out. The department acknowledged it was falling short of the identity and reputation it desired; leaders engaged in candid self-examination of institutional data; and they revisited standard operating practices and mindsets that justified those practices. The capacity to work not only on one's image and outward behavior, but to identify and question embedded values characterizes double-loop learning, and without it, diversity work will never be more than impression management.

Change is complex, reality is multidimensional, and academic organizations must disabuse themselves of the notion that impression management is a sufficient pathway to creating more equitable environments. Diversity cannot operate for long as a matter of numbers or optics when members who represent the "diversity" feel they are being used or abused. Leaders should not settle for goals of increasing the numbers of students from certain groups or reducing gaps in enrollment; there is no less than a moral obligation for leaders to ensure a high quality of education and life for every student who enrolls. Putting people first means designing not only for objective statistics, but also subjective inclusion and well-being. In the next chapter, we will see an example of a department that did just that.

5 Inclusive Design and Disciplinary Boundary Work in Applied Physics

DESCRIBING HIS VISION TO ME, PROFESSOR ROY CLARKE TILTED HIS head, lowered his eyes, and explained, "The academic structures are very, very old. They're older than two hundred years. They go back a thousand years. They're medieval. What we wanted was to knock down the walls."[1] The applied physics program that he founded at the University of Michigan had in its very DNA the image of an academic community whose boundaries would not pose undue barriers to intellectual interests and demographic groups that had been traditionally excluded from advanced training and work in physics and who would not take medieval structures of higher learning for granted as their norm.[2] Rather, its founders and subsequent leaders—faculty and others—would choose for themselves how they wanted to define their intellectual scope, set up curriculum and assessments of learning, and relate to one another.

Having portrayed the limits of employing primarily top-down or bottom-up approaches for sustaining reforms, this applied physics (AP) program is a case study that outlines a third approach—designing for inclusion from the inside out. In creating this program from scratch, faculty and other leaders make explicit the empirical and ethical grounds for assumptions and everyday practices that are the basis for symbolic boundaries, which were introduced in Chapter 2. As part of this process, they redesigned key aspects of their intellectual paradigm, admissions and other organizational processes, curriculum, and mentoring, as well as their general social relations. They were explicit with one another, prospective students, and other stakeholders about the high value they placed on equity and inclusion and the close relationships this value motivated.

The chapter represents learning obtained over a year of fieldwork with this program from 2014 to 2015.[3] As with the research design for case studies presented in Chapter 4, a group of research assistants and I conducted focus groups with current students and interviews with individual students, professors, administrative staff, and alumni. We also participated in a variety of events in the program to observe how members interact with one another, with prospective students, and with the broader university community. The latter two types of observations were especially important in drawing out how the program defines itself in relation to—or, more specifically, distinguishes itself from—physics. From the full ethnographic case study that resulted from our analyses (published elsewhere for readers who may want additional methodological details, analysis, and discussion of the data), four core patterns emerged in data collected with students, faculty, administrators, and alumni alike.

Specifically, there were four ways that this program tried to distinguish itself and its boundaries from other physics programs through its policies, practices, and interpersonal relations. Indeed, the willingness to alter traditional intellectual, organizational, social, and professional boundaries was at the core of the program's success facilitating access and inclusion in a field known for its inequality. The program institutionalized a flexible, interdisciplinary intellectual paradigm; it reformed admissions and recruitment to align with their distinctive vision of the ideal student; it empowered administrative staff to serve as cultural translators across racial and faculty-student boundaries; and it worked to create close relationships that would set the program apart from the more hierarchical, impersonal dynamics they saw in other physics programs. "The family" was a shared identity within the program and served as more than just a cliché or tagline. It created an environment that provided their program with a competitive advantage over other physics departments around the country.

These themes illustrate what in sociology we identify as boundary change mechanisms. Common across all four themes was the program's willingness to erase, relocate, or deactivate boundaries that had implicitly created barriers to access and inclusion for underrepresented students. Building on the work of Tilly, I propose boundary translation as an additional boundary change mechanism. The chapter concludes by relating these findings back to the notion of designing for inclusion through a summary of how the department's activities align with the seven principles of universal design—an established interdisciplinary framework for making environments and products more accessible and inclusive. My hope is that in addition to advancing our knowledge about the social construction of boundaries, that the AP story will encourage readers to engage in their own inside-out analysis about the symbolic boundaries operating in their own departments, and that they will work with colleagues to consider steps toward (re)designing for inclusion.[4]

Disciplinary Culture in Physics

Physics occupies a high status within academe and society as the oldest and most mathematically informed of the scientific disciplines. It commands respect for its intellectual intensity, financial resources, and contributions of such iconic scholars as Galileo, Newton, Einstein, and Hawking.[5] A well-established field, physics has relatively strong norms, both organizationally and epistemologically. For instance, although there is a culture of celebrity, the fact that few physicists today conduct purely independent work reveals the field's reliance on collaboration.[6] Another norm associated with the discipline's maturity is its high level of knowledge codification. Knowledge in physics is tightly packaged into a series of interconnected, widely held topics that the majority of the disciplinary community accept.[7] Possession of this canonical knowledge has become an important basis for judging who is "prepared" for graduate study and a career in the field. Physics theories, and the means of developing and testing them, have been described as constituting the core of the discipline's epistemic culture.[8]

The high degree of consensus required to achieve physics' high degree of intellectual codification may also compel more widely shared beliefs than most disciplines have about other aspects of professional life, such as what the criteria should be for professional success and recognition.[9] Neither consensus nor achievements in physics come about easily, however. Rather, Traweek's ethnography of three major physics labs evocatively portrays disciplinary advancements as the result of "elaborate and stylized combat" across lines of difference and disagreement.[10] With boundary work commonplace in this high-consensus discipline, boundary processes should also be expected to be important for any prospects of cultural change with respect to equity or inclusion.

With this perspective on the high-consensus physics disciplinary culture as a backdrop, it is useful here to remind readers of several core findings from the scholarship on social boundaries. These findings inform the current research in three specific ways. Knowing how organizational actors define, negotiate, and perform boundary work provides a glimpse into taken-for-granted cultural norms that pattern behavior in ways that can create social inequalities.[11] Second, how groups conceive of themselves and others as similar and different—and then work across the differences—is at the heart of organizational diversity work. Finally, recent theory and research on boundaries clarifies not only how they can be manipulated to institutionalize exclusion and inequity but also how boundary change may lead to more expansive notions of excellence and belonging.[12]

The same mechanisms that change symbolic boundaries may therefore also function as mechanisms affecting access and inclusion. Tilly developed a typology of processes that precede boundary change (e.g., encounter, imposition, borrowing, conversation, incentive shift) as well as mechanisms that constitute changing boundaries: inscription-erasure, activation-deactivation, site transfer, and relocation.[13] *Inscription* describes how relations on either side of a salient boundary can become more sharply differentiated; *erasure* occurs when differentiation is weakened or reversed. Next, *activation* highlights how context primes some identities and associated boundaries to be more salient than others, whereas *deactivation* occurs as a particular boundary loses salience. As an example, Tilly noted how when writing, the boundary between his disciplinary identity and other disciplines was activated, and how his roles as teacher and father faded into the background. Under *site transfer*, the third boundary-change mechanism, the existence of a boundary does not change but actors' positioning relative to the boundary does. Examples of site transfer include racial passing and religious conversion, in which one moves across categorical racial or religious boundaries. Last, *relocation* combines two of the previously named mechanisms, resulting in alterations to "the major boundaries that are organizing action and interaction."[14] As outlined in the following sections, this typology provided a useful framework for understanding organizational access and inclusion efforts as boundary work.

The University of Michigan Applied Physics Program

The University of Michigan's applied physics program has a record that is unusually successful by the standards of the discipline in its record of training

Black PhDs. By the program's own reports, about 10 percent of the Black PhDs in physics nationally for the previous decade have come through this program. Its enrollment and graduation record with women and students of color is especially notable given its location in a state with an affirmative action ban. In 2011, 33 percent of the program's PhDs awarded went to students who identify as Black, Latinx, and/or Native American versus a national average in physics of just 5 percent for these populations. In addition, 33 percent of those who enrolled and graduated were women, double the national average of 16 percent in physics. It also received formal White House recognition under President Obama for excellence in STEM mentoring.

As with the chemistry and psychology departments described in Chapter 4, we set out to identify in applied physics the efforts and organizational conditions to which faculty, staff, and student members attributed their record of enrolling and graduating Black and Latinx PhDs. In this case, knowing they were intent on creating an environment that would be different from a typical physics department, we also sought to define in specific terms how they sought to distinguish their program.

The AP program enrolls about eighty doctoral students and boasts a 77 percent PhD completion rate, far exceeding the national average for both physics and engineering. To date, fifty-three Black, Latinx, or Native American students have entered the program. Of these, twenty-three graduated with a PhD, twenty were enrolled at the time of the research, seven graduated with a master's degree as part of a program described below, and three left without a degree. The average time to degree for students of color in this program (5.8 years) is shorter than the national average in physics.[15] So successful has the program been on multiple outcomes that several institutions have replicated its model.

Physicist and professor Roy Clarke founded the AP program in the 1980s to push back against qualities of physics' disciplinary culture and that of the institutional culture at Michigan. He was struck by the lack of support for students pursuing innovative research outside the traditional disciplinary core, for example, and by a university culture that he described as "remote" and "uncaring." Roy envisioned an interdisciplinary program to correct these conditions and their potential effects on students' access, persistence, and satisfaction. He wanted to offer a "small community within a big community," encourage collaboration, and emphasize "intellectual and social diversity."[16] More fundamentally, he wanted to "knock down the walls" between disciplines, departments, and people—which he hypothesized were a source of continuing racial and gender inequities in physical sciences. He might not have used the language of boundary work to describe these efforts, but it was nonetheless the work he sought to carry out.

Social, financial, and organizational factors converged to enable the program's establishment in the late 1980s. A state grant provided seed money, and the university president at the time, James Duderstadt, was an applied physicist himself. He saw the creation of an AP program as a strategic opportunity to bridge the geographically and intellectually separate Central (liberal arts) and North (engineering) campuses, and to build support in STEM for the Michigan Mandate. Sparked by student protests, the Michigan Mandate is acknowledged as "one of the most comprehensive diversity initiatives ever undertaken by a predominantly White research university."[17] It resulted in the University of Michigan doubling its minority student enrollment over fifteen years and significantly increasing the number of faculty of color.[18] The initiative also encouraged interdisciplinarity and an agenda linking academic excellence and racial diversity—both of which gave the nascent AP program some legitimacy. In time, the AP program also established a master's-PhD bridge program in cooperation with the American Physical Society. It procured federal grant support for that program, saw its students win NSF fellowships, and garnered accolades for its diversity work.

Considering the relevant forces for change, the Michigan Mandate was a force for top-down bureaucratization of diversity throughout the university, while establishment of AP in association with that bureaucratization can be thought of as successful case of bottom-up institutionalization of Clarke's visionary leadership. Strong institutional support, along with state and federal funds, provided necessary resources for the top-down actions required to build diversity into a major public research university's bureaucracy. At the same time, the Michigan Mandate's framing of academic excellence in relation to diversity (as opposed to presenting them as competing values) helped build a culture that supported the program's mission. In addition to these top-down and bottom-up forces, the department engaged in four areas of inside-out effort—critically analyzing typical norms about "how things work" in physics and mindfully designing with a more expansive, inclusive vision. Let's consider each of these four areas, which include the program's intellectual paradigm, its conceptualization of merit and means of assessing it in admissions, its empowerment of staff as cultural translators, and the interpersonal relationships it cultivated.

A Flexible, Interdisciplinary Intellectual Paradigm

Two features of the intellectual paradigm distinguished AP from a traditional physics PhD program and helped the program attract underrepresented students: an emphasis on cross-disciplinary collaborations and application of physics knowledge to real-world problems. Program founders defined working across disciplinary boundaries as normal and expected—and they modeled it in their own scholarship. Practically, they developed connections with units throughout campus, including engineering, environmental science, medicine, social work, and more. A prior director recalled how AP's development as a field of study also pushed other disciplines' boundaries, with engineers routinely using quantum mechanics, for example. At the university, they found that transcending the usual disciplinary boundaries that separate physics forged collaborations, transformed scientific practices, led to significant inventions, and reshaped doctoral students' experience.

Program founders also observed that, structurally, departments' tendency to operate as intellectual and organizational silos tended to impede collaboration. Therefore, when establishing the program, founders opted for a "loose programmatic structure rather than formal departmental status." They developed flexible curricular requirements that enable students to develop an individualized course of learning with 130 faculty in over a dozen departments. In one faculty member's words, AP drew students in by giving them "wider options" and "a flexible means of exploring and expanding core knowledge" of physics. It was unconventional by design.

Third, whereas physicists' communication and scientific practices traditionally place high value on the production of theory,[19] AP faculty emphasized possibilities for enhancing the public good through application of physical knowledge. Across the country, AP as a field links physics, knowledge from other fields, and real-world problems. As a former program director put it, "The great power of physics is it can be used to solve problems, to develop new technologies, to understand complicated interactions." Founders saw the program as a site of "connections between physics and other places where physics is used," and felt that this structure enabled students to develop with "more freedom."

Faculty, staff, and students alike attributed the program's ability to attract women and students of color in part to this intellectual paradigm. The "flexibility and individualization" afforded by the program's interdisciplinary orientation was described as "a big selling point" for female, Black, and Latinx students. Faculty shared a common refrain they heard from prospective students: "I want to make a difference in the world. I want to be able to find a job. I don't want to go into theoretical physics because it is too disconnected from the real world." Making it easy for students to fulfill their "desire to help with societal problems" also made it "much easier to recruit minorities." These findings are consistent with recent evidence in the sociology of science that suggests one way scientists may advocate for emerging interdisciplinary intellectual fields is by framing monodisciplinary work as insular.[20] As the program institutionalized this intellectual paradigm as their normal, it came to affect both whom they attracted and whom they admitted.

Rethinking the "Best Students" and Reinventing Admissions

As cohorts of students progressed through AP, faculty and other leaders observed a record of success among students whose profiles differed markedly from the conventional achievers privileged in graduate admissions. Recognition that the odds of success do not depend on the possession of a single set of characteristics was powerful in helping broaden faculty members' conception of the "ideal" applicant's profile. Yet from the beginning, program faculty insisted they had employed "more flexible admissions criteria than comparable physics departments." Staff corroborated faculty claims, noting admissions committees "downplayed the standardized tests" and "jettisoned the physics GRE." Instead, they closely "looked at the transcripts and . . . the research experience of students," as well as their fit with the program's multidisciplinary focus. A director explained:

> We brought in the best students we could find. Now these are not like the typical definition of the best student that . . . did their undergrad degree in Harvard or Princeton or Yale, and they had a 4.0 or 3.99 GPA, and they had GRE scores up the wazoo. That wasn't kind of what we were after. We were after people who would be willing to take a big risk. They hadn't necessarily got the best grades because people who take risks when they're undergrads

very often don't have stellar GPAs. They're usually very solid, but they may have taken a really difficult course because they wanted to learn about that topic, but then they only got a B-plus instead of an A. So we wanted to look for those kinds of people who were intellectually adventurous, were willing to learn about other disciplines, and willing to integrate themselves.

Redefining "the best students" as those who are "intellectually adventurous" was one part of a broader process of inside-out change: it involved clear understanding of the program's distinctive identity and the students who might help them embody that identity, willingness to question the value attributed to traditional credentials, and open-mindedness about reasons capable students may not receive top grades.

Recruiting the Intellectually Adventurous

In building cohorts of intellectually adventurous students, program leaders have worked hard to build and sustain a critical mass who identify as women, Black, and Latinx, both for "social justice reasons" and "the health of the field," given their emphasis on developing innovative technologies. They have also revisited their multifaceted recruitment plan every year. Especially since the passage of Proposal 2—Michigan's ban on affirmative action—their recruitment plan has included cultivating relationships with affinity groups in physical sciences and engineering (e.g., National Society of Black Engineers, National Society of Hispanic Physicists) and traveling to minority-serving institutions (MSIs). The program director developed a tradition of visiting at least one new MSI each fall to catalyze outreach and another MSI with which AP had an established connection.

Bridge Program

Within the past ten years, program leaders made visible a commitment to reinventing doctoral admissions by establishing a research-based master's-to-PhD bridge program for underrepresented students. Inspired by the Fisk-Vanderbilt bridge program (Chapter 6) and financially supported in its early years through the American Physical Society (APS), admitted students join a master's degree cohort and, over one year, receive financial support, research experience, credit-bearing courses, and mentoring. These activities are intended to build what one professor called students' "scientific foundation," recognizing that some applicants with strong potential may benefit from time to focus their interest or build academic preparation before embarking on the

PhD. Although a few students and program-affiliated faculty murmured to us that the bridge program runs the risk of creating a "second-class citizenry," both leaders and student participants alike remain firmly persuaded of the bridge program's net benefits.

Within the PhD program, program leaders contrasted their approach to holistically reviewing and supporting students with the "stylized combat" typical in physics.[21] Roy reflected: "We made it clear that people who come here succeed. So it is not hand-to-hand combat. The weeder system is where you look to your right and to your left; one of you is going to be gone. That was not us. We've always had very high success rates." Each professor expressed, in some way, that AP's unusual success enrolling women and students of color was tied to both purposeful reevaluation of "the best students" and focused investment in recruiting students who might grow to reflect their ideal.

Empowering Administrative Staff as Cultural Translators

The story of AP would be incomplete without discussing the unconventional work of their administrative support staff. Administrative staff typically have limited authority in academic departments and are often invisible in research on higher education. However, staff members in this program played instrumental roles as translators between students and faculty. In this role, they were also agents of faculty learning and student support in serving a racially diverse population of students.

For depth, I discuss Joe, whom every single participant mentioned as important to the program's success with underrepresented students. Joe is a gregarious Black man, a first-generation graduate of the University of Michigan, and was a popular local DJ at the time of our research. When he was hired as a full-time program assistant after working with the program in a work-study capacity, he was younger than most of the program's students. As he put it, "You know I was in my early twenties. I was like everybody else. I had the chains. I had the big earring. . . . I was wearing jeans and a T-shirt." Although Joe assumed that he should change his dress for this full-time position, Roy was adamant that he be himself. Joe said that Roy's first instructions to him were : "I don't want anything about you to change. You stay who you are. That's why I want you in this position." Recognizing the cultural gap between most professors and the Black and Latinx students they wanted to better serve, department leaders explicitly encouraged him to speak freely about what he felt was needed to bridge the gap. And indeed, that's just how it worked out, although as I discuss, this expectation required Joe to take on emotional labor that was not part of his job description and for which he was not compensated.

Joe also recalled that Roy had a "vision" for his role that stemmed from the almost-effortless way he connected with students of different backgrounds. Such comments may sound as though hiring Joe was part of a calculated strategy for increasing student diversity, and it was true that Roy and his colleagues recognized the overwhelming whiteness of the scientific community as a serious barrier to recruitment. They knew the faculty did not yet represent the diversity they sought, that as a program (versus a department) they would not have control over faculty hiring, and that they wanted to create a climate in which students from underrepresented backgrounds felt they belonged. Roy saw in Joe an opportunity to introduce youth and Blackness into the culture of the department—indeed, Joe was the first person with whom visitors entering the program suite would interact. Hiring staff who embodied some facets of the diversity they sought was a calculated move.

Formally, Joe's job was to provide administrative support and record keeping for admissions and recruitment, but from his work-study position, program leaders knew his "way with students," so they gave him responsibilities and influence exceeding that of his position. Shortly after transitioning to his full-time role, he began traveling with the director to MSIs for recruitment visits and providing informal support to enrolled students. Joe became a go-to person for both faculty and students, serving as an intermediary who helped members of these groups understand one another. One professor said of him:

> There are many things students will not tell the director . . . because you don't want to tell the director, "I'm not doing well in this school." . . . But Joe was the eyes and ears of the program; he was the contact with *all* students. He will be able to tell you aspects of the program that no one else will be able to tell you.

As the program's "eyes and ears," he informally monitored students, particularly those whose behavior or academic performance fluctuated. The trust he engendered, his passion for nurturing community, combined with his ease working across race and professional role boundaries enabled Joe to serve as a cultural translator.

Joe's perspective as a Black man at the university enabled him to shift how the program director at the time interpreted various Black students' engagement with faculty. In one case, Joe advised him that this was a student who would not proactively ask for help, saying: "You don't understand. This is not how an African American male would act. He would just never do it." For these reasons, the director specifically highlighted the value of Joe's cultural knowledge and his willingness to translate it for him, describing him as a "boundary spanner" and "my pipeline to the students and particularly African American students."

Joe also volunteered that students would occasionally come to him, upset about difficult patterns of interaction with faculty outside the AP core. He shared with us how he approached the program director in these situations:

> I had some real heart-to-hearts with Professor Cagliyan in the first year. . . . He didn't quite understand. I would just go in his office and close the door and talk to him. I would tell him, "You know as much as I know that you care about students. But I don't quite think you're getting it." . . . And at the end of the day he would tell me, "Thank you."

For better or worse, I could fill pages with student testimonials of Joe's advocacy. Students trusted him as "really serious about having your back" and providing support for "serious departmental political-type problems."

It is worth pausing here to ask why cultural translation is necessary. Decades of research indicate that it is not uncommon for white faculty to hold different expectations from doctoral students of color about what constitutes good mentoring and student performance, especially surrounding notions of rigor and support.[22] These expectations are just one of many areas in science and graduate education where symbolic and social boundaries meeting can generate misunderstanding and friction. In Chapter 4, we saw that even in numerically diverse departments, students may read the climate very differently than faculty do. Until the academic community institutionalizes a shared belief that "good science" involves awareness of the ways that subject matter and social dynamics are entangled, those at the core of the academic community need cultural translators: people who make plain the social dynamics that are hiding in plain sight, who are empowered to speak up when issues arise, and who advocate and provide support to students whose professors do not fully appreciate how race, gender, identity, or power may be operating.

In this department, a growing share of the student population entered doctoral education with different norms than those to which the faculty were themselves socialized. Cultural translation by Joe, another administrative staff member Wendy, and selected faculty of color equipped white faculty to better mentor Black students. Although in the long run it would be ideal for all members of scientific communities to have sufficient consciousness of social issues, the importance of work that helps faculty "get it" with respect to advising across race, gender, and other social identities cannot be overstated in departments that are striving for diversity and equity. It can mean the difference between a student dropping out, barely making it through, and thriving.

There are complexities here that have to be acknowledged. Joe was emphatic that the program cared about creating an inclusive environment, commenting, "They didn't just talk the talk; they walked the walk." Yet he also noted that creating and maintaining a fully inclusive environment did not always come naturally for program leaders, and that some students needed advocacy or support specifically because faculty failed to provide it. Relatedly, it bears noting that like other examples of cultural brokering that scholars have studied, Joe's efforts were a form of emotional labor carried out without financial reward, by a worker of modest positional authority within the organization. At the same time, the work was incredibly meaningful to Joe. He valued this part of his role so much so that when we asked him to describe a highlight of his experience with the program, he relayed a story of successfully advocating with faculty to retain a student who had failed his qualifying exam. Involvement in high-stakes situations like this and in governance issues highlights his credibility and how we might reconsider the leadership that administrative staff are empowered to hold.[23] However, it also raises critical questions about the justice of asking anyone—especially individuals from historically marginalized or professionally subordinate groups—to take on responsibilities beyond their role without commensurate rewards or positional authority.

When Roy and the AP program received an award from the Obama administration for their commitment to diversity and mentoring, however, Joe was the colleague whom Roy invited to join him at the White House. In an emotional moment of our interview, Joe shared: "I can't even tell you what that felt like. . . . I guess that goes to show you how much I meant to him and the program." President Obama's recognition was a point of pride for everyone in the program, and a large framed photo and certificate marking the event hung in the main office, directly above Joe's desk.

Rethinking Relationships to Attract and Support Diverse Students

A fourth area in which AP tried to distinguish itself was in creating a community that differed markedly from the "remote" and "uncaring" relationships that the program founder perceived in physics. The program director, when asked what he does to encourage underrepresented students' success, said, "Maybe more than *any*thing else from the founding of the program, we tried to institute an atmosphere which was what I call 'like a family.'" My research team and I were initially skeptical about how "the family" played out in reality. Was this just a cliché? Over our year with the program, however, we saw over and over again how staff, core faculty, and students worked to make the family metaphor a lived experience. Nearly every single student mentioned the "family" as important to their educational experience, and we observed program administrators at all levels going above and beyond what was expected or necessary, driving three hours to attend a parent's funeral, for example, standing up in student weddings, and hosting dinners for women in the department to build a sense of community in a predominantly male field.

Program staff and core faculty strategically used the family metaphor with prospective students because they knew it would call to mind closeness and intimacy that would give them a "competitive advantage" over other PhD programs. All but one of our focus-group participants indicated that the family-like climate was central to the program's recruitment narrative and their own decisions to enroll. William noticed it right away: "The thing I noticed the most was that it was a much warmer environment than other schools that I had applied to. . . . When you come in, the administrators say, 'Welcome to the family.' And it seems like they've said that years and years in a row." Emma and Jamal also recounted their campus visits:

EMMA: The day I visited, they kept saying things like, "Applied Physics is like a family." I didn't know what that meant, but I heard it a lot. . . . And I didn't know about the diversity when I applied.

JAMAL: Everyone I talked to in the program kept saying, "It is a family." . . . And it was a smaller group, and I felt I would be supported and cared for well.

Describing the program's climate, students added such language as "comfortable," "supportive," and "cohesive."

A focus group facilitator probed participants to describe "an experience that made you feel this really is a family . . . [that] it is not just a tagline." Brad recalled his campus visit, which had been set up separately from the usual campus visit day. That faculty and staff went above and beyond typical roles and work hours to ensure he had a positive visit "was the experience for me that was like, 'These guys put their money where their mouth is.'" Emma reported a similarly positive campus visit, and Robert added: "The first time I'd actually spoken to anyone from the university was Wendy. When I talked to her I was like, 'This is the place.'" The roles that students attributed to Wendy and Joe—"mother figure" and "big brother"—reflected the program's desire for family-like relationships. "Wendy and the others work wonders over there," as one student put it. Joe commented that together, he and Wendy "tried to do a lot to foster a place where they [students] really are comfortable."

That the quality of key academic relationships affects student belonging and well-being is hardly a surprise, but this program's collective, conscious attention to relationships must not be overlooked. Many STEM graduate programs find themselves stuck in a negative feedback loop, in which poor representation of women and students of color raises red flags for prospective students about departmental climate and the quality of day-to-day life. It can deter those students from matriculating, which perpetuates the feelings of isolation and tokenism that those who are enrolled may experience. AP has interrupted this cycle by talking openly and honestly about their field's problems—and those within the program. Students shared that it was a major draw to discover the diverse, warm relationships that so many in the program tried to encourage. Perhaps the strongest evidence of student satisfaction, though, was their pride in playing a recruiting role themselves, welcoming prospective students into "the family."

Equity Efforts as Boundary Work

What does the AP program's story teach us about equity in science and about how we can encourage it through boundary work within scientific communities? Tilly's mechanisms of boundary change—erasure-inscription, activation-deactivation, site transfer, and relocation—are instructive here.[24] They illustrate how efforts to improve Black and Latinx students' access to and inclusion in physics graduate education involved basic alterations to traditional intellectual, organizational, social, and professional boundaries in the field. Consistent with the notion of designing for inclusion, this interpretation also makes clear that such boundaries are subtle "products of action" that can be manipulated and managed to achieve particular ends.[25]

Manipulating Disciplinary Boundaries
The AP program's interdisciplinary, applied intellectual identity served as a backbone to many other facets of community life and educational program design. They deferred to their intellectual paradigm in making decisions, and it provided flexibility for faculty and students to pursue innovative research. Their interdisciplinarity represented the partial erasure of a cultural boundary that separates physics from other disciplines.[26] Professors prided themselves on collaborations through which students could appreciate the relevance of physics knowledge outside the discipline. And yet by blurring the cultural boundary with other fields and acknowledging how real-world problems compel interdisciplinary entanglement that requires knowledge and expertise throughout campus, faculty inscribed a distinction between applied and traditional physics. They repeatedly emphasized to prospective students the incredible potential of physical knowledge to solve real world problems, particularly through cross-disciplinary collaborations, relative to a vision of physics that privileged theory alone.

Efforts to recruit underrepresented students were relevant to both of these boundaries. When underrepresented students described commitments to "making a difference," finding employment, and staying connected to the real world, it resonated strongly with both the weaker boundaries between physics and other disciplines and the real distinction between applied physics and traditional physics. Their sentiment deactivated, or made less salient, the physics-other boundary, because interdisciplinarity provided grounds for exploring how physics might fit into their vision for social change. Simultaneously, however, students' sentiment activated the applied-traditional boundary by casting traditional physicists' focus on theory as disconnected from real-world problems.

Manipulating Organizational Boundaries by Rethinking Merit
The mental models that faculty members hold about their fields of study, what it takes to succeed in those fields, how much support they are willing to provide, and about merit more broadly inform gatekeeping activities like admissions and hiring.[27] Such practices are ipso facto forms of organizational

boundary work, and the evaluations made in the interests of determining membership reveal symbolic boundaries about what it means to be desirable, capable, intelligent—to belong. Often such evaluations force leaders to ask normative questions: On what grounds should one have an opportunity to be allowed in? What signals define a prospective member as a "good fit"?

AP worked assiduously to counter prevailing assumptions about merit that undercut the admission of students from underrepresented backgrounds. Admission to most physics doctoral programs depends on deep training in the discipline and quantitative methods used to bring about theoretical advancements. Under that model, extremely high GRE scores are interpreted as a sign that students' quantitative skills extend beyond those covered by the test. In contrast, AP's flexible intellectual paradigm, paired with its strong commitment to building social diversity in physics, motivated program advocates to redefine who "the best students" are.

In defining their own vision of the ideal student, applied physicists deactivated the boundary that implicitly separated those scoring in the top percentiles of the GRE physics and quantitative sections from everyone else. Program leaders marshaled evidence from the literature and their own students' performance that test scores could not predict who might grow to become a successful scholar. At the same time, by examining transcripts and records of research experience, faculty inscribed a boundary separating applicants who were conventionally "risk averse" from those deemed "intellectually adventurous." These two processes—deactivating the distinction between those who earn very high GRE scores versus everyone else, and inscribing a boundary between the intellectually adventurous and risk-averse—relocated the boundaries on what should count as merit for admission.

Manipulating the Boundaries of Program Roles and Relationships

Consideration of boundaries enables a closer analysis of how we define people as similar and different to ourselves and one another—and how we judge who should be deemed of higher and lower status. "Hidden assumptions concerning the measuring sticks used by higher and lower status groups" are especially useful for understanding the prospects of cultural change in organizations.[28] For departments and disciplines striving to become more inclusive, a new type of status seems to be emerging—that of the boundary spanner who possesses the knowledge and savviness to serve as a cultural translator. So it was in the AP program, with its highly influential administrative staff. Whereas the norm in academia may be for students and administrative support staff to have subordinated status and minimal influence, they were critical players in the AP program. With traditional boundaries in place, we would expect significant cultural distance between Joe, the faculty, and program directors. Instead, directors strove to minimize the hierarchy implied by their official roles, encouraging shared leadership and admitting they had learned much from Joe about how to better serve students.

The activation of a racial boundary was most explicit in our data in Joe's role as a cultural translator and advocate for Black students. When a former director commented that Joe was the "eyes and ears" of the program and "my pipeline to ... African American students," he was evocatively conveying Joe's ability to connect across both the racial and role boundaries that often separated faculty and students. Graduate programs striving to diversify would no doubt benefit from having someone who serves the role of cultural translator, but they should also work toward an organizational culture in which all faculty possess skill and commitment to support students from diverse backgrounds.

Finally, weakening the typical role-based hierarchy opened the possibility of warm, family-like relationships that set the program apart from other physics departments. The supportive environment and trust fostered through "the family" allowed faculty, staff, and student relationships to break down fronts and interact as human beings.[29] As "mother" and "big brother," Wendy and Joe created a community of support that extended well beyond typical staff-student relationships, emphasizing dimensions of their identities to create this community. Wendy stressed her shared gender identity with female students through "girls' night out" and similar activities; Joe emphasized a shared identity with students as a Michigan alum and his shared racial identity with Black students. Both effectively deactivated the staff-student boundary to connect in a way that students discussed as integral to their well-being and success.

"Herding Cats"

Searching for evidence that contradicts prevailing themes—that is, what social scientists call disconfirming evidence—turned up challenges that AP's leaders have faced as they strive to select and serve students of color. The constraint on affirmative action in admissions that comes with Proposal 2 prevented them from recruiting underrepresented students using the generous funding packages they know other institutions offer. A few students also shared with us that, despite the warm relationships in AP, the racial climate outside the comfort of the AP family can be difficult. And consistent with other research on graduate education, some students mentioned that they wanted opportunities for more honest conversation about the realities of race in science.

The data also raise lingering questions about institutional change. Although AP has been successful in catalyzing change in faculty assumptions and routines in some parts of the university's STEM community, they have struggled to diffuse the view that intellectual adventurousness—not conventional achievement and affiliation with elite universities—is really what characterizes great graduate students. Founders had hoped that by operating as an interdepartmental program rather than a free-standing department that their values would more easily seep across the boundaries of the departments with which its faculty associate. Organizational theory that describes universities as loosely coupled systems supports this logic. Karl Weick observed that weak intraorganizational ties across units produce a tendency toward stasis, but that change can occur as influential individuals—for example, the AP program's core faculty—working at the interface of multiple networks press colleagues in one network to learn from the culture of another.[30]

A program director admitted that it has been difficult for core AP faculty to galvanize support among the program's 130 total faculty affiliates—in part because not everyone is as comfortable practicing critical reflection or discussing race openly. Comparing the challenge of building faculty consensus to "herding cats," a program director noted that the program structure limited his ability to shape faculty hiring, which restricted his ability to fully bring about the sort of learning community and student experience he envisioned. What he aspired to offer was a community in which students could be matched with faculty mentors from similar racial and gender backgrounds, and in which open conversations about gendered and racialized aspects of academic life would be routine. Although it may be impossible for any leader to prevent all negative faculty-student interactions, any student reports of feeling "like a second-class citizen" in a program that prides itself on equitably serving diverse students indicates room for growth. Effort and capacity to "herd cats" will undoubtedly shape the potential of the program to expand its influence.

In the meantime, the program's impressive enrollment and completion statistics have generated national attention, with its directors recognized figures in the national movement for diversity in physics. Cagliyan, for example, was a panelist on the topic of sustaining institutional change at a 2015 American Physics Society meeting, and a physics magazine recently wrote a long profile about Roy's contributions. With other well-regarded graduate programs in the physical sciences having adopted the AP model, program leaders find themselves confronting a new kind of competition in attracting prospective students.

Cultural Translation and Changing Boundaries

The findings about administrative staff members' critical work of cultural translation suggest that translation may represent an additional boundary change process not articulated in Tilly's framework. Joe's role as cultural translator for Black students and mostly white faculty was prompted by honest conversations with both faculty and students in which he came to know students' everyday struggles and then gently brought them to the attention of faculty. Through these interactions, he activated race as a social boundary by naming it as salient in situations where faculty had not recognized it as such. By explaining cultural norms with which faculty were unfamiliar, Joe provided access to actionable information about Black students' educational experiences. This knowledge altered subsequent faculty-student interactions, partially deactivating the role of race as a factor affecting engagement across the faculty-student boundary. Ironically, it was only through his willingness to be explicit with colleagues about race being a line of social difference across which misunderstanding is possible and then translating cultural norms about Blackness and whiteness to people on either side of that line that Joe helped weaken racial difference as a barrier to student learning and belonging.[31]

Critically for the relevance of cultural translation in other diverse educational settings, we found that the process of translation and faculty learning hinged upon the ability to have honest conversations. These conversations reflected and cultivated trust between Joe and students and between Joe and faculty. His doing so evokes Carter's landmark study of diverse classrooms, in which "cultural straddlers" employed a variety of cultural practices and skills to "broker the boundaries among multiple cultural environments."[32]

Joe, as a cultural straddler himself, likely possessed an ability to broker tradi-tional boundaries by using conversation to translate students' cultural codes for faculty.

How Can Educators Design for Inclusion?

A practical way of looking at what the applied physics program did to de-sign for inclusion—and considering the relevance of those decisions in other educational environments—is to compare the details of its efforts against the seven principles of Universal Design: equitable use, flexibility in use, simple and intuitive use, perceptible information, tolerance for error, low physical effort, and size and space for approach and use. In 1997, Ronald Mace led a working group of engineers, architects, and designers to identify principles that can guide the design process, evaluate existing designs, and educate de-signers and consumers about what characterizes inclusive environments and products. Although developed with an eye to improving access for people with disabilities, this framework is intentionally transferable for practitioners designing for other types of inclusion as well. Addressing the same rigidity, complexity, and opacity that present physical barriers can also be applied to policy and practice to improve the overall accessibility and inclusiveness of organizations. Here, I use examples from the AP program to outline the reso-nance of several universal design principles for organizing PhD programs as inclusive learning environments.

Equitable Use

The principle of equitable use ensures that a product or organizational design accommodates a range of abilities, defined as present preparation or profi-ciency in skills, irrespective of aptitude to learn. For example, given the ineq-uities in our educational system, designing an introductory PhD curriculum to rigidly require courses with extremely high levels of prerequisite learning would violate the principle of equitable use. In contrast, creating a curricular structure in which students may enter with a broader range of prior prepara-tion, including from related majors, and still complete degree requirements in a reasonable amount of time is more aligned with the principle of equitable use. Another guideline of equitable use advises designers not to stigmatize or segregate users. In the case of applied physics, the bridge program was an auxiliary mechanism for accessing graduate education that allowed some students to take additional classes and obtain research experience. But to avoid the risk of their stigmatization, bridge students were integrated into the same day-to-day courses, office spaces, and research labs as students who had been admitted through traditional means.

Flexibility in Use

To accommodate a wider range of preferences and abilities, flexibility in use makes options available to users and enables adaptability with the pace consumers engage with an environment or product. AP was proud of the individualized courses of learning that students and their advisors designed to meet their specific goals. The program was also proud of its flexibility in what counted as required curriculum. These forms of flexibility both enabled the program to admit students who might need a bit of additional preparation in a core area or—as most did—who wished to substantively engage with other departments as they explored the application of physics knowledge to real world problems. And, as mentioned earlier, the bridge program's separate funding stream enabled flexibility that allowed admissions decision makers to take seriously a small group of students each year with exceptional potential but who might require an additional year of coursework.

Simple and Intuitive Use and Perceptible Information

The final two principles I discuss here both reduce the complexity of design so that something is more approachable and user-friendly. Against the backdrop of a hidden curriculum in graduate school that often requires students to have or quickly develop sophisticated social and cultural capital to navigate the PhD process,[33] programs can design for inclusion by clearly communicating critical information—both upon entry and on a regular basis. They can be consistent with expectations and provide prompt feedback following key tasks. Indeed, the importance of mentors and students regularly checking in to ensure steady progress—which AP considered a cornerstone of the bridge program experience—has emerged as one of the most important characteristics of high-quality doctoral education for all students.

For many graduate programs, applying these and other principles will be a matter of revamping current systems, which will compel the need to assess and change existing processes, official policies, and everyday practices. In special cases, however, faculty may be in a position to design a graduate program for inclusion from the ground up, as did applied physics. In both cases, the process should itself embody the inclusiveness that leaders strive to create in their programs: leaders and stakeholders should represent the types of communities whom they wish to better include, status distinctions should be minimized to the greatest extent possible, labor and resources should be equitably distributed, and trust should be cultivated to facilitate healthier working relationships.

Noticing Symbolic Boundaries in Our Midst

I visited the universities of Oxford and Cambridge for the first time shortly after interviewing Roy Clarke and hearing him discuss the vision of "knock[ing] down the walls" that had emerged from medieval structures in academe and that have historically excluded women, Black, Latinx, and Native American students. I saw for myself medieval and Gothic architectural and landscape designs still intact that present a fortress as much as a campus to an American visitor's eye. In addition to the physical barriers posed by gates at seemingly every turn, and ivy- and moss-covered walls in various states of crumbling and stability, I learned at Oxford and Cambridge about some of the medieval customs that survive to this day as symbols of varying degrees of inclusion in these universities' cultures. In those universities, for example, only tenured faculty members of a particular college are allowed to cross the line separating gravel paths from carefully manicured lawns. Indeed, in places with long-standing histories, there can be a fine line between tradition and exclusion that must be acknowledged in our equity efforts.

Hidden in plain sight within American academia, too, are a host of symbolic boundaries created in traditions that have become routine. We create boundaries through the knowledge and student qualities deemed valuable through our admissions practices, through ways we construct the roles and status of community members in allocating responsibilities and rewards, and through the nature of their relationships with one another through everyday interactions. Founding the applied physics program may for Roy Clarke have been a project of knocking down the walls in physics at its most advanced levels. However, applied physics' history demonstrates that that designing an organization to support inclusion—and then enacting that design—is not a onetime event but an ongoing learning process.

6 Advocacy and Management in Astronomy and Physics

I N THE PREVIOUS CHAPTER, WE OBSERVED HOW LEADERS OF AN APPLIED physics PhD program designed for a more racially inclusive culture of excellence by defining key program qualities more expansively than those of a traditional graduate education in its parent discipline, physics. Following the insights that a singular STEM label belies variation in departmental and disciplinary cultures, and that those cultures matter much for the definition and implementation of equity efforts, I now take the level of analysis up from departmental diversity and inclusion efforts to that of disciplinary societies. I examine resources and barriers to these efforts within the American Physical Society (APS) and American Astronomical Society (AAS). Physics and astronomy are two fields that, though adjacent to the point of overlapping in many universities, have distinctive qualities that manifest in how their societies have sought seek diversity, equity, and inclusion at a field level, especially in graduate education. The comparison is also useful in highlighting the need for distributed leadership, given the potential and limits of change that comes about from the top down and the bottom up. As will become clear, the managerial culture of diversity and equity work by the American Physical Society comes with resources and constraints very different from those of the advocacy culture in the American Astronomical Society.

Disciplines are self-replicating knowledge communities, "groups of professors with exchangeable credentials collected in strong associations."[1] The American system of disciplines developed as an outgrowth of higher education's rapid expansion in the early twentieth century. The establishment and decentralization of new colleges and universities fueled rapid growth in faculty hiring and the desire for internal organization. Leaders sought a common credential by which expertise could be recognized, which institutionalized the PhD in specific subject areas as a prerequisite for faculty hiring. It became the "medium of exchange" among universities for scholars. Sociologist Andrew Abbott describes how the relative resilience of today's disciplinary system can be traced to its "dual institutionalization." Disciplines institutionalize the macrostructure of the academic labor market, on the one hand, through national meetings of professional societies and networks through which scholars move. On the other hand, they also institutionalize the microstructure of universities, insofar as lists of departments and disciplines are nearly one in the same. Abbott notes, "This duality means no university can challenge the disciplinary system as a whole without depriving its PhD graduates of their academic future."[2] Students strive to solidify their status in the labor market through educational credentials,[3] and even though they go on today to a broader range of positions than they did when the disciplinary system coalesced, faculty perpetuate the disciplinary system through academic hiring processes and the system of graduate education that produces candidates for that market.

Disciplines operate, however, as both knowledge markets and as knowledge communities. One of the most fundamental distinctions between and within disciplines pertains to the forms and foci of knowledge in which scholars practice their expertise. Kant distinguished pure from practical reason (practical in this case refers to action, not to utility), and over time, disciplinary communities have continued to subdivide along such lines, resulting in the persistence of those identified as pure disciplines and the steady growth of those thought of as applied. We have, in effect, a continually changing game board of knowledge and knowledge communities with predictable patterns of subdivision. Within the field often dubbed the queen of the sciences—physics—cohorts of graduate students may initially enroll together in entry-level courses, but via admissions processes have already begun sorting themselves as theoretically or experimentally focused—another example of the pure-applied distinction.[4] Concomitant to this intellectual specialization, physicists come to identify themselves as theorists or experimentalists. There are also within the physical sciences a number of disciplines—astronomy and astrophysics, geophysics, materials research—that broadly represent applications of physics. And within each of these fields, the theory-experiment divide repeats itself. In astronomy, we see the self-repeating pattern of pure-applied work manifest as theory-observation, with yet another subdivision within application: instrument development.[5] Disciplinary cultures also can be distinguished from one another in other important ways, including the conventional wisdom and practices by which they go about approaching equity and inclusion efforts.

Disciplinary Societies and the Potential for Isomorphic Equity

Graduate education has a dual organizational structure. It is organized by universities that award degrees, with schools or colleges hosting departments within which graduate programs that provide education and one's closest intellectual network. Graduate education is also organized by disciplines; fields of study are held together by disciplinary societies and professional associations with affiliate graduate programs, whose graduates are usually eligible for positions in that field. Disciplinary societies and professional associations are thus taking a growing interest in shaping the graduate education landscape. There is growing recognition that by what they choose to publish in their journals, and in the tone and content of conversations they encourage (or discourage) at major meetings and other communications channels, societies define and set disciplinary standards. Publications and convenings provide a context for people to come together from across affiliated departments to learn certain knowledge. Along the way, members observe and absorb certain behaviors and ways of thinking as fitting within the discipline—or not fitting. Likewise, that which early career scholars do not gain exposure to from a society may be come to be understood as outside the scope of what is acceptable. In this way, disciplinary societies are vehicles through which the hidden curriculum of academia is learned and fields' cultures are negotiated.

To date, though, disciplinary societies have been a largely underutilized lever for improving graduate education, perhaps because the levers for changing faculty behaviors and practices that affect graduate student training depend, to some degree, on awareness of what other graduate programs are doing—awareness that is currently lacking in this highly decentralized system. By bringing together scholars to interrogate and discuss field-level issues such as inequalities and the changing labor market for PhDs, however, there is growing recognition that disciplinary societies are well suited to convene discussions about current practices, to diffuse more innovative ones, and to coordinate agendas for change. In one of the few studies to examine the role of professional associations as arbiters of institutional change, Greenwood, Suddaby, and Hinings observed that they can also "legitimate change by hosting a process of discourse through which change is debated and endorsed."[6] Indeed, when controversies emerge at or around national meetings, it is usually a signal that some disciplinary boundary—whether related to subject matter or individual organizational members' behavior—is under debate.

There are other reasons to believe that disciplinary societies have untapped potential, especially for encouraging discipline-wide change toward more equitable graduate training. These reasons are suggested by the conditions under which organizations within a field tend to converge on new models, a phenomenon that DiMaggio and Powell dubbed *institutional isomorphism*.[7] They identified three such conditions.

Coercive isomorphism describes tendencies of people and organizations to conform to the expectations of high-status resource providers. Indeed, to varying degrees, disciplinary societies serve a soft regulation function that may be employed toward equity-minded objectives.[8] When the American Psychological Association determined that all PhD students in accredited clinical psychology programs must have training in serving diverse populations of clients, for example, programs in the field moved quickly to provide such learning opportunities. More recently, when the NSF and AGU recently articulated policies and expectations about sexual harassment and assault by people serving as principal investigators and faculty advisors, it was with the hope it would serve both preventative and enforcement functions.[9] Particularly in fields where scholars rely on a disciplinary society or other organization for resources (e.g., financially, reputationally), new organizational policy may encourage field-wide redirection toward more equitable behavior. A strength of coercive isomorphism is the ability to obtain field-wide, measurable outcomes; however, insofar as it comes about by changing the rules of a given game, there will always be risks of symbolic adoption and of manipulating the appearance of compliance.

Normative isomorphism is a second process by which organizations within a field may converge on new models. Professional socialization processes shape what whole new generations of members understand to be acceptable standards of practice and, thus, adopt as their own. On a day-to-day basis, graduate students not only absorb subject matter but also observe their advisors' and other mentors' typical work-life habits, research ethics, attitudes toward students and teaching, and much more. As I have suggested throughout the book, when graduate students encounter socially conscious conduct of science and witness inclusive or equitable practices during their graduate studies, the quiet socialization process of graduate school itself may hold potential as an intervention to create more equitable futures. Disciplinary societies have a role to play in this because, although PhDs are awarded by universities and their PhD programs, meetings of disciplinary societies are one of the few sites where program leaders regularly meet and have opportunities to exchange ideas and innovations. The convening and discourse-shaping power of professional associations should not be ignored as a means of institutionalizing new forms and norms.[10] Change that leads to the collective adoption of more equitable forms and norms, however, may be more likely in combination with the third mechanism, mimetic isomorphism.

Mimetic isomorphism captures the tendency of people and organizations to model their behavior on the most powerful within a field. When leading organizations adopt equity-minded practices, for example, mimetic isomorphism may foster a broader tendency to the same. One way that a disciplinary society can contribute to field-level change is by nudging or supporting change efforts by the most prominent members. Indeed, we see examples of this with respect to graduate admissions reform in physics and astronomy in some highly ranked doctoral programs. Elimination of GRE requirements for admission to Harvard's astronomy PhD program around the same time that the American Astronomical Society recommended removing such requirements induced other astronomy PhD programs around the country to the same. In physics, the American Physical Society was part of launching the Inclusive Graduate Education Network to stimulate more equitable admissions practice in six large, selective PhD programs. It recognized that if change could be achieved in these well-regarded programs, other PhD programs might follow suit. I describe both of these examples in greater detail in this chapter.

With these isomorphic mechanisms in mind, I explore more deeply the possibilities of change for equity in disciplinary cultures of physics and astronomy, through analysis and reflections about initiatives sponsored by disciplinary associations aimed at diversity, equity, or inclusion in graduate education.[11] I have been honored to be part of these efforts in roles that include research director, workshop facilitator, task force advisor, and conference attendee. Work is ongoing in three of the projects, which has permitted an opportunity to work within and across the physics-astronomy boundaries and to appreciate cultural variation in their equity work. In contrast to previous chapters in which I reported findings from specific studies, in this chapter I present pictures of these fields obtained while embedded in them as a social scientist. I engaged as an expert on equity in graduate education with colleagues via in-person and video-based meetings, workshops, and conferences while also taking copious notes when returning to my home, office, or when traveling for these meetings, other accommodations. In the classic typology for qualitative researchers of complete participant, participant as observer, observer as participant, and complete observer, I classify my involvement as that of a complete participant.

Physics and Astronomy: Disciplinary Entanglement

One could make a solid case that relationships between physics and astronomy represent both a case of disciplinary entanglement and a case of symbolic boundaries' power. Physicists and astronomers defer to the same scientific laws, often belong to the same departments, and astronomers in particular may swing in identifying with one, the other, or the hybrid affiliation of astrophysicist. Yet members of these communities also define themselves against one another, drawing symbolic boundaries and judging the other group to be inferior or themselves to be superior on particular dimensions. Despite their social similarities and intellectual dependencies, the organized equity efforts of their disciplinary societies have been independent until very recently.

Both recognize the size of the communities as a structural distinction, for example, and in formal and informal discussions alike displayed in-group preferences about the size of their own discipline. I heard physicists dismiss astronomy as numerically "small" and "too small" to be influential. Likewise, astronomers described physics as oversized—"a dinosaur of a discipline," in one person's words and "a behemoth" in another's. One Canadian astronomer I spoke with compared the populations and power dynamics between astronomy and physics to that of Canada and the United States.

They also note cultural and quasi-moral qualities of the scholars in their fields. Physicists take pride in the status of their field and its reputation for difficulty, usually choosing to identify with physics if their credential permits it over other adjacent, applied fields like astrophysics or materials science. I saw no evidence of such posturing in astronomy about its status. As one said: "Astronomers aren't as uptight about how difficult it is to do our work.

There's more of a sense of humility and humor than physicists have." Another quipped, "Yeah, we don't do lab experiments like they do, and yet we are trying to understand how the complicated universe works."

Astronomers also draw a symbolic boundary with physicists in their use of money. Charges that physicists are "cheap" or "stingy" arose repeatedly, albeit informally, in reference to the facilities and meals that physics professional societies provided for community meetings and their lack of compensation for service roles.[12] It bears noting, however, that at least one of the several societies in physics, the American Physical Society, has been revisiting its standard practice for compensating participation on national advisory boards and for such groups as its Committee on Minorities.

Whether the symbolic boundary pertains to size, status, difficulty of the work, financial shrewdness, or other qualities, the patterns are clear: disciplines operate with the same in-group and out-group biases of any social group and cultural distinctions with near disciplinary neighbors may emerge alongside the formal knowledge distinctions that motivated historic splits from a parent discipline. The boundaries can become tools. Group members use them to organize their work, reinforce identity, and provide a source of pride in one's work, community, and choices. Where the boundaries between disciplines are indistinct in terms of theories, training, funding, or other key resources, friendly competition between them can ensue.

The comparison of these two fields' efforts in this chapter therefore continues the thread of examining how symbolic boundaries shape scientists' work toward equity, diversity, and inclusion. Relational sociology asserts that groups and organizations are defined as much by as how they relate to others as by what goes on within them. I explored in the first several chapters how interactions and relationships among scientists within courses and within departments are defined, formed, and maintained. I argue in this chapter for the value of similarly examining interactions and relationships among scientific disciplines. Disciplinary societies' work on equity in graduate education provides a window into their past and present organizational cultures and the potential for the kind of change that might be expected going forward with respect to equity and inclusion.

Equity Work and Organizational Culture

Partnerships with and observations of one another across the disciplinary boundary help nudge both physics and astronomy forward in efforts to reduce inequities. Indeed, some of the most determined reforms to the structure of access to graduate education that I know of have come not from the social sciences but from these fields. Their disciplinary societies are actively involved in reconsidering the transition to graduate school, and they have each established successful programmatic efforts that create bridging opportunities between undergraduate and graduate education.[13] The cultures of these efforts are instructive in revealing the possibilities and limits of discipline-level movements for change.

The efforts of astronomy and physics to broaden participation reflect qualities of advocacy and managerial organizational cultures. An advocacy culture in astronomy is reflected in a decades-long, bottom-up movement toward equity and inclusion led by what a number of participants in my research have dubbed "faculty activists." This movement is supported by the primary professional association, the American Astronomical Society (AAS). Physics as a field has a more hierarchical culture (in part because of its very large size) and a number of societies; my focus is on efforts to shift the opportunity structure at the graduate level that are being pursued through projects led by the American Physical Society (APS). The positioning and power of faculty change agents relative to AAS and APS, respectively, also distinguishes the fields. In astronomy, faculty change agents direct efforts, with AAS staff playing a supporting role. In physics, faculty change agents are incorporated into disciplinary society efforts that are directed by staff who are not currently faculty members.

Managerial and advocacy are two cultural styles among six types of organizational culture that Bergquist and Pawlak frequently found in the higher-education system,[14] with the other four being collegial, developmental, virtual, and tangible. The managerial-advocacy distinction may help explain why two fields that are so related in many respects might engage so differently in equity and inclusion work. Table 1 outlines core cultural beliefs of each field, mapping them on to Bergquist and Pawlak's core cultural qualities. I introduce these cultural types, how their inherent relationship may reveal why astronomy and physics seem to interact in some ways as "frenemies," and then examine their limitations—why, on their own, the two fields are likely to continue struggling to meet long term goals if they do not broaden their cultural repertoire.

Managerial cultures in higher education have emerged through a combination of internal (i.e., endogenous) and external (i.e., exogenous) forces. The

TABLE 1. Comparing the cultural beliefs of physics and astronomy diversity efforts

Cultural beliefs	Physics	Astronomy
Core quality	*Managerial culture:* "A culture that finds meaning primarily in the organization, implementation, and evaluation of work that is directed toward specified goals and purposes; that values fiscal responsibility and effective supervisory skills; that holds assumptions about the capacity to . . . define and measure its goals and objectives clearly; and that conceives of the institution's expertise as the inculcation of specific knowledge, skills, and attitudes in students."	*Advocacy culture:* "A culture that finds meaning primarily in the establishment of equitable and egalitarian policies and procedures . . . ; that values confrontation and fair bargaining among constituencies . . . ; that holds assumptions about the ultimate role of power and the frequent need for outside mediation."
View of faculty	Governance processes and meetings that privilege collegiality are inefficient and a waste of time.	Faculty governance is critical; debates usually surround procedures for fair participation and respect for faculty judgment; conflicts between "old guard" and "young rebels" are common.
View of learning	Strong belief in a central, core curriculum that must be inculcated in all students, through a specific sequence and specific texts.	Learning is both a mechanism for advancing the discipline and for institutional change.
View of leadership	Shrewd supervision of money and people through bureaucratic management; "respect and work in a formal, hierarchical structure."	Leadership comes not only from positional authority but also from moral authority.
View of students	Professionalized students: "Efficient, competent learners. They have demonstrated a high level of achievement in specific knowledge, skills, and attitudes."	Students are community members, and thus their participation is a worthy focus of advocacy; they can also be allies in equity efforts when structures are established for their inclusion.

NOTE: Bergquist and Pawlak, 2008, p. 66, 68, 111.

growth in size and complexity of postsecondary organizations compels a need to coordinate activity at scale, whereas declining external financial support may compel cost-cutting strategies and judicious organizational management. Efforts to define and measure goals and objectives mark the managerial culture, and it privileges competent, efficient management of people and budgets toward those outcomes. Students in this culture are highly professionalized, prized for knowledge and skills that fall within a well-defined canon. In this culture, "respect and work in a formal, hierarchical structure" reflects a view of leadership as bureaucratic management. Leadership tends to focus on running the organization as it is, at the cost of attention to what could be if more attention were paid to members' development (i.e., learning), collegiality (i.e., relationships), or advocacy (i.e., values)—three other cultures of the academy. Leaders operating in the managerial mode may thus appear unduly political or simply hostile or insensitive. Employees are not immune from these appearances and impressions. Alienation and discontent often follow organizations and groups growing in size and complexity. The rise of the managerial culture—and, with it, bureaucratization and professionalization—indeed sparked discontent within higher-education institutions that gave rise to the advocacy culture.

Advocacy cultures support activism to ensure well-being and fair participation within managerial structures. They, too, emerged through endogenous and exogenous influences, first as a "response to the inability of the managerial culture to meet the personal and financial needs" of its members.[15] Concerns about compensation and workload often develop in large, complex organizations, threatening members' sense that the organization is protecting its end of an implicit psychological contract between administrators (managers) and faculty (employees). Amid violations of "expectations about mutual respect, autonomy, and status,"[16] forms of collective action become normalized in order to protect core norms that serve faculty interests, protect members of the community who have the least clout, and seek justice for those who denied opportunity under currently institutionalized rules. It is not difficult to see the ties of an advocacy culture in the academy to social activism, and the leaning toward this work by groups that are numerical minorities—either within a larger intellectual community (i.e., as astronomy is within the physics community) or with respect to their social identities.[17] For their bottom-up, principled, faculty-led qualities, advocacy cultures are, in effect, countercultural to the top-down, bureaucratic efficiency of managerial culture.

Astronomy: "A Social Movement Is Taking Over the Field"

The American Astronomical Society has commissioned a series of task forces, reports, and convenings over the past twenty-five years, each speaking to the issue of racial representation in the field. Looking at PhD production in astronomy relative to the student population and labor market, and examining the number of PhD-granting programs nationally, a 1996 report concluded that it would be "not wise" to reduce either the population of astronomy graduate students or PhD programs, and it made the unusual claim that practicing "birth control" in astronomy via more restrictive graduate admissions would compromise their "stated goal of enhancing diversity." However, fifteen years later, astronomy's Decadal Survey acknowledged that "little progress has been made increasing the number of minorities."[18] It therefore recommended the creation of partnerships between research universities, which produce the most PhDs in general, and minority-serving institutions (MSIs), which produce the most bachelor's degrees awarded to students of color.

Innovating Access

The recommendation by AAS to support MSI–research university partnerships emerged largely from the success of the Fisk-Vanderbilt Bridge Program, which was started by Fisk University physicist Arnold Burger and Vanderbilt astrophysicist Keivan Stassun. The partnership was motivated by a combination of facts: fully one-third of Black baccalaureates are awarded in historically Black colleges and universities (HBCUs); underrepresented minority students in STEM are about 50 percent more likely to obtain masters degrees on the way to a PhD; and the top producers of Black masters degrees are HBCUs.[19] In the Fisk-Vanderbilt Bridge Program, students with a completed undergraduate degree who are interested in a PhD but may need or be interested in obtaining additional coursework, research, or professional development complete a carefully mentored research master's degree at Fisk with the intention of transitioning to PhD programs at Vanderbilt. Through individualized mentoring, course selection, and research, students have space to both develop their potential and develop relationships with prospective PhD advisors.

One cannot understand the landscape of activity in STEM graduate education today without understanding the Fisk-Vanderbilt Bridge Program. Although it was not the first such postbaccalaureate program in the academy,[20] it was the first in the physical sciences, preceding the University of Michigan applied physics bridge program profiled in Chapter 5 and others associated with APS. Fisk-Vanderbilt started as a physics program specifically, and it was first funded through an NSF early career award to Stassun. To my knowledge, it was the first to partner with minority-serving institutions to enhance recruitment. Today, throughout the physical sciences, a widening array of bridge programs inspired by the Fisk-Vanderbilt Bridge Program are improving enrollment rates of underrepresented groups by facilitating promising students' passage into PhD programs. Bridge program models come with varied benefits and drawbacks for equity, and given their increasingly widespread adoption as a strategy for broadening participation of underrepresented groups, they are worthy of refining as part of a systematic assessment of how college students make the transition to graduate school.

In one of my interviews of Stassun, he observed that bridge programs' diffusion throughout physics and astronomy highlights that, at least in the long term, "You *can* have grassroots projects filter up in physics." He hypothesized that it had something to do with a quality that astronomy and physics share: "reverence for individual actors who come up with a big idea and go for it." There is, indeed, a culture of celebrity and hero worship in these fields (e.g., Richard Feynman, Albert Einstein, Stephen Hawking, Neil DeGrasse-Tyson), and Stassun's innovation for broadening access in physics gained him widespread respect and notoriety, especially in astronomy. He explained that, "pretty organically, other astronomers who wanted to be allies for social justice actively sought out affiliation with the Fisk-Vanderbilt Bridge Program or to learn from the model." My interviews with six other bridge program leaders in physics and astronomers support this observation, with every one of them mentioning Stassun and/or the Fisk-Vanderbilt Bridge Program as an influence on their work. One of them even commented that he was so inspired the first time he heard Stassun speak publicly that his eyes filled with tears. Astronomers welcomed the sense of moral authority that accompanied his values-based approach, and NSF itself took notice. The Division of Astronomical Sciences created the program Partnerships in Astronomy and Astrophysics Research and Education to encourage bridge programs throughout the country that would facilitate access to graduate education through research experiences.[21] Stassun recalled, "There was a real sense that, even within NSF, astronomy was doing this for themselves," apart from its larger parent Directorate for Mathematics and Physical Sciences.

The spread of this model into physics was not so simple, however. Stassun reports that he "quickly ran into a wall with physicists, because moral authority would not carry it [the argument] there." By this time, he was hardly the only person striving to raise attention to and redress inequities that prevailing approaches to admissions had "perpetuated and legitimized" in physics.[22]

One collaboration that developed was between Stassun and an experimental physicist, Casey Miller, who was leading an APS-affiliated bridge program at the University of South Florida. The two published a paper in *Nature* that today is widely known in both fields.[23] Graduate admissions reform, it would turn out, was a time whose idea had come, but the case for it needed to be translated into physicists' own language: quantitative data.

The 2014 paper, provocatively named "A Test That Fails," analyzed publicly available data about the Graduate Record Examination from Educational Testing Service and revealed large differences in the distribution of quantitative GRE scores by race and gender. The findings were made especially compelling alongside evidence from the National Research Council that a widespread tool for culling pools of applicants to physics PhD programs was setting a GRE cutoff score of 700, which disproportionately filtered out of the pool applicants of color and women of all race/ethnicities. The paper closed with a summary of the Fisk-Vanderbilt Bridge Program's model, its success in admitting and graduating PhDs, and its selection process, which included structured interviews that gauge socioemotional competencies. They concluded: "This is not a call to admit unqualified students in the name of social good. This is a call to acknowledge that the typical weight given to GRE scores in admissions is disproportionate." From start to finish, Miller and Stassun's intent to raise attention to a social problem through a focus on quantitative data is clear.

Stassun reflected that this manuscript's importance was in "the combination of the paper, visually—I mean, it centers on a graph—as well as the authorship of two physicists sharing an interesting pattern in the data, *not* sharing stories about people, lives, or values." In another example of cultural translation, authors Miller and Stassun interpreted the numbers into a message for a specific audience with whom they would have credibility: fellow scientists who are more driven by data than by values, who value seeing the data for themselves, and who would be compelled by publication of that data in a top-tier journal (see Figure 3). In an interview, Miller suggested that the *Nature* paper laid a foundation to get people to "think differently about the *status quo* in admissions." It is partly due to the empirical authority—not moral authority—afforded by critically examining social trends that Miller and Stassun have each come to provide strategic leadership in propagating and diffusing new admissions models within their respective fields of physics and astrophysics.

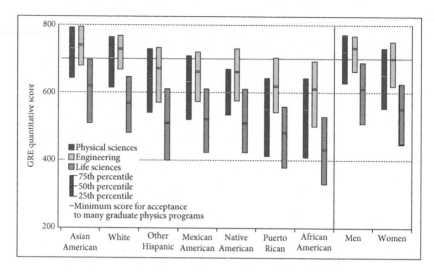

FIGURE 3. Scores earned on the quantitative GRE by physical sciences, life sciences, and engineering test takers, by race and gender.
SOURCE: Reprinted by permission from Springer Nature Customer Service Centre GmBH: Springer Nature, "A Test That Fails," by Casey Miller and Keivan Stassun, *Nature* 510, no. 7504 (2014).

Promoting Inclusion

Alongside efforts to change systems of access to graduate education, astronomy has a particularly well-organized grassroots movement. The AAS has institutionalized this to some degree through committees focused on specific populations: the Committee for Sexual Orientation and Gender Minorities in Astronomy, the Committee on the Status of Minorities in Astronomy, the Committee on the Status of Women in Astronomy, and the Working Group on Accessibility and Disability. Led by community members who embody these identities, these committees organize in online blogs and social media as well as in person. Today, when new initiatives and task forces seek legitimacy in the association, representation from these affinity groups is a must.

In addition to these groups, four times (in 1992, 2003, 2009, and 2017) women in astronomy have organized for national meetings aimed at equipping one another and male allies with knowledge, perspective, research, and skills about advocating for more equitable workplaces. I had the privilege of attending the 2017 Women in Astronomy (WiA IV) meeting, along with hundreds of others. Never before had I been in the presence of so many natural scientists who were also so conversant with dynamics of power and privilege, so outspoken about injustices, and so thoughtful about the range of identities that intersect with gender to affect experiences of women in science.[24] However, the WiA meetings had not always been this way. Concerns about an undue focus on gender to the neglect of its intersections with race and other social identities produced meeting programs, speaker lists, and a tone that drove away women of color.

In response to these concerns about the early WiA meetings, the 2015 Inclusive Astronomy meeting was a convening at Vanderbilt University that brought together 160 astronomers, social scientists, and policy makers to highlight issues facing marginalized communities, but from an explicitly intersectional perspective. As described in *Astrobites*, a blog written by and for astronomy graduate students:

> Inclusive Astronomy was about recognizing issues that the astronomy community faces from structures of oppression and discrimination, as well as offering robust solutions. To make astronomy more inclusive, this group of amazing people chartered a living document, known as the Nashville Recommendations. These recommendations include not only a vision of the field in the future, as well as active steps that physics and astronomy departments all across the USA (and the world) need to take in order to improve the working conditions of disenfranchised astrophysicists!

They identified sixty-five specific actions to take in four areas: removing barriers to access; creating inclusive climates; improving inclusion and access to power, policy, and leadership; and establishing a community of inclusive practice. Within each area, they specified short-, medium-, and long-term goals and actions, gave each a numeric code, and identified target stakeholders. For example, RBA1S referred to the first short-term action under removing barriers to access and recommended that universities and departments "develop and deploy best-practice, research-based tools for evaluating graduate school applications holistically and equitably; Eliminate the General and/or Physics Graduate Record Exams (GRE) for graduate school admission (see the AAS statement of endorsement), and integrate holistic measures of scientific talent into graduate admissions procedures (see, e.g., the Fisk-Vanderbilt Bridge Program toolkit for sample protocols and rubrics)."[25] Other short-term recommendations to remove barriers to access included making graduate school applications affordable by reducing or eliminating application fees; developing, publicizing, and following equitable criteria for hiring and evaluations; and elevating attention to disability issues within the community to "the same level as minority and gender issues." Recommendations like these and others involve complex policy decisions, but others in the full set of Nashville Recommendations are everyday social justice behaviors for individual astronomers and leadership. For example, medium-term goals and actions under creating a community of inclusive practice include the following: "Learn and use best practices for discussing racism and its intersections; Reduce the negative impact of power imbalances in a given situation; Speak to your own experience; Use both/and rather than either/or thinking . . . ; Use inclusive language; Recognize that intent does not equal impact; Allow space for unexpected responses; Lean into discomfort; and Respond constructively when someone tells you that your words and actions are harmful to others."[26] In sum, the Nashville Recommendations were intended to provide a comprehensive "roadmap for equity and inclusion in astronomy," advocating actions for people, organizations, and the field as a whole—a vision for what the community could do to overcome intersectional power asymmetries.[27]

Members of the community recognized the Inclusive Astronomy meeting and articulation of the Nashville Recommendations as a turning point for the field. Co-organizer Stassun wrote on the AAS blog, "We can commit together to make astronomy the scientific profession that leads by example in becoming a truly diverse and inclusive professional community."[28] Another attendee, Kim Coble, shared with me during a meeting of the AAS Task Force on Graduate Education and Diversity, that Inclusive Astronomy connected like-minded scholars, made the grassroots movement visible, and pointed to the need for a community of practice. In an interview, she commented, "Inclusive Astronomy was a watershed moment for all of us who had been feeling like points in the darkness."

Top-Down Advocacy for Bottom-Up Recommendations
Graduate education was a prominent theme in the Nashville Recommendations, and organizers sought the commitment of individuals and organizations to implement them. Later in 2015, AAS president C. Meg Urry—who had given the introductory remarks at the first Women in Astronomy meeting in 1992—wrote a first-of-its kind letter encouraging department chairs throughout the discipline to rethink the role of the test in their admissions processes. The final statement, ratified as a resolution by the AAS board at their annual meeting in January 2016, "recommends graduate programs eliminate or make

optional the GRE and PGRE [i.e., the GRE's Physics subject test] as metrics of evaluation for graduate applicants. If GRE or PGRE scores are used, the AAS recommends that admissions criteria account explicitly for the known systematics in scores as a function of gender, race, and socioeconomic status, and that cutoff scores not be used to eliminate candidates."[29] Since that time, seventy-four physics and astronomy departments have logged their use of test-optional or no-test PhD admissions on a publicly viewable spreadsheet.[30]

The association has also issued statements and resolutions on other occasions in support of members organizing for equity and inclusion. One statement expressed support for recommendations emerging from a Women in Astronomy meeting (the Baltimore Charter), and another centered on outcry in the field around faculty sexual harassment. AAS also issued an official statement of support for women speaking out about an incident that became known online as #ShirtStorm and #Shirtgate. At a European Space Agency media conference, a male participant had worn a shirt with sexualized images of women carrying guns, and he later compared to a woman the spacecraft that was the focus of the meeting. Women who spoke up about this found themselves faced with abusive responses including insults, complaints of "overactive feminism," and threats against their physical safety. According to an AAS leader I interviewed, its resolution in response to this incident and to other issues of gender equity have been intended to communicate both the Association's own stances and to make clear their support for individual-level resistance of status quo gender relations in the field.

It is not hard to see why some say that, as a recent early career award winner in astronomy put it, "a social movement is taking over the field." A few specific calls for change generated through grassroots support have taken hold across the field. We also see that leaders of the early movement to change astronomy have become leaders of the AAS, although as in any movement or complex organization, there are factions. And no disciplinary society to my knowledge has been as vocal as AAS in advocacy for specific practices surrounding graduate education or creating a more inclusive climate.[31] AAS is small compared to its counterparts the American Physical Society and American Chemical Society, but its relatively small size and lean administrative structure do have benefits; for example, it enables more nimble action when an official word from the organization can send a timely, politically important message to the field. Urry's and AAS's advocacy on GRE policy is a perfect example of this. The push to eliminate GRE requirements started outside official

AAS channels, but the AAS resolution—combined with early adoption from about six prominent PhD programs, including Harvard—has facilitated a bandwagon effect that is having ripple effects throughout STEM disciplines. By contrast, a formal statement about GRE policy has languished for years within American Physical Society's byzantine committee approval process.[32]

Coordinated Advocacy on Equity in Graduate Education

Recognizing the potential for influencing the field, a group of faculty convinced AAS to convene a task force in 2017 dedicated to diversity and inclusion in graduate education. The year before, members of an astronomy education task force had recognized the centrality of graduate education to the field's ongoing dialogue about equity and inclusion, as well as to the momentum for change following the Inclusive Astronomy meeting and the AAS statement on the GRE. Among its top-three recommendations was the creation of a second task force specific to graduate education "to repackage the Nashville Recommendations in a form that departments could use to implement real change." Proposed originally by Alex Rudolph at Cal Poly Pomona, it was ultimately led as a partnership between him and Gibor Basri, a professor at University of California, Berkeley, and former vice chancellor for equity and inclusion. Its charge was to create a targeted list of recommendations that collectively would create workable agendas for PhD student admissions and retention reform, focusing on Nashville Recommendations with a strong evidentiary base in either research or community practice. To strengthen the credibility of recommendations, they brought in advisors with relevant social science knowledge and broke out efforts into an admissions working group led by Keivan Stassun and Marcel Agüeros, a working group on retention led by Kim Coble and Angela Speck, and a working group on data collection led by Ed Bertschinger and Jackie Monkiewicz. The latter group was dedicated to looking at the data infrastructure that would be needed to measure and track progress at the field and departmental levels.

Following the model of initiatives like the Leadership in Energy and Environmental Design, or LEED, certification, Athena Swan, and SEA Change, the task force sought to incentivize inclusive or progressive practices by offering a certification or seal of approval for PhD programs that would become a signal of quality in the field. Task force leaders envisioned working with the AAS to compel adoption of key recommendations field-wide by creating an online platform on the AAS website where prospective students and members of the community could see which departments used inclusive practices.[33] In doing so, they wanted to stimulate the market for inclusive practices like high-quality mentoring, recruitment from minority-serving institutions, and holistic admissions.

In January 2019, the report was presented at the annual meeting of the AAS and the board of trustees endorsed the recommendations. It is too soon to say whether their more targeted recommendations, the AAS imprimatur, and the hope of positive publicity for those departments that take up their recommendations will lead to more widespread adoption than when the recommendations came through the grassroots movement. They are, in effect, striving to leverage the forces of mimetic and coercive isomorphism to coordinate advocacy for practices that have been on the agenda for years, under the assumption that the field is ready to associate inclusive practices with excellence and that field-level facilitation will aid in it.

Barriers to Implementation in the Advocacy Culture

The advocacy culture and its associated movement to adopt a wide variety of more and less evidence-based recommendations emanate from a holistic understanding of equity and inclusion, from commitment to changing the status quo, and from an astute recognition of the power that everyday practices have to shape climate and culture. I see more positive pressure for equity-minded change in this field than any other STEM field of which I know. The movement also supports a need for community and solidarity among change agents across the country. However, it has not been as strong in developing capacity for implementing changes at the department level. Facilitating local dialogues that develop context-specific agendas from AAS-endorsed recommendations may be especially crucial for astronomers working in departments that house both physicists and astronomers, given differences in their disciplinary cultures and differences in the depth of buy-in for AAS-endorsed recommendations. The graduate education task force has therefore called for strategic planning by department, including the development of locally resonant rationales for prioritizing and adopting specific recommendations, phasing activities, and ensuring adequate resources are available. It is too soon to say whether this particular recommendation is being implemented or what its impact may be.

A second and related drawback of astronomy's advocacy culture has been the emergence of such elaborate sets of recommendations that community members struggle to engage with them.[34] Not every good or necessary idea for action is feasible, and will for institutional change is uneven within the very organizations that need it most. As a result, there is a tension between being clear and honest about the many areas of work that need improvement and the press for a focused agenda that might actually be implemented. In recent years both the AAS and the broader field of astronomy have recognized this issue and they are trying to address it. At the 2017 WiA IV meeting, organizers of a session titled "Engaging the Nashville Recommendations" acknowledged that preparing for their session had revealed to them that the set of recommendations may be too large to be useful to institutions. One described the meeting's impact: "Inclusive Astronomy was a transformative event, seeing people come together and develop so many recommendations. But that's also been a drawback. There are so many recommendations. How do you implement them?" To one audience member's question: "What should I do with the long list?" one panelist suggested sending colleagues to a website dubbed "The Hidden AAS Community." Another suggested that "every department should be doing at least one thing." More recently, at the 2019 AAS annual meeting, members of the graduate education task force presenting recommendations in a plenary session were urged to remind audience members that they need not adopt the entire set of recommendations but start by identifying just one, two, or a small handful that resonate with colleagues. A far cry from the wholesale transformation implied in the Nashville Recommendations, improvements of *any* sort are now being portrayed as "building the culture of change that so many of us are excited about."

Physics: Diversity Work as Project Management

If the culture of equity work in astronomy has been sustained advocacy through a grassroots movement aimed at innovating access and inclusion, in physics the culture of equity work has been top-down management of sponsored projects to reduce racial—and sometimes—gender gaps in participation. The APS Education and Diversity office has directed considerable effort to stemming the loss of Black, Latinx, and Native American students from undergraduate to graduate education.

Following conversations with Stassun regarding the Fisk-Vanderbilt Bridge Program, Ted Hodapp, then the APS director of education and diversity, has been reworking the bridge program model so that it could be facilitated not by individual universities but by the disciplinary society itself. APS established its bridge program in 2012 with the goal of "increasing the number of UREM [underrepresented racial-ethnic minority] students [in PhD programs] to the level where there is no difference in attainment rates by such students between bachelor's and doctoral degrees."[35] The gaps between BS, MS, and PhD attainment rates and the number of additional graduate students it would take in various fields to equalize the rates are represented in Figure 2 in Chapter 1. Unlike the Fisk-Vanderbilt program, the APS Bridge Program does not facilitate partnerships between research universities and minority-serving institutions. Rather, APS hosts a common application portal from December to late March to six bridge program sites, located within departments that already have PhD programs which have been vetted by the APS Committee on Minorities for their use of inclusive practices. Students from underrepresented racial/ethnic groups who did not obtain PhD admission through usual channels are eligible to apply. Students submit a single application, and APS makes their applications available to all of the bridge program and partnership sites, which may then extend admission offers on a time-specific schedule. "We become the national recruiter," Hodapp explained to me. "Departments appreciate that. We're just being a matchmaker to get them into the right place." Once the programs have successfully recruited bridge students, APS expects that they will support them through completion of the PhD. Indeed, this has mostly proved to be the case. The program has exceeded its targets, and if currently enrolled students continue with their presently high rates of persistence, it will more than close the gap between the number of Black, Latinx, and Native American students earning baccalaureate degrees and those earning PhDs.

Nucleating a Network

My first connection with the APS graduate education agenda was in fall 2015, when I shared my research on graduate admissions as an invited plenary speaker at the APS National Bridge Program Meeting at Florida International University. Never before had I attended a conference where the gender dynamics were so different from those within education—both numerically and culturally. Women earn less than 20 percent of PhDs in physics, and I estimated that this conference's attendees approximated this distribution.[36] So striking was the experience that, flying home from the meeting, I could not help but think of the famous line by Robert Frost: physics would have "miles to go before we sleep," regardless of how quickly APS and its constituents could change rates of participation.

In 2016, I collaborated with APS staff Erika Brown, Ted Hodapp, and Monica Plisch, along with physics professors Geraldine Cochran and Casey Miller, to design a project to improve access to physics graduate education. We obtained a design and development launch pilot grant through the newly established NSF INCLUDES program, which is a national network designed to enhance STEM nationally through innovative, ambitious projects aimed at broadening participation. The vision, we told ourselves and NSF, was to nucleate a paradigm shift in the evaluation and education of PhD students in physics, based on a triangulation of evidence from the APS Bridge Program and research we had personally conducted about the need for change in graduate admissions processes. Cochran, Hodapp, and Brown had found, for example, that although that APS Bridge Program students were succeeding in graduate education, the students believed GRE scores had presented the single biggest barrier to their entrance to graduate school—either in preventing their admission or in deterring them from applying because they worried their scores would disqualify them. Miller had coauthored the influential paper in *Nature* described earlier in this chapter about the detrimental effects for racial and gender diversity of using GRE score cutoffs in admissions. He was also engaged in other research to examine GRE scores' validity and, with industrial-organizational psychologist Joann Quinn, was working toward the development of a quantitative assessment of noncognitive competencies. And over two different research projects, I had conducted ethnographic research on doctoral admissions—including case studies of physics PhD programs' admissions processes—which found that faculty mindsets about merit, diversity, and intelligence were a root cause of inequities.[37]

Through the NSF INCLUDES pilot award, we created the Inclusive Graduate Education Network (IGEN). Whereas the APS Bridge Program was aimed at jump-starting Black and Latinx student enrollment using an alternative enrollment method, IGEN—also administered through APS—has been predicated on the need for systemic, long-term institutional change alongside an accelerated access in the short term. We partnered with six large, selective PhD programs in physics (University of Chicago, University of Illinois at Urbana-Champaign, University of Michigan Applied Physics, Ohio State University, University of Maryland, and Rutgers University) that opened themselves to reconsider their recruitment, admissions, and retention practices under the following assumptions:

1. Consistent with the tenets of mimetic isomorphism, well-respected programs' adoption of more inclusive practices could nucleate a field-wide shift.

2. Sustained changes in who enrolls in graduate education in physics called not only for alternative pathways in, but also a cultural change that shifts how faculty think about and practically assess merit. Faculty mindsets affect how students are evaluated not only at the point of admission but also once they enroll.

3. Admissions reform represented a reasonable goal given the momentum for change in astronomy, the research evidence, and the expertise within our group.

Given the discipline's strong orientation toward data and research, we also recognized that any such change would necessarily involve faculty reflecting upon the best available data and research about admissions, reconstructing established practices accordingly, and then tracking their outcomes. Therefore, the primary IGEN project activities during the pilot stage were facilitating on-site faculty professional development workshops in each of the six participating programs,[38] gathering data from the programs about their admissions practices before and after the site visits, and conducting original research in collaboration with doctoral research assistant Theresa Hernandez to advance the literature about access to graduate education.[39]

A Day in the Life of an Equity Project

To take you into the culture of IGEN, I offer the following "day in the life" description of one in-person IGEN project meeting at which we gathered to discuss project outcomes near the end of the pilot period. The principal investigator team, additional APS staff, directors of the six partner PhD programs (all of whom were men), and representatives from affinity groups like the National Society of Black Physicists and the National Society of Hispanic Physicists all gathered at the American Center for Physics, in suburban Washington, DC, in a large, sunny boardroom. The day started with good news: a message in email inboxes of about half the people in the room from the National Science Foundation indicating a high likelihood that the next-generation version of the pilot project would be funded for the next five years to the tune of $10 million. Spirits high, the meeting started with the usual confirmation of the agenda and ensuring connections with those who were calling in through video conference. Ted, who presided over the meeting, gave a twenty-minute report about the APS Bridge Program, followed by fifteen-minute PowerPoint presentations from each of the participating PhD program chairs.

The first program director who presented shared that the program's "diversity numbers" were up by 50 percent, and three other chairs similarly mentioned significant increases in "URMs" and "students of color." Another meekly commented, "Well, a student whom we took a chance on is doing well." I caught a furtive glance between two people at the table at this comment, and later learned that the two people who exchanged it thought the comment represented a misunderstanding of IGEN's aims—that is, that they should move away from thinking of students in terms of risk and of defining progress in terms of single students.

Last, David Reid, of the University of Chicago, noted that although his faculty had initially been skeptical of holistic admissions, they had successfully implemented an evaluation rubric and women had come to represent 44 percent of the incoming class—a fourfold increase over previous years. He presented the graph shown in Figure 4, which plots the department's progress since 2009 in admitting women and underrepresented minorities. Interpreting the figure and how much progress it signified yielded a lively exchange between two participants, whom I will call Bill and Carl:

BILL: This is an amazing graph.

CARL: It's half amazing.

BILL: But look at the desert of zeros!

CARL: It's half amazing. I'm sticking with that.

BILL: OK, it's a step toward amazing.

CARL: But if you accept it, you're normalizing a situation that was bad to begin with.

At this point, David interjected: "The way I read it, after four cycles in a row of nonzero, there's something happening." The three of them stopped short of discussing what that "something" was.

The discussion highlighted that even when it comes to quantitative data, interpretation and subjectivity matter. One's perspective is like a measure-

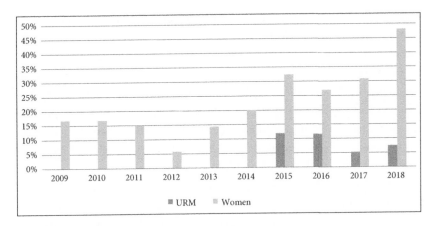

FIGURE 4. Admission of women and underrepresented racial minorities to the University of Chicago Physics Department, 2009–2018.
SOURCE: University of Chicago Physics Department.

ment apparatus, determining whether light appears as wave or particle. A person whose project funding depends on demonstrating "progress" may be more inclined to notice the increase over time in participation and insist that something "amazing" is going on, whereas a person wearied by the slow pace of change may notice "the desert of zeros." Who's right? Technically, they both are, although both interpretations are partial. By putting them together and accepting the empirical basis for both claims, we can piece together the more complex reality—yes, change is possible, and it will almost always seem to be occurring more slowly than key community stakeholders want.

Following Bill and Carl's exchange, Jesús Pando, IGEN's partner from the National Society of Hispanic Physicists, shifted the topic to encourage David and the other PhD program directors not to be upset that they had not seen all of the progress that they wanted since the start of the project just eighteen months before: "To expect a sea change in one year isn't reasonable. It's going to be an ongoing process." David agreed, then moved to comment on how the faculty development workshops had changed thinking about the meaning of GRE scores within the department:

> Those already leaning against the GRE used the data that was presented to us as fuel for their position. They now say, "And as the data says . . ." Those who were in the middle have moved toward feeling scores have less value, citing the workshop. And those who felt the GRE had value are less vocal, and less confident.

He also stated that "there has been a shift in diversity consciousness in graduate admissions. Everyone's thinking about diversity during admissions without pushing or prodding. People are recognizing that their definition of who's
best may be biased." Also important to consciousness-raising within Chicago's physics department he said, was a new department chair—Young-Kee
Kim—a particle physicist committed to making diversity and inclusion the
theme for her leadership. To that end, she has taken to personally telephon-
ing every woman and person of color who is admitted, to welcome them and
make a recruitment bid. She produced a glossy code of conduct that hung
prominently throughout the department. "Each day the department works
to build a campus where there are no others," it read. Thus, as with the PhD
program case studies in Chapters 3 and 4, the physics program at the University of Chicago suggests reform can catalyze change in admissions practices,
but sustaining it takes leadership, faculty learning, and consciousness raising.

Drawbacks of the Managerial Culture

Physics illustrates how disciplinary societies have unique power to convene
and sponsor large-scale projects. They also have infrastructure enabling
them to coordinate and facilitate activities that constituent members or small
groups of them cannot. However, while the top-down impulse helps get some
things done, like the advocacy culture, it has limits.

In part to satisfy perceived expectations of NSF, and in part due to the ontological legitimacy of numbers within the physical sciences, project outcomes
and thus perceptions of progress were often cast quantitatively. The bar chart,
as Figures 2, 3, and 4 all indicate, is a favored format in this community for
justifying movement toward equity. However, the meaning of the numbers for
faculty and project members working on the ground entailed stories about real
students' presence and absence, their lives in the profession and discipline, and
the same practical and political dimensions of changing faculty colleagues'
minds and practices that compelled advocates in astronomy. From the standpoint of APS, equity work in IGEN was mostly a matter of project management and aggregating department-level outcomes, but for the PhD program
chairs and affinity groups associated with the project, it also involved significant policy-changing, consciousness-raising, mindset-shifting work among
their colleagues. Support for this type of equity work could have been incorporated more effectively into the project. Thus, it is understandable that IGEN's
research activities with PhD program directors and affinity group partners re-

vealed two perceived needs: to open the project's goals to discussion, and for more formal opportunities to communicate across organizations in the network. PhD program chairs, in particular, wanted more contact with each other; more resources to reform admissions, recruitment, and retention practices; and ongoing professional development for their colleagues. Of course, only so much is possible with a small grant during a two-year pilot period, but a significant challenge was that project communication suffered as its leaders were stretched thin. IGEN was only one in an array of APS education and diversity projects, and staff members' energy and attention were often divided between projects that had already been awarded and the next major grant on the horizon.

I present this candid critique for two reasons. For one, I am confident that the IGEN Alliance is committed to improvement in the design of its work, including learning from lessons of the APS Bridge Program and the pilot described earlier. The collective impact model that NSF INCLUDES projects are encouraged to use calls for strategies that create a more inclusive approach to project management, such as regular revisiting of goals, the use of shared metrics, and a network model of governance to reduce status hierarchies.[40] As Cathy Mader, a physicist at Hope College and lead of the IGEN Alliance backbone, put it:

> Many of us that have survived in this field have surrounded ourselves with folks that, like us, are willing to learn how to transform our institutions and remove barriers that push folks to the margins. For the first time in a long time, I don't feel like I'm doing it alone *and* I feel like there is convergence on this idea from so many different communities I work in.

For scientists whose training does not include social science but who are seeking equity through institutional change, "willing[ness] to learn how to transform our institutions" is a critical component of equity work. I would therefore argue the value of complementing the managerial culture with aspects of a developmental culture, which centers the role of individual and collective learning and growth.

I also present this critique toward a broader goal of all the case studies in this book: that by unpacking the complex realities of equity work in science, readers can more wisely design and carry out such work themselves. It should be clear by this point that grounding in noble intentions does not mean that the design or implementation of a given effort cannot be improved. Indeed, given the investments of time and money that increasingly flow into work toward equity, diversity, and inclusion, their improvement is a necessary focus of attention. This work will always benefit from management and advocacy, as well as from managers and advocates. And it needs those managers and advocates to learn as much as they can, just as work directly advancing understanding of physical science phenomena benefits from its leaders' expertise and continuous learning on those topics. In equity work, it marks a step in the right direction when management and advocacy activities are carried out according to more inclusive, equitable norms than those that animate the communities they are trying to change. For this to occur, many scientists will have to look beyond their existing networks and the mainstream of their communities for knowledge and perspective.

Reflections on Engagement in Equity Work in Astronomy and Physics

In the spirit of the ethnographic practice of reflexivity, a few words are warranted about my own experiences working in this landscape. My collaborations with APS (as conference speaker and co–principal investigator tasked with leading research and facilitating professional development workshops) and with AAS (as conference speaker and senior advisor on its Graduate Education Equity and Inclusion Task Force) incline me to see particular facets of these disciplines' equity efforts. My view would no doubt be different as a student in one of the bridge programs, for example, or as a professor helping to convene one of the Conferences for Undergraduate Women in Physics. Indeed, my initial invitation to collaborate in designing IGEN and advising the task force can be understood as a reflection of managerial culture—that diversity work is organized in projects, and project management includes assembling teams so that work can be carried out with reasonable division of labor, and delegated to people with specific expertise and perspective.

One PhD program director affiliated with IGEN recently joked with me, "You're practically a physicist now," but the truth is that nothing has revealed the boundaries between natural and social sciences to me like being the sole social scientist on teams otherwise constituted by natural scientists. We work together effectively, but in addition to the need to negotiate philosophical differences about goals, strategies, and tactics, we vary in the forms of data and other knowledge we tend to bring to bear, the ways we interpret that knowledge, and the language we use for shared concepts. What physicists call parameters, I think of as variables, to name just one example. At the beginning of the collaboration with physicists, I found myself frequently looking up physics concepts to keep up with the metaphors my colleagues used—thanks be to Google for the provision of translation across disciplinary languages. For that reason I laughed to learn that one of the other co-PIs had bookmarked the website Dictionary.com for quick reference during meetings, so often was I using social science language that was new to him. Engagement across disciplinary boundaries may not come easily, but it is intellectually and professionally rewarding when people on in different discourse communities are committed to learning, translating, and putting new understandings to work toward shared goals.

My socialization into education and sociology has given me a different way of knowing and a different language. It has also given me the instinct (some might call it a bias) to encourage collective learning as part of our work and to develop sensitivity to issues of power—topics that are atypical to discuss for most physicists and astronomers given their disciplinary logics and training. For example, I have been jokingly called a "trouble maker" by one physics PhD program chair for occasionally "surfacing issues that everyone has noticed and is thinking about, but no one acknowledges." My engagement no doubt generates some creative tension.[41] I am confident, though, as numerous collaborators have affirmed, that this creative tension is a positive feature of my participation; indeed, research shows that effective teams benefit from "outsider" perspectives.[42] Scott Page found that the core of diversity's intellectual benefits is variation that people with heterogeneous backgrounds bring about the nature of problems and strategies for their solutions.[43] I have thus learned to embrace that my personal and disciplinary standpoints provide a check to the central tendencies of scientific groups,[44] and to engage with care and thoughtfulness when I choose to speak up.

My hope, as a collaborator across disciplines, is that making explicit some of the implicit, social dimensions of our own work together contributes to cultural translation of social knowledge into the natural sciences. Expanding scientists' vocabularies for communicating about the social aspects of their worlds and work can expand common sense about what is acceptable, logical, or necessary engagement.

Revisiting the Relationship Between Managerial and Advocacy Cultures

Although my focus has been diversity and equity efforts in graduate education, we have hints that physics and astronomy as disciplines—not just their approach to addressing inequities—map on to the managerial and advocacy cultures. For example, that the managerial culture positions students as competent acquirers of an established canon aligns well with physics' well-codified curriculum, reflected in the widespread use of the same small handful of textbooks across the country.[45] An advocacy culture among astronomers would be expected in departments that house both physics and astronomy. There, astronomers typically account for a small share of overall faculty, students, and course offerings, and astronomy faculty may find themselves in ongoing negotiations with physics departmental leadership about their status and autonomy. It could be that the cultures of their equity work serve as windows into wider cultures; however, I cannot make definitive claims in this regard with my current data, which are centered on their equity projects.

Perhaps the most interesting thing about the cultures of equity work in physics and astronomy mapping so well on to the managerial and advocacy cultures is that the original theory positing these cultures suggests that the two are inherently interdependent. Bergquist and Pawlak note that advocacy activities keep administrative power in check, making it "a worthy opponent to those in the managerial culture." At the same time, this style of engagement effectively reinforces administrative power as dominant.[46] When an advocacy culture is aggravated as a result of a domineering managerial influences, it strengthens the identity and passion of the advocacy culture, which aggravates the managerial culture in response. Over time, each side doubles down on its distinctiveness relative to the other rather than finding pathways forward together. This "mutually aggravating spiral" ensures the continuation of both the managerial and advocacy cultures, drives them to look tacitly to each other for their own definition and makes conflict between the two inevitable, expected, and therefore a normal part of how the academy as a whole operates.

This analogy—while helpful for understanding cycles of engagement between activists and administrators—breaks down in application to physics and astronomy. At least with respect to specific equity projects, astronomy— though smaller and more advocacy oriented—does not defer to physics. The various bridge programs across the two fields have effectively carved out their own student markets and their own domains of influence through which expansion can be pursued—into other regions of the country, other disciplines, and other important student transitions. The Fisk-Vanderbilt Masters to PhD Bridge Program has influenced other bridge programs, as mentioned, and the formation of another regional network, Cal-Bridge, that links physics and astronomy departments in the California Community College system and California State University system with PhD programs in those fields on the University of California campuses. Meanwhile, one component of the IGEN Alliance is to scale out its bridge program into other disciplinary societies (most immediately, the American Chemical Society and American Geophysical Union). The AAS and Materials Research Society are also involved. And following the work of the AAS task force on equity and inclusion in graduate education, the American Institute of Physics is following suit. Today, it seems, there are more opportunities than ever for the advocacy and managerial cultures to rub off on one another and, perhaps, to bring some balance. Advocacy can point out problems and recommend solutions, while managerialism has a role in implementing change.

Implications: Questions to Ask in Balancing Top-Down and Bottom-Up Influences

That the equity efforts in each of these fields reflect to some degree the broader disciplinary cultures in which they are situated reveals the type of institutional inertia that may need overcoming in order to accelerate change. No doubt within other fields, the managerial and advocacy cultural tendencies may be represented, as may be the tendencies toward other organizational cultures that Bergquist and Pawlak identified: collegial, developmental, virtual, and tangible.[47] When originating from the center of the community and its most powerful people, organized equity efforts are likely to reflect the cultures they are trying to change. The same preferences for certain types of data, prevalence of community-wide biases and blind spots, and styles of leadership and participation that drive the discipline are likely to carry forward into equity efforts—shaping both the likelihood of their impact and the experience of those who participate in them. It becomes important to ask what defines the agenda and who is leading and participating in it.

What (and Who) Defines the Agenda?
Whereas the advocacy culture tends to permit too elaborate an agenda in the name of inclusiveness, the managerial culture may fail to appreciate how identities, ideology, and power *should* matter for defining social agendas. Exclusively top-down efforts risk setting priorities that do not map on

to community concerns, and that means some people may disengage if they think their ideas are insufficiently represented in the agenda. Heterogeneous groups need ways of developing agendas that ensure everyone feels like their ideas, partnerships, and needs matter to the conversation. Bottom-up efforts risk creating so broad an agenda that it becomes unwieldy to enact, much less to institutionalize at scale. What both the AAS graduate education task force and the collective impact model driving IGEN acknowledge is the need for shared goals and metrics. Coming to such shared understanding is hard work that requires skills of listening, negotiating, and sometimes translating across boundaries.

Disciplinary Cultural Tools Get (Some) Things Done

Professional associations in physics and astronomy demonstrated the potential and limits for working within prevailing disciplinary cultural norms. The managerial style of APS diversity activities has worked from the top down to set an agenda of activities and carry it out to meet specified numeric objectives. APS has significant convening power, and its strong ties with constituent departments and chairs has facilitated communication with leaders and data collection on a variety of matters. Professional associations often hold formal or informal regulatory functions, and this may be especially so in strong paradigm fields like physics, where members are accustomed to working within hierarchies. In such environments, faculty in the decentralized graduate program landscape may be more likely to accept recommendations from central entities, particularly when those recommendations are clearly grounded in data or research—another prized value of physics' culture. But can adoption of programs and practices change culture? Indeed, we can think of it as a reflection *of* the culture that there is even a question about *whether* culture should be identified as part of the problem to be addressed. Traweek's ethnography of high-energy physics labs persuasively argued that many physicists deny that physics has a culture at all or that it influences their work.[48] If this is true today, it surely presents a fundamental barrier to cultural change of any sort.

The growing movement for inclusion in astronomy takes a very different approach. The advocacy culture harnesses passion and energy from the ground up to set agendas of recommended behaviors as guidance for the broader community. A combination of public statements by the AAS, reform in well-respected programs, and a growing group of scholars organizing and meeting to articulate an agenda for change have converted the potential energy of a quiet network into collective action and, today, clear momentum for specific changes to graduate admissions. The advocacy culture itself makes conversation about grievances and norms more commonplace, which may also create conditions in which recommended actions will be taken. However, that the recommendations are read by some in the field as an idealistic vision or a new orthodoxy of behavior suggests that additional mechanisms, such as the learning focus that the developmental culture asserts, may be needed for advocacy to become reality.

Both advocacy and management are necessary, but neither is sufficient on its own to realize lasting change. Just as organizational culture provides tools to get things done, it also puts bounds on what is possible. You cannot use a Phillips-head screwdriver on a screw with a flat head. Culture narrows human actions to those that will be considered natural or appropriate—and my work in these communities suggests this includes the perceived appropriateness of tactics for equity and inclusion. Advocacy cultures engage culture, and their attention to principles and practices aligns with the ground-level, grassroots work required to change how people think and act. They keep power in sight and in check. Managerial cultures provide structure and organize activity to narrow the scope of action to that which can be coordinated. Ultimately, equity work benefits from both.

7 Retooling Science for Equity Through Cultural Translation

> There must exist a paradigm, a practical model for social change that includes an understanding of ways to transform consciousness that are linked to efforts to transform structures.
>
> —*bell hooks*, Killing Rage

ANTHROPOLOGISTS KNOW THAT IF YOU WANT TO DEEPLY UNDERSTAND a culture, two things are especially revealing: how people are socialized to it and how the people who do the socializing think and act on a daily basis. To understand cultures within the academy today, and those of initiatives to make it more equitable, it is therefore instructive to look closely at graduate education. Useful insights for change emerge from departments, programs, and disciplines where leaders have committed to building diversity where there has been homogeneity, reducing inequities where gaps have been stubborn, and creating more humane and inclusive environments. In these spaces, which occupy a liminal space between the central tendencies of what science has been and the glimmers of what it might become, we see barriers and possibilities, cautionary tales and inspirational examples.

Although I began this research with a desire to more deeply understand the conditions, trajectories, and priorities of graduate programs that are enrolling more diverse students, what became clear is that even in these places—not unlike the country as a whole—the work is in progress. The work will always be unfinished, in part because change agents in science are products of the communities they are trying to change, just as scientists are part of the reality they try to understand. Socialization within racialized organizations gives white folks, in particular, a narrower view than the goal of equity demands. For example, to the extent people have been socialized to think of racism as an individual attitude or bias—and not also a feature baked into

most American organizations through routine practices and policies that—
they will have a limited view of what dismantling racism in science looks like.
Similarly, to the extent that the next generation of change agents is socialized
to think of equity only in terms of representation or closing gaps—and not
also in terms of reconfiguring systems so those gaps stay closed—they are
likely to select strategies and tactics that yield short-lived progress at best.[1]

In this chapter, I synthesize findings from across the case studies and sum-
marize implications—first for graduate programs, then for the design and
implementation of collaborative equity efforts more generally. I present two
key mechanisms, cultural retooling and cultural translation, as relevant both
for groups seeking to reduce inequities within academic departments and
for cross-sector collaborative change efforts. I then make a series of concrete
recommendations for practice. First, I identify two particularly high-leverage
opportunities for retooling graduate education: I present recommendations
for how we admit and support students as cases of the need for more equitable, holistic approaches to evaluation and interactions in academia generally. Then, recognizing the growing number of people who are working on
equity efforts like those described in the book, I present recommendations for
improving the equity and effectiveness of such collaborative efforts, including
ways to manage resistant, recalcitrant colleagues. I finally close with implications for theory about entanglements and boundaries across disciplinary and
other cultural differences.

Case Studies' Crosscutting Themes

The need for a relational, multi-level approach to change emerged through
fieldwork in a variety of disciplinary settings that converged on a common
pattern of findings: First, equity and inequity were constructed at the micro level, from moment to moment and person to person, by enacting unspoken but widely held community norms and values through the minutiae
of everyday evaluations and interactions. Obtained often through their own
socialization as graduate students, professors' norms and values predictably
aggregated to legitimate certain policies and practices within organizations.[2]
Here is where the micro and macro were linked—through institutionalized
practices at the meso level of organizational activity that formed the basis for graduate students' experiences and learning of particular rules and
knowledge—that is, its hidden curriculum. Those who imagine transforming

systems and structures to reduce disparities and empower historically marginalized groups therefore have good reason to design change efforts with
relationships and behaviors at multiple levels in mind.

In addition, as an open-systems view of organizations and a view of agency
as entangled and embedded would predict, the environments (e.g., organizationally, temporally, institutionally) in which specific equity efforts occurred
mattered much for how they played out. Change efforts did not occur in a
vacuum. Actions of other departments on a campus or within one's discipline
shaped departmental trajectories and the cultures of change efforts. Within
specific organizations, faculty, graduate students, and staff would join while
others would leave (academics are a relatively transient population after all,
and departmental "homes" do not often operate as such for more than about
five years). This fluidity and associated turnover in governance and committee participation influenced what new or improved actions could be deemed
reasonable and appropriate, and how difficult it could be to institutionalize
them as the new normal.

Creating equity was therefore less like reaching a single goal and more
like an iterative practice of system redesign. Positive steps made through individual projects and initiatives that change practices were small wins that
built momentum, sustained motivation, and helped quiet skeptics. Figure 5
summarizes themes from the practices identified in the PhD program case
studies, any one of which might be thought of as a small win.

Entanglements are normal within complex systems, and within STEM
graduate education, domains of practice like recruitment, admissions, teaching, and mentoring were entangled with one another. Orchestrated combinations of small wins at the level of practice were definitely possible, but they
took time and intention, and there were no silver bullets. We saw in the psychology program, for example, the unsustainability of changing recruitment
and admissions without concerted attention to the quality of classroom experiences, lab climates, and mentoring relationships. It implies that we need to
think of systemic change as not only adopting an especially long checklist of
more inclusive practices, but also attending to the system that provides them.
We need the perspective to recognize couplings, anticipate feedbacks, identify
high-leverage interventions, and grapple with the cultural, environmental,
and other engrained barriers to change.

In this system, small wins that redefine engrained assumptions are especially high-leverage opportunities. Changes at this level matter both in

Recruitment

- Ensure online presence communicates commitment to diversity, equity, inclusion
- Engage with MSIs
- Attend to cues sent at campus-visit weekend
- Timely responses to email inquiries from prospective students
- Bridge program
- Recruit undergraduates directly from their institution as appropriate
- Diversity fellowships
- Coordinate with graduate school outreach and recruitment
- Create a climate in which current students gladly serve as ambassadors

Admissions

- Downplay or eliminate GRE
- Fine-grained read of transcript (not use of cumulative GPA)
- Value research experience
- Intentionally assess non cognitive competencies
- Emphasize potential over absolute achievements
- Contextualize achievements
- Revisit committee composition
- Discuss meanings of criteria to check misperceptions
- Develop, refine, and use rubric to systematize evaluation
- Define merit in relation to what makes program distinctive

Mentoring and Support

- Individual development plans
- Develop a lab manual
- Attend to quality of relationships
- Empower staff
- Same-identity faculty available for mentoring, even if not formal advising
- Support student organizations
- Include students in faculty decision making
- Appoint ombudsperson or means to report harassment, bias, and/or assault
- Encourage multiple mentors
- Make support and resources for mental health explicit

Creating Conditions Conducive to Equity

- Attend to social relevance of science
- Coordinate with university and disciplinary leaders, to leverage resources
- Create processes that support reform
- Shift from diversity champions to collective engagement
- Critical mass of women faculty and faculty of color
- Track program-level data, disaggregated by race/ethnicity and gender
- Empower a department diversity, equity, or inclusion committee

FIGURE 5. Inclusive practices in high-diversity STEM PhD programs.
SOURCE: Adapted from Posselt et al. (2017).

their own right and because they signal to stakeholders that cultural change is under way.[3] Rethinking, for example, what merit means, whether curriculum ought to be common or individualized, and the acceptability of talking openly about race and gender all affected not only single domains of practice but also how people moved through them and interacted with one another informally. Going so far as to rethink norms that had motivated previous generations of diversity efforts (i.e., the chemistry department's recognition of costs associated with thinking of hiring women as diversity hiring) was a critical aspect of embedding double-loop organizational learning, because it enabled shifts in organizational discourse, conventional wisdom, and strategy.

In sum, change of a sort happens when new practices are adopted, but this is just one dimension of institutional change, defined as "changing structures, understandings, and beliefs that have come to be taken for granted as normal, neutral, and legitimate."[4] To change the system means aligning changes in specific areas of practice with changes in the mindsets of individual practitioners. Those mindsets are a function of community-wide norms and values—many of which scholars learned in and are therefore institutionalized by graduate education.

Orchestrating Systemic Change: From Policy Reform to Reimagining Boundaries

My research indicates that where cultural change is occurring in STEM graduate education, scientists and scientific organizations are involved in, but going deeper than, a technical process of policy reform. This conclusion is consistent with research on more than a century of reform efforts in various sectors of American education, which makes clear that reforms focused on closing gaps through policy and programs rarely succeed—and when they appear to do so, rarely stick.[5] Either they lack community buy-in or fail to change the fabric of the community.

Rather, as we saw in applied physics, the best chances for deep and lasting change come with reimagining the community's boundaries of what constitutes good science and the practices and qualities we associate with good scientists. These boundaries shape identity itself. As such, they govern what community members think of as acceptable and compel the organization—not just the advocates, activists, or "champions" within it. How can boundaries be broadened? The quantum insight that scientists are part of the realities they strive to understand and the communities they try to change highlights the fundamental need for fresh perspectives. Two mechanisms, cultural retooling and cultural translation, explain how fresh perspective makes its way through existing boundaries and into organizational practice.

Cultural Retooling: Expanding What
Counts as Tools of the Trade

I argue that such boundary work constitutes serious *cultural retooling*, or learning new cultural knowledge (e.g., concepts, skills, practices, norms) in order to broaden the boundaries of effective professional practice, with the needs of particular student populations in mind. Where once a professor might be lauded for a certain approach to teaching, cultural retooling for equity may mean incorporating new knowledge and skills, such as culturally relevant pedagogy, into lesson planning or assessment. In disciplinary and departmental cultures, tools may come from academia generally, the wisdom of marginalized groups, the institutional culture, and disciplinary subject matter and methods. They constitute a cultural apparatus that people use in both everyday science and in change efforts.

When working on any project—home improvement or organizational—one's natural instinct is to use the tools at hand for the job. However, a "do-it-yourself" approach to disciplinary cultural change is unlikely to yield outcomes with the same depth or longevity as change that works across conventional boundaries, where there are different and more resources and tools available. For example, in STEM, experimentation is a tool of the trade. It is an excellent starting point in building support for short-term innovations, but other common cultural tools (e.g., individualism, value neutrality, comfort with hierarchy) are mismatched to social, relational, and equity-minded work.[6] People, after all, are not particles, and social systems do not change in the same way that natural systems do.[7] Mismatch between the set of existing and necessary tools helps explain some of the common barriers to change that people and teams encounter.

To effectively select and serve a more diverse student population takes additional, different cultural tools from those with which most graduate programs equip scholars.[8] Three specific activities enable retooling: critical reflection about how implicit standards, priorities, and practices have been racialized and gendered; acquisition of new knowledge; and experimentation with it in the context of their work and organizations. In the case studies, I found common patterns in the resources that facilitated reflection, acquisition, and experimentation with new tools: perspectives of community members from historically marginalized groups, institutional or field-level data, professional development, social science research, and varied supports from disciplinary societies and graduate schools.[9] These resources enabled retooling by allowing change agents to carry out self-study, see inequities in their midst, negotiate differences, create community buy-in, and ultimately adopt and analyze new practices.[10] Reform that tinkers at the margins of education has been a stable feature of American education for a century. Cultural retooling, however, is something new for higher education, particularly toward culturally responsive practices that center the knowledge and voices of people from historically marginalized communities.[11] For marginalized and outsider knowledge to permeate community thinking (with its varied power dynamics that tend to impede change of any sort) and enable retooling of policy and practice, however, also required cultural translators who make new knowledge, norms, and practices intelligible and persuasive. Only with new understanding enabled by cultural translation will cultural retooling in areas like admissions and mentoring make sense.

Cultural Translation: Spanning Boundaries to Build Understanding

There was at least one cultural translator within each of the organizations I studied, regardless of whether change efforts better resembled reform or retooling. These individuals used the language and sensibilities of the existing culture to communicate and collaborate across boundaries—decoding, valuing, and applying perspectives different from those to which long-standing members had been socialized. Without this translation and the learning it enabled, those who held the reins of the status quo were unlikely to loosen their grip on it because they simply could not see reality from a perspective other than the worldview to which inequitable institutions had socialized them. I have therefore argued that translation is an educative process that is especially needed by people with privileged social and professional identities, which is consistent with previous research about the role of perspective taking in higher education.

Whether it was Bonnie translating student concerns across a gender divide to male faculty in the geoscience course, applied physics staff enabling the chair to interpret interactions with Black students differently, or IGEN workshops translating the social science of admissions to physicists through disciplinary-relevant metaphors, the cultural translators who facilitated this learning were boundary spanners.[12] Their work played a powerful role toward equity in cracking entrenched mindsets so that a fresh perspective could make its way in. In deciphering what seemed like outsider perspectives into language that was intelligible to insiders, cultural translation deactivated boundaries by facilitating the realization that our thinking and intentions may be more aligned than we think.

By building bridges, forging psychic bonds, and otherwise serving as intermediaries, cultural translators eased frictions at the boundaries of cultural communities that were just learning to work together. Tools used by translators included racial literacy, interpersonal savvy, moral authority, and clear personal commitment, and their work resembled that of what anthropologists have called cultural brokers.[13] For leaders of organizations striving for diversity, equity, and inclusion, practical steps may be identifying community members with the knowledge, skills, and dispositions to span salient boundaries within the organization; actively creating spaces to interpret and translate across those differences; and validating and compensating such contributions.[14]

Retooling and Translation in Practice: Reexamining Evaluations and Interactions

Where might a department or discipline start if it wants to seriously consider retooling for equity? The case studies here suggest two fundamental targets are the norms and practices by which faculty evaluate excellence and interact with students. Ubiquitous and fractal-like, our subconscious justifications for evaluations and interactions are replicated over and over throughout institutional life, from such apparently inconsequential judgments as whether and when to reply to an email from a prospective student, to structures for dyadic mentoring and advising relationships, to the bureaucratic systems that allocate admissions, fellowships, and access to skilled mentors.[15] Evaluations and interactions communicate our priorities to students, shape access to opportunities, and have implications for productivity and persistence via belonging and well-being.

Typical mindsets that guide evaluations and interactions in many science cultures—for example, that merit can be gauged by our impressions of scholars' brilliance, or that our interactions should tip toward challenge more than support—institutionalize racial, gender, and other barriers. In this section, I therefore present models of holistic review and holistic support as general models that can be customized with the needs of specific organizational and evaluation or interaction contexts in mind. From a systems design perspective, keep in mind that changing structures of evaluation like admissions to increase access for racially minoritized groups without ensuring the availability of culturally aware mentoring and interactions may set students up for a bait and switch experience akin to that described in Chapter 4.[16]

Equity-Minded Holistic Review

To change admissions requires a conversation and negotiation of cultural values and priorities that most of the time remain latent. Changing admissions therefore both reflects and requires some modicum of cultural change. Criteria for admissions reflect priorities, and priorities reflect values. My previous research revealed that many of the priorities that faculty hold in admissions are not rooted in the best available evidence or a commitment to shared principles; rather, they are rooted in tradition, flawed conventional wisdom, or professors' personal beliefs about what facilitated their own success. Therefore, as I investigated science cultures working toward diversity, equity, and inclusion for this book, I was not surprised that each organization I studied had reexamined its selection processes, was innovating on typical admissions models, or had designed its selection processes from the start with holistic review in mind. In these spaces, changes involved dropping certain criteria and practices to deinstitutionalize bias from formal evaluations, evaluating new criteria to capture potential and a broader conception of merit, and creating new steps for the players involved to check themselves at a process level.

Not unlike "diversity," holistic review is an idea in increasingly wide circulation, but one that people interpret and implement in so many ways that a singular meaning is hard to pin down. That doesn't mean we should be satisfied when people tell themselves or one other that they "do holistic review." Like any technology, it is not the claim to use of holistic review, but rather the way it is designed and implemented that determines how well it can contribute to an agenda of organizational activity toward diversity and equity. Even ETS now advocates holistic review—as long, of course, as you continue using the company's product.[17] I am persuaded that if equity is not at the heart of the thinking and practice of holistic review, it will simply become the next tool that perpetuates inequality.

To that end, the model I am collaboratively refining, studying, and enabling adoption of through the Inclusive Graduate Education Network and California Consortium for Inclusive Doctoral Education (an NSF-funded partnership of faculty and administrators throughout six California universities dedicated to collective research and experimentation with new forms of admissions and other practices in graduate education) urges critical reflection about evaluation criteria, decision-making processes, and participants in the review process alike—recognizing each of these as a pillar of equitable evaluation. Holistic review should be rooted in clarity about the current legal landscape for race in admissions; awareness of how gender and racial bias manifest in individual judgment, committee deliberations, and institutionalized criteria; and knowledge of current evidence about how inequities are institutionalized in various aspects of the admissions file. In addition to being equity minded, holistic review should be comprehensive, contextualized, and systematic. I detail each of these three characteristics.

Comprehensiveness involves assessing numerous, diverse criteria and considering the whole person and multiple indicators of their potential—not only achievements and skills to date. It means accounting for the unique perspectives an applicant may bring, which may improve scholarly work, as well as socioemotional competencies.[18] Skills like initiative, conscientiousness, creativity, and leadership have positive relationships with professional performance and show little, to any, differences by race and gender.[19] In some respects, comprehensiveness is the easy part of a move toward holistic review because a variety of types of information are already collected and, at least when judging among finalists, faculty do not reduce review to a single criterion. However, in my research, I have found a need for comprehensiveness is motivated by the long-standing tendency to unduly rely on GRE scores as an indicator of merit—sometimes to the neglect of everything else in one's file.

The second characteristic of holistic review, contextualization, is so critical to creating more just forms of admissions that in the United Kingdom affirmative action goes by the name contextualized admissions. In US graduate education three types of contextualization are important. Thinking about academic metrics in context means remembering that, like all statistics, grades and test scores have error.[20] One source of this error is disparate access to educational opportunities and resources from elementary school through college, which accumulates to produce racialized, classed, and gendered variation in the records represented in graduate school applications.[21] As those who investigate and advocate holistic review at the undergraduate level also advise, contextualization therefore means considering a person's credentials and achievements relative to the opportunities that person has enjoyed and the barriers that person has faced.[22] We have to stop confusing access to educational opportunities with potential for excellence in scholarship. Finally, a third form of contextualization is to evaluate prospective students in the context of the program and what makes it unique. At the University of Michigan, the applied physics department's linking of its applied, interdisciplinary intellectual paradigm with a notion of merit that emphasized intellectual adventurousness, which was then applied in admissions, is an excellent example of this sort of contextualization. In Latin *ad mission* means "toward the mission," and a closer linking of admissions criteria and practices with educational mission can create congruence that serves both a program and its members.

Systematic review is necessary as part of being holistic, because unstructured, undisciplined consideration of any and all information that strikes a reviewer is inequitable (i.e., different people are evaluated on different criteria) and opens the process to unconscious biases. Under what committee members in my prior research considered holistic review, I heard manifestly racist, sexist, and classist comments about applicants' hairstyles, hobbies, and hometowns.[23] Basing evaluations on shared, predefined criteria using structured protocols reduces this risk and redresses several other common drawbacks in traditional decision-making processes: Efficiency is enhanced by expediting review. Structure is enabled for comparing many applicants along the same dimensions, the necessity of which is part of current Supreme Court precedent for admissions. Specificity about what reviewers should be attending to in the application may reduce implicit bias, and the transparency, reliability, and accountability enabled with rubrics protect interests of decision makers, their colleagues, and prospective students alike.[24] To be systematic is to ensure that we are doing more than succumbing to instinct, and it elevates admissions as a process that reflects collective instead of idiosyncratic values.

So You Want to #GRExit?   In every PhD program and disciplinary society this book has described, policy around the GRE was a starting point and, in some cases, a lightning rod for conversation toward holistic review, given the national conversation about test-optional admissions at both the undergraduate and the graduate levels. Each one, as well as those specific physics departments that were part of the IGEN project in Chapter 6, controlled and reduced the weight of the GRE, eliminated score submission as a requirement for admission, or stopped collecting scores altogether.[25] Two of the four cases had gone through a process over a few years in which reducing weight of the GRE one year enabled the realization that scores were not needed at all to identify the students they wanted. Upon making scores optional to submit, they grasped it would be more equitable to not accept them at all, to ensure they had the same types of information about all applicants. In all cases of admissions reform, changes were developed and gained credibility among department faculty through open dialogue and through a willingness to experiment while looking at both their own data and that in published research.

Current evidence does not persuade me that potential benefits for selection that come with using GRE scores outweigh the varied costs and risks, and this is especially so for programs that wish to tout diversity, equity, or inclusion as goals. I address the details of this position in other publications. And yet I recognize that thoughtful people may come to different conclusions about what is best at a given point in time for their organization. I strongly support faculty having principled and data-driven conversations about this issue, in part because it surfaces cultural assumptions that deserve more discussion than we give them.

Just as we need to think systemically about graduate education writ large, we need to design admissions systemically. I would, therefore, never counsel a program to drop GRE requirements without developing a clear plan for the selection process that will replace their current approach. If not implemented with care, test-optional and no-test admissions come with risks and costs to equity of their own. Similarly, I would never advise a department or graduate school to eliminate GRE requirements as its only tactic for reducing inequalities; nor would I advise my own students to apply to such PhD programs. Nevertheless, if a department is unwilling to even consider letting go of a single one of the criteria within just one of its evaluative processes—namely, one with mixed evidence of validity and one that presents specific barriers for underrepresented students—it may well be a red flag about that department's willingness to loosen its hold on other institutionalized practices that preserve inequities. Whether to use GRE scores and, if so, how is just one set of issues that merits revisiting within graduate admissions and the broader graduate education system, but it is proving a useful litmus test for the general change readiness and evaluative cultures of faculty groups.

A valid question is whether eliminating test scores from consideration will simply lead to greater weight being placed on other biased credentials (e.g., college reputation), or whether introducing a rigorous holistic review process might still favor students from historically overrepresented backgrounds. The truth is, it depends. Empirical research on these questions is limited, although more research is currently under way at both the undergraduate and the graduate levels. Here is what we do know: research on contextualized and holistic review in undergraduate admissions comes to mixed results about whether—on its own—it increases enrollment from specific, underrepresented groups. Much appears to depend on how holistic review is defined and put into practice and what the motivations for it are. Is it aimed merely at reducing access disparities introduced with conventional admissions criteria? Or does it also assess qualities that may directly or indirectly boost odds for underrepresented groups? Is it part of a coordinated strategy for creating a more equitable and inclusive learning environment? Does a test-optional strategy define how those who do and do not submit scores will receive fair review?

With respect to motivations, we see at the undergraduate level test-optional admissions being used in some places as a tool of enrollment managers to increase selectivity (i.e., to increase the number of applications received while holding constant rates of admission, and thus, to reduce the acceptance rate), which is part of rankings algorithms.[26] I do not see this impression management tactic and effort to game rankings algorithms being used as frequently in graduate programs. There, decisions to eliminate GRE requirements usually start with questions about the test's implications for diversity and equity, and those questions are asked amid other change efforts (e.g., recruitment, student organizations, qualifying exam reform). However, there is an emerging bandwagon effect for GRE-optional policy in some fields that merits attention and research. Programs that have eliminated GRE requirements mainly as a result of field-level pressures may not, like the psychology program whose students felt a bait and switch, be ready to equitably and effectively serve more diverse students, even if the environment has pressed them to do so. Regardless, this much is clear: it is in departments and disciplines that are both retooling evaluative cultures and their cultures for supporting students that the greatest chances of equitable outcomes are to be seen.

Retooling Evaluation Regimes.   Equity-minded holistic review in graduate admissions is simply one case of the need for attention to equity, comprehensiveness, contextualization, and systemization in academic evaluation and decision-making contexts more broadly. Racial, gender, and other types of inequities are institutionalized as normal through evaluation regimes for qualifying exams, hiring, tenure, promotion, and more. To retool evaluations toward equity means attuning ourselves to engrained—and sometimes highly personal—norms about how we define excellence and merit, what we value and prioritize, and what criteria and processes we use to arrive at decisions that reflect those ideas, values, and priorities.

Processual issues, including selection, training, deliberation, and data use among reviewers contribute to both equity in the process and its outcomes. *Selection of reviewers and committees* matter much to the patterns of preferences that are likely to emerge. As Jesús Pando from the National Society of Hispanic Physicists observed, "If the committee is composed of people who don't have a broader perspective or life experiences, then their discussion is more likely to ignore those factors that enable you to see potential." *Training*, or at minimum norming, of all who participate in evaluation enables more consistent review of different people and the strengths they bring. *Deliberation* during training and following file review permits an opportunity for misperceptions to be corrected and differences in norms to be negotiated. In those deliberations, *use of available data* for equity checkpoints "may include whether known biases are revealed in the information or criteria being used for judgment, whether decision processes or rules are reinforcing or interrupting power asymmetries, and whether intermediate outcomes preceding the ultimate outcome reflect inequities or reduce them."[27] In addition to adopting a more holistic approach to evaluation, attention to the selection and training of reviewers, and the use of data for equity checks as part of their deliberations are practical actions for enhancing the quality of review toward goals of more equitable access.

Holistic Support for Healthier Students and Academic Communities

Interaction is the second core area in which lessons can be drawn from the outliers studied in this research. Case studies reported here suggesting several potential types of retooling for norms on interactions may be needed, including the gendered occupation of sonic space and patterns of communication, poor accountability for advising women of color, and failure to talk openly about race in coursework and graduate education more broadly. In addition, to better understand both positive and problematic student interactions with faculty, my students and I conducted a study-within-the-study across student perspectives in these high-diversity PhD programs. We focused data collection and analyses on seventeen individual interviews with current students or alumni and three additional focus groups. The twenty-nine total PhD students across the four STEM programs included women from a mix of ethno-racial backgrounds, men of color, LGBTQ-identifying students, and military veterans.

Our goal was to use phenomenological methods to unpack meanings and experiences of faculty support when it did occur.[28] Perhaps counterintuitively, students saw their advisor as a last resort for academic support. Indeed, they would actively avoid their primary faculty advisor for as long as they could when the going got rough. A woman of color in psychology admitted: "My first years were very rough for a lot of different reasons, and one of them was I didn't—you know, this impostor syndrome. I didn't know how to ask for help. And so I remember my mentor as intimidating, not because he was not friendly or helpful; I was just scared." With social comparison among their peers endemic, fear deterred some of the very students who needed academic support from seeking it.

Rather, when facing academic and other struggles, students described professors providing psychosocial support by normalizing the difficulty of graduate school and talking openly about its racialized and gendered dimensions. More than half described professors offering alternative interpretations of challenging situations or themselves as scholars. Consistent with research on the value of a growth mindset, I found that in the face of significant struggles, students could see a path forward for themselves when professors placed performance in the context of a learning process. By validating that they had necessary professional qualities quelled anxieties, and by "keeping it real" about the challenges of race and gender in the academy, faculty helped ensure that students would not conflate feelings of being an impostor or isolation with their ability to handle graduate school's rigors.

With doctoral research assistant Theresa Hernandez, I also conducted a negative case analysis of ample evidence in our data that students felt unsupported in these diverse programs. We found great variation in the quality of students' day-to-day experiences and unsupportive interactions with faculty along a spectrum of behaviors, from failure to ensure clear expectations, to benign neglect, to overt racism, sexism, intimidation, and harassment.[29] Students also described a range of unsupportive interactions with the program itself.[30] Negative program interactions surrounded the liminal state that each of the programs occupied between pasts from which they wanted to pivot and their aspirations for a more equitable future. Uneven commitment among faculty and students for diversity, equity, and inclusion goals contributed to this sense of liminality, combined with students' perceived need to perform a certain degree of satisfaction with the program (so that few could fully discern how happy or unhappy another might be).[31]

This data were well suited to analyzing from the perspective of emotional labor. We found that students in each of the departments suppressed their emotional responses to discriminatory interactions with peers and faculty. They didn't want to come across as hostile or angry because it might reinforce negative stereotypes or compromise their working relationships, but neither did they want to simply accept insults about their worth or abilities. In addition to the emotional burden of "being the diversity," we found a tendency for diversity efforts to lean more than they should on students for programming and coordination.[32] The combination of needing to suppress frustration with microaggressions, while being relied on both to "be the diversity" the program sought and to increase diversity for the program, exacted a cumulative burden that frequently manifested in exhaustion and depression. A Black woman student who was heavily involved in recruiting students of color for her department despite a poor advising relationship reflected, "I think I'm just so tired; I don't feel like fighting anymore." To relieve this emotional dissonance and burden of performing what they thought people around them expected of them (a phenomenon the emotional labor literature calls surface acting), students in three of the four programs were actively involved in graduate student organizations, especially for students of color. These counter-spaces, in providing an outlet for revealing feelings of anger, confusion, and being minoritized, provided students with a break from the surface acting and a means of resolving emotional dissonance.

From these findings and the results of prior research, the value of a holistic, culturally responsive approach to supporting students—especially students from backgrounds historically marginalized in the academy—becomes clear. Students need academic support to acquire core subject knowledge and advance it through their research. They also require that we who serve graduate students make more explicit the sociocultural rules of the academy (i.e., the hidden curriculum) as well as strategies for navigating and, in some cases, resisting those rules. Understanding the current cultural rules may be especially important for doctoral students of color, who often experience dissonance between academic and personal values.[33] Racialization within the academy, STEM disciplines, and departments and labs can amplify insecurities, leading to false inferences about the reasons a person might feel like they are struggling. Third, given the rigor of graduate-level learning and the necessity of developing comfort with the nonlinearity of research and experiences of rejection and failure, psychosocial support is needed to cement students' sense of self and belonging in academia. The value of a growth mindset for student development and mastery supports this view.[34] Finally, recent empirical application of the cognitive apprenticeship model in doctoral education suggests cognitive foundations to these other forms of support.[35] In particular, the notion—originally proposed by the Carnegie Initiative on the Doctorate—of "making thought visible" makes explicit the many implicit rules and expectations of scholarly life.[36] Distinct but overlapping sets of supports are needed for graduate student well-being—academic, sociocultural, psychosocial, and cognitive supports.

Not even the most skilled and committed advisor is likely able to meet every student's need for all these types of support. Multiple mentors, developmental networks, and peer mentoring are all valuable models for department and program chairs to explore in order to ensure student well-being, progress, and productivity. That being said, given the oversized role that interactions within one's lab and program have in a graduate student's life, anyone tasked to supervise, teach, or advise will likely benefit from research-mentor training.[37]

Common to holistic review and holistic support is validating and engaging the whole student. In holistic review, it takes the form of recognizing how students' professional potential is revealed only with multiples types of information and is a composite of many different qualities. This variation, alongside the multiple types of challenges students face in graduate education, compels a multidimensional, holistic notion of support that faculty and the organizations that administer graduate education can provide. Retooling mindsets and practices along these lines is more easily facilitated under some cultural conditions than others.

Diagnosing and Managing Common Forms of Resistance

In a world where whole books have been written about faculty resistance to innovation and change, some ambivalence and resistance to equity-based change can be expected. Every organization has limits to the change it is willing to pursue at a given point in time, and anthropologist Sara Ahmed uses the metaphor of a brick wall to describe that within a university "which keeps its place when an official commitment to diversity has been given."[38] In different organizations, the wall derives its durability from different sources. The large size and complex structure of the psychology department in Chapter 4, for example, ensured that very little ever happened in a coordinated way within the department; this would come to include diversity-related activities. Within the geosciences, the wall of the intense schedule derived strength from the discipline's culture and history. Any change in the schedule to accommodate student needs or create a more inclusive climate for everyone came up against deeply embedded norms that privileged togetherness and intensity. In short, even organizations with the best intentions are likely to have a certain comfort zone with respect to change. Those striving to bring about change may enable better negotiation through a clearheaded understanding of what "the wall" is in a given context and from what it derives its strength. Before shifting to discuss implications of this work for the design and implementation of collaborative equity efforts, readers may appreciate what to do about three common forms of resistance that can arise. With greater clarity about the kind of resistance that one is facing, a person can more effectively engage with it—or perhaps, undermine it.

Nihilism: "But the Privileged Always Find a Way"
Some faculty resist making change because they are convinced that what appears in principle to be more open and equitable is nonetheless likely to be gamed and therefore uphold the *status quo*. This is a reasonable concern: transparency can help level the playing field to some degree, but as studies applying the theory of effectively maintained inequality have found time and again, people with privilege effectively use transitions that appear to become more open to preserve a competitive edge. Nevertheless, the proposition that people will game a more equitably designed system should not be used to legitimate an inequitable system. Equity can and should inhere not only in our outcomes but also in our organizational designs and processes.

Embedded Bias: "But Now That He Says It . . ."
A common sign of racial and gender power asymmetries in organizations is for ideas or change recommendations to be dismissed or critiqued when members of underrepresented backgrounds express them, only to be affirmed thereafter when a person who is white and/or male expresses them.[39] It is just

one example where the same micro-level communication patterns I observed in the field course—of men dominating the sonic space and institutionalizing women's silence—reappear regularly in academic life.

What explains this behavior? One reason people have hypothesized is that it performs status and reiterates who holds power. Another view suggests that people tend to be less critical of their own views than they are of people from groups that are different from their own. Charles Darwin is infamous for incorrectly concluding that women are intellectually inferior to men because, as he looked around Victorian society, he observed their achievements were fewer. Although meticulous in his research, Darwin's failure to apply the same care and scrutiny to his own inferences about women and the social world contributed to damaging stereotypes and gendered hierarchies that persist today.[40] If people or organizations do not recognize the voices and ideas of people from the backgrounds they say they want to attract, they arguably do not deserve to have such individuals in the first place.

Skepticism: "But We Need More Evidence First"

After fifteen years of research on graduate education and engaging with practitioners, it is my contention that we cannot and should not wait for a convergent base of research evidence to emerge that creates a field-wide consensus about how best to admit and educate our students. Just as Bill and Carl could come to very different interpretations about what the same, simple bar chart means, graduate education stakeholders will always be able to look at both the bodies of research and evidence from practices and come to different conclusions about which actions are best supported by the data. At some point, debates that split hairs about methodologies are, at best, delay tactics and, at worst, obfuscatory.[41] For some people the right data will, indeed, compel action or experimentation. Others will need to see data they already know presented differently—such as the Miller and Stassun paper striving to convince physicists about problems with their GRE use through a compelling visual figure. Yet like all humans, scientists are apt to confirmation bias: reading new information through the lens of their current assumptions.

We need research using a variety of methods and theories to gather evidence about innovations in selection, recruitment, and educational practices.[42] But we ought not to let the desire for widely generalizable evidence get in the way of experimenting locally. After all, people have used existing graduate admissions processes for decades with little research basis other than mixed findings on the GRE's validity—and this despite PhD completion rates that top out at 60 percent for most fields and most racial-ethnic groups.[43] If we have been performing barely better than a coin toss in selecting and serving students for this modest form of "success," the average program has little to lose in stepping out and experimenting with new methods. Well-resourced programs with much higher completion rates usually have limited evidence that their admissions processes are primarily to thank for their outcomes. Such programs are poised to experiment for a different reason: rather than citing their resources and prestige as cause that they have the most to lose, they could view their resources as evidence that they have the most responsibility to provide leadership for equity. It is an interesting thought experiment to imagine what the conversation about improving STEM would be if scientists in America's most elite PhD programs came together with shared conviction, will, and courage to use their resources toward racial and gender equity.

Equity in Science as Convergence Work

Pursuit of social aims in science continues a thread in the philosophy of science that is more than 2,500 years old—the integration of what previously has been thought of as distinctly social knowledge with scientific subject matter.[44] In 2017, the National Science Foundation described this as disciplinary convergence and, recognizing its potential, identified it as one of their ten "big ideas." The NSF defines convergence as occurring when experts from varying disciplines engage in common research challenges and their "knowledge, theories, methods, data, research communities and languages become increasingly intermingled or integrated."[45] As a result of sustained interaction across disciplinary differences, new perspectives and paradigms can emerge.

Convergence builds on other movements for disciplinary entanglement like multi-, inter-, and transdisciplinarity,[46] but two characteristics make it distinctive: shared commitment to addressing a compelling problem and effective communication across disciplinary differences. Consistent with the notion that cultural translation can facilitate new understandings and paradigms, NSF proposes that using common frameworks and language on pressing challenges "may, in turn, afford solving the problem that engendered the collaboration, developing novel ways of framing research questions, and opening new research vistas."[47] The turn of disciplinary knowledge in a more socially conscious direction is already under way with the institution-alization of NSF's broader impacts criterion, the burgeoning discipline-based education research community, and new journals to support dissemination of their work.

Factors and Tensions in Collaborative Change

Effective collaboration improves the quality of work on complex social problems by pulling together individual actors' own, partial perspectives to collectively develop better, more complete understandings and strategies for addressing them. Effective collaboration also enables us to spot and manage gaps, connections, and feedbacks among people, among activities at different levels, in varied domains of practice, and through change emerging from multiple angles. But collaboration isn't easy. It involves a certain scientific logic and engineering or design thinking, but it is much more than a technical activity. Any effort tied to equity, diversity, or inclusion is also a political activity that will come with emotional and relational challenges; as such, its success will be subjectively judged. The case studies in this text highlighted four distinct but overlapping factors that affect how different people may view the same collaborative equity effort:

- *Perspectives:* Views and associated background knowledge (i.e., often taken for granted) based on multiple, intersecting social and professional identities.
- *Foci:* Attention to individual experiences, organizational practices, institutionalized norms, and/or group outcomes.
- *Priorities:* The relative emphasis placed on equity, diversity, or inclusion generally, as well as indicators of and activities toward these goals.
- *Narratives:* Implicit and explicit theories of change, power, inequality, and climate.

Just as cultural conditions make some organizations more conducive to equity work, generally, the perspectives and knowledge held by its members may condition their focus, priorities, and narratives. Collective activity requires teams and organizations will need to negotiate and weigh these factors. I observed that two specific areas generate tension within collaborative efforts, with implications for the design and implementation of projects aimed at equity, diversity, and inclusion.

Defining Success Beyond Participation Metrics

Looking deeply into a field course and PhD programs in which women of all backgrounds and Black and Latinx students were present at greater rates than typical for their field revealed that goals and actions that affect access and structure were necessary but not sufficient for creating an inclusive climate, for cultural change, or for equitable participation in the long term. Representation matters, but the success of change efforts must not stop with numeric indicators; we also need to know whether we are creating communities that can sustain gains.

The departments that maintained diverse enrollments in this study worked to create inclusive communities, actively replacing hierarchical tendencies in how people relate with networks of mutual support and actively mentoring students within and across generations. They centered students as learners and took care to support them as whole individuals. The chemistry faculty in Chapter 4 worked their way into a virtuous cycle in which conscious organizational learning about improving representation and climate for women faculty yielded both a better environment for graduate students that organically attracted women and confidence on the part of faculty leaders that they could similarly take steps to improve representation and climate for graduate students of color. Their analytic, democratic approach to revising GRE policy is one marker of that department's approach to institutional change.

Communities need to define goals for themselves to ensure alignment with local needs and to cultivate support for their pursuit. However, the case studies here demonstrate that it is shortsighted and ultimately unsustainable to center efforts only on processes affecting access or objective measures of participation. It is not enough to reform pathways into organizations and institutions built on biased assumptions of legitimate culture and behavior.[48] What Joanne Martin cheekily calls "the 'add women and stir' approach" is a naïve view of gender equity and inclusion,[49] and so, too, would be the ethno-racial equivalent. The enterprise itself needs changing. Without this, the tendency will be to reengineer systems of access into environments whose cultural norms and practices still privilege groups that have been historical insiders. It is not just the gates of academe and how we manage them that need changing, but also the everyday work and interactions that take place within them.

In groups that are as complex as the nine-area psychology department or as large as physics—where jockeying for recognition, authority, and resources is a way of life—leaders may understandably prefer the apparent clarity and precision of numbers over nuance. Quantitative reasoning is the basis for their way of knowing, and it was not until the twentieth century's engagement with quantum theory that physicists seriously questioned their own ontological assumptions about reality as measurable and impersonal. Further, belief in a world that can be observed, defined, measured, and captured numerically—and thus controlled—aligns well with and subtly reinforces the logic of a depersonalized, managerial approach, which undoubtedly feels like a safer path to repair in a broken system. And yet we also need to know about the stories of individual experiences, which, even as outliers, cannot be tolerated, such as Lydia's experience with unchecked harassment and assault by her doctoral advisor.

In sum, an important implication of this work is that people, projects, or organizations endeavoring to advance equity, diversity, or inclusion in academia need focused, measurable goals as part of a multifaceted vision that includes both participation or other representation rates and how people from the groups who represent "diversity" experience the environment. Clarity about what we mean when we say climate, culture, change, and metrics may prevent miscommunication in this respect.

Defining Standards for Leadership and Decision Making

Clarity about standards for leadership and decision making also emerged as a common source of tension within the change efforts that I observed. Who leads and participates in science conditions its character and impact in important ways. To that end, Harding argues that we ought to "include in scientific decision making the groups that heretofore have been excluded from participating in decisions about research that has effects on their lives."[50] This core principle of democratic ethics means that "those who bear the consequences of decisions should have a proportionate share in making them."[51] However, most tenured faculty, principal investigators on major research projects, administrators in universities and foundations, and a surprisingly large share of those who lead diversity and equity projects are men, white, and/or have well-educated parents. These forms of social privilege, individually and in combination, lead people to see, define, and address problems of inequity differently than people without such advantages. Those from disadvantaged groups are more likely to feel the weight of power asymmetries, are thus more likely to expect equity projects to address power and identity explicitly, and are more likely to address both structural and cultural foundations of inequity. They may also run projects differently. What may be lost when equity projects themselves are led by people with privileged identities? What opportunities for shared leadership exist across salient identities? Although on paper or in practice most projects benefit from appointing one or two people to be at the helm, collective leadership within equity projects is vital to avoid reproducing the same problems we see in the communities we are working to change.

Equity projects will always need allies from privileged communities, and yet ally work can be fraught. Intersectionality scholar Patricia Hill Collins points out that even within activities to improve the "STEM pipeline," the people with the deepest personal knowledge of inequities due to their intersecting identities—such as queer Black women—often find themselves marginalized.[52] Unless proactive steps are taken, equity efforts themselves will reflect white and/or male biases, norms, and preferences. Paulo Freire explained this point with such clarity that I quote him at length:

> Certain members of the oppressor class join the oppressed in their struggle for liberation, thus moving from one pole of the contradiction to the other. There is a fundamental role for them, and has been so throughout the history of this struggle. It happens, however, that as they cease to be exploiters or indifferent spectators or simply the heirs of exploitation and move to the side of the exploited, they must always bring with them the marks of their origin: their prejudices and their deformations, which include a lack of confidence in the people's ability to think, to want, and to know. Accordingly these adherents to the people's cause constantly run the risk of falling into a type of generosity as malefic as that of the oppressors.... [They] truly desire to transform the unjust order; but because of their background they believe that they must be the executors of the transformation.[53]

Freire's words highlight the importance of centering the voices and wisdom of people who might usually be at the margins or outside of it entirely. We need all hands on deck to deal with systemic challenges, and efforts in this area must do a better job of amplifying the voices, knowledge, and influence of women of color. Whether diverse voices contribute to design, decision making, and implementation is one marker of power dynamics within a group. At minimum, leaders and advisors should ask how open the opportunities are for participating in different ways, and how design, decision making, and implementation might look differently if community members—rather than community allies—were at the helm.

The contested standards for success and leadership within equity efforts make clear that new research and theory on these matters are needed, especially as practitioner-led equity work of the sort detailed in this book becomes increasingly common in colleges, universities, and other scientific institutions. More research is also needed about patterns of participation in this work and how to democratize it so that equity and inclusion work is itself carried out equitably and inclusively.

Theoretical Implications

Boundaries provide a sense of identity, security, connection, and belonging. In *Consilience*, E. O. Wilson writes: "People must belong to a tribe; they yearn to have a purpose larger than themselves. We are obliged by the deepest drives of the human spirit to make ourselves more than animated dust, and we must have a story to tell about where we came from, and why we are here."[54] Community provides this sense of purpose, and this includes scientific community. We are responsible to a large degree for how and why people from particular groups often become part of some academic tribes and not others, and are excluded from particular intellectual territories and not others. I have argued that micro-level values, everyday interactions and behaviors, and larger organizational and technological systems are all framed by cultural boundaries that have consequences for inclusion and exclusion. These human and nonhuman processes are the stuff of culture, so it is easy to lose sight of their influence. This is a deeply rooted cognitive, cultural aspect of social life. We need more research on cultural activities and cognitive apparatuses that enable translation across boundaries, retooling of activities that are governed by symbolic boundaries, and what it takes to transform extant boundaries to reduce barriers to access and belonging.[55]

By looking at the relationships present between and across social boundaries at multiple scales, we can come to better understand social groups and phenomena as discrete and connected—as a system of interdependent entities and activities at individual, organizational, and institutional levels. Given this complexity, and the fact that the work is not immune from the same power dynamics that characterize larger academic communities and society, equity work may always be work in progress. Just as natural scientists are constantly advancing knowledge about specific phenomena and their relationships, knowledge is continually advancing in the social sciences about the nature of inequality, power, and race within organizations. Innovation most frequently appears within organizations that can value, assimilate, and put to use new knowledge, a set of abilities that organizational theorists call absorptive capacity. One study of 285 different projects found that as a project's complexity increases, so do the risks of overspending and delays, but a project's absorptive capacity mitigated these risks. The ability to learn and apply what is learned are tools for managing complexity, and I have proposed cultural translation as a critical mechanism for this learning.

Revisiting Cultural Translation

In quantum theory, Werner Heisenberg's uncertainty principle asserts that there is a limit to what we can simultaneously know about pairs of physical properties, such as particles' momentum and position. Michael Frayn's play *Copenhagen* envisions a meeting of Heisenberg and fellow quantum physicist Niels Bohr in the afterlife. In it, Frayn reimagines the uncertainty principle from a social standpoint, proposing that there are limits to what we can know about mental states like motivation, including our own. The best chances we have of catching a glimpse of ourselves, he suggests, is through another person's eyes. Perhaps this is the real value of cultural translation. When translation facilitates understanding across discipline, identity, professional role or any combination thereof, it is because another's perspective permits us to see ourselves and experience our familiar world from a new angle. With this perspective, we can question what was once taken for granted, including beliefs we were socialized to hold without our realization.

Translation thus creates useful distance between self and others. Distance, according to French philosopher Paul Ricoeur, "is not just a gap in space-time. It is 'the principle of a struggle between *otherness* that transforms all spatial and temporal distance into cultural estrangement and *ownness* by which all understanding aims at the extension of self-understanding.'"[56] Reexamining our assumptions as knowers, our interactions with students as mentors, and our organizations and institutions as advocates for equity begins with appreciating just how much of the scientific and academic enterprise is not natural but rather a product of history. This appreciation is uniquely enabled when those with privileged positions actively listen to and mindfully learn from those who have been marginalized in ways that those with privilege have not. Such acts of solidarity and humility enable a person to step outside of themselves, enlarge their viewpoint, and transcend boundaries that otherwise would divide us.

Possibilities of Equity Mindedness: Listening, Learning, and Humility

In a practical sense, cultural translation provides new ways of experiencing and seeing what once had been familiar. The ability to re-view the familiar is important for those engaged in institutional change work, enabling us to question inherited structures that we might otherwise have taken for granted.[57] Cultural translation is therefore a fundamentally educative practice that permits more critical thinking. It paves the way for what Bensimon and colleagues call equity-mindedness, and what Paulo Freire and other scholars call critical consciousness, the ability to recognize and analyze systems of power and inequality and the commitment to intervene in those systems in order to change them.[58] Recall that for Joe's translation across the student-faculty divide in the applied physics PhD program, honest and open conversations in an atmosphere of trust enabled the PhD program chair to receive messages about where his own practice was falling short and to adopt a posture of learning. Conversations were the medium for communication, but honesty and humility cultivated trust so that listening and learning could take place.

In decoding another perspective to improve how two parties can relate, the importance of listening, learning, and humility cannot be overstated. Rorty defined learning as "our ability to engage in continuous conversation, testing one another, discovering our hidden presumptions, changing our minds because we have listened to the voices of our fellows."[59] Yet barriers to listening, learning, and humility are deeply engrained in academic culture. Academia rewards not the humility of learners but accomplishments, achievements, and performances of expertise—beginning with the awarding of grades for performance and degrees for mastery. The routinization of rewards for demonstrated expertise elicits, over time, a psychosocial link between perceived knowledge and pride, that most powerful drug. Thus, it is understandable that academia would set scholars up to embody Harry Truman's definition of an expert: "someone who doesn't want to learn anything new, because then he wouldn't be an expert."

I would also be remiss not to reiterate that for those with privileged social identities there is a special obligation to learn and engage with humility across boundaries. Thinking about how to communicate effectively across boundaries is something that people from marginalized and minoritized backgrounds do every single day to simply exist within institutions and organizations that were founded by and run on routines that privilege people from groups other than their own. Through years within educational institutions, people of color become "cultural straddlers" who are conversant and fluent in a variety of communities.[60] One way social privilege operates is that those with it do not have to engage in boundary-work activities for the sake of their own advancement. Any time we are working across lines of social difference, including team-based science research and collaborations required to create equity, the work benefits from effective translation across differences.

For scholars, there is another psychic barrier to learning that enables more effective engagement in change. Whereas learning one's subject matter is typically cast as mastery and acquisition of depersonalized facts, developing knowledge that improves one's work as a change agent requires self-reflection and synthesis of knowledge that exists "out there" with knowledge of oneself and what one does in the world (i.e., praxis). It is a fundamentally different epistemology and one that can be uncomfortable. I speak from my own experience to say that it takes intentionality and, ideally, connection with others who will both encourage and challenge us.

Conclusion: Sink, Swim, or Learn to Tread?

"Are you going to take it up to the microscope?!" Alicia asked me excitedly. "Come check it out you guys!" Suddenly, I was swarmed by a group of about five students, all women, all eager to see the scores of glowing plankton that stuck to my surf shirt and swimsuit after I climbed out of the water. We had been night swimming in bioluminescent waters, and they were exhilarated by the cold, plankton-rich water and the bliss of being immersed in it, the Milky Way spread out above us like a canopy. It was completely dark, so that I only could tell who one or two of them actually were, and as soon as someone walked up with a flashlight, the group made them turn it off so they could continue investigating.

"Aw, they're fading."

"Check her back."

"Good idea."

"They really are like little jewels, aren't they?"

I, who had been studying these women for three weeks, was now their re-search subject, or at least the medium for observing their phenomenon. It was a nice turning of the tables, so I played along.

One asked, "Are they on the inside of her shirt, too, or just the outside?"

I checked, peering closely at the underside of my shirt's edge. "Both sides!"

There was a chorus of "Oooooooh!" They were intrigued and immediately added their interpretations.

"It suggests how small they really are!"

"The plankton's really right in the water, though of course concentrated at the top."

"I wish they weren't fading, we could go up to the lab."

"But how would we sample them?"

"We'd have to turn out the lights in the lab and get a slide or something."

As in other times during the field course that I spent in groups that were only or mostly composed of women, people rarely interrupted one another. They built off of one another's ideas. Questions, answers, and observations flowed as freely as their beer did at the end of a long day in the sun. This self-selected group of adventurers literally jumped into the additional opportuni-ties that TAs and professors created for them to engage with the field station's resources, science, and recreation. In addition to the night swimming, a group of us woke at sunrise one day to kayak to and through sea caves. Another day I joined six or eight people in swimming against the ocean tides to a rock out-cropping. There, I observed a student have a lightbulb moment as a TA gave us a mini-lecture in structural geology while all of us were treading water.

I personally had a great time and learned some science in the night swim-ming, the sea kayaking, and the swim against the tides, but I could not get my mind off the students in the class who were excluded from these course high-lights—who did not have swimming experience and therefore could not join us. The absence of a learning curve built into these activities reminded me of how graduate education, especially STEM disciplines, have famously operated with a "sink or swim" mentality, one that implies that the water quality needs no attention and that getting in and staying afloat are individual endeavors. Fish in this cultural water—that is, the scientists who know how to swim and are adapted to its conditions—may or may not even remember what it was like to enter the water. They may not notice how their sink-or-swim culture not only legitimates drowning but also keeps many others from even climbing in.

However, more and more departments and disciplines are taking notice that this mentality is part of a pattern of exclusion, one that hurts the health of their communities. Our learning environments and workplaces are racially and sexually coded spaces, not the meritocratic, objective institutions that those who have benefited from its rules might like to imagine. From routine interactions and communications in the field course, to the reform of policy and practice in PhD programs, to the coordinated efforts of disciplinary societies, the portraits of culture and change here have revealed a range of ways that actors in higher education create, maintain, and can rework boundaries. I have argued that the best way for science as an institution to move toward equity involves the following:

- Systemic action in the multiple contexts and levels at which equity is created or impeded
- Leveraging bottom-up, top-down, and inside-out forces for change
- Cultivating, expecting, and rewarding knowledge, skills, and labor that support equity as new generations of scientists are trained and enter the labor market
- Equity-minded retooling, facilitated by cultural translators who span social, professional, or disciplinary boundaries

To this point, most organizations that constitute the academy have not placed expectations on professionals to possess or develop the pertinent knowledge or skills to facilitate these necessary changes. A 2018 report from the National Academies pointed out STEM graduate education has, to our society's detriment, failed to prepare graduate students with the leadership, communication, and other social skills needed by twenty-first-century scientists—much less skills to make science more inclusive.[61] Add to this the rigidity of incentive structures, and it is no wonder science is evolving so slowly.

And yet academia can change—is changing—and the lessons from outliers presented in this book highlight actions and mechanisms that may accelerate this change. There are spaces in STEM where rising scholars can learn about the social dimensions of the scientific enterprise, empowering the next generation with a more critical perspective on the professions they will eventually lead. Graduate schools, disciplinary societies, and a variety of other initiatives are providing professional development to students, postdocs, and faculty that enable racial literacy, skills in mentoring, and advocacy for change, among other skills.[62] Critically from the standpoint of institutionalization, some universities are incorporating demonstrated experience and commitment to serving diverse students into their admissions, hiring, and other evaluation structures.[63]

The dynamics of equity-based change in graduate education include both interventions aimed at closing representation gaps and efforts to improve the climate and center the voices, needs, and cultural sensibilities of people from historically marginalized groups. This dual agenda is mutually reinforcing— and necessarily one of both broadening scientific boundaries and of transforming them. To the extent holistic review and holistic support have begun to resonate in higher education, it is due to a growing recognition that students in a diverse society are ill-served by conventional, narrow definitions of excellence and conceptions of support. When we recognize that the rules by which educational institutions have selected and served students are the product of social construction—for a time and population that is different from our own—then we open ourselves to designing a dynamic, student-centered system rather than resigning ourselves to replicate the one that we received.[64]

Acknowledgments

My gratitude as a researcher is always first and foremost to my research participants, without whom the data do not exist. Spanning every time zone in the United States and beyond, they shared their time and expertise in a culture where these are two of the most important currencies. A special thanks to those participants who also discussed portions of the findings with me to confirm their veracity or resonance. Their input, as well as that from the outside reviewers of the book manuscript and the peer reviewers for journal articles that contributed to two chapters of findings, helped ensure that trustworthiness. I would also like to thank Marcela Cristina Maxfield and Sunna Juhn at Stanford University Press for shepherding the manuscript through to publication.

I carried out this research individually, in partnership with faculty colleagues around the country, and in collaboration with vibrant and dedicated teams of doctoral students at the University of Michigan and the University of Southern California. My research teams have been my anchors during these years and my greatest teachers. Students at Michigan were integral to the data collection and analysis in Chapters 4 and 5: Aurora Kamimura, Kamaria Porter, Kelly Slay and Kimberly Reyes. My team at USC has held me up and supported studies reported in Chapters 3 and 6: Aireale Rodgers, Cynthia Villarreal, Deborah Southern, Lauren Irwin, Román Liera, Steve Desir, and Theresa Hernandez. Special thanks to Theresa, who was research assistant during the pilot phase of the Inclusive Graduate Education Network. My project specialists Yasmin Kadir and Steve Desir, as well as project manager Monica Raad, have been a blessing with their administrative and editorial work, as well as their sunny attitudes.

Faculty colleagues at USC have inspired and challenged me with their work and encouraged me with their friendship, especially Adrianna Kezar, Bill Tierney, Estela Bensimon, Morgan Polikoff, Shaun Harper, Tatiana Melguizo, and Zoe Corwin. I'm also grateful for colleagues around the country who have become friends and a network of mutual support via our shared work on equity and inclusion in STEM higher education: Anne-Marie Núñez, Casey Miller, Chris Pfund, Leslie Gonzales, Kimberly Griffin, Melissa McDaniels, Rosie Perez, and Sara Xayarath-Hernandez.

The Spencer Foundation and National Science Foundation (Awards 1645465, 1649297, 1834528) have generously supported the research reported in this book, and although I speak only for myself, I hope the ideas and evidence in this volume advance their efforts for improving education and science. A fellowship from Spencer and the National Academy of Education was integral in enabling me to broaden my intellectual focus from the evaluative cultures affecting access to graduate education to include also how the culture of science affects the well-being of aspiring members. It was through this fellowship that I first arrived at the core insights in this book, and my mentors during that time—Anna Neumann, Sarah Freedman, and Maresi Nerad—enabled me to see the potential for a book in the work I was doing.

Through NSF and disciplinary society-sponsored projects, I have been fortunate to meet and work with some wonderful scholars who are working for change in their fields. There is so much they have taught me that is between the lines of this book. Thanks to Corey, Julia, and Lora; to Anne-Marie, Carolyn, Darrin, Gillian, Lisa, Mary, Peggy, and Wendy; to Casey, Cathy, Chris, Dave, Erika, Geraldine, Jaclyn, Joe, Joerg, Melissa, Monica, Pranoti, Stephanie, and Ted; to Cagliyan, David, Jon, Lance, Rob, and Weida; and to Alex, Gibor, Keivan, and Marcel. I look forward to continuing work that translates social science for maximum usefulness to natural scientists.

Finally, for their encouragement of me and of this work, thanks to my first science teachers, Janet and Gary; my comic relief, Karen and Greg; my running partner, Derek; and my pastry chef, Danny.

Methodological References

Please see the following papers for additional methodological detail.

Chapter 3

Posselt, J. R., & Núñez, A. (2018, November 16). Cultural boundaries in scientific field-work: Mapping dynamics of inclusion and exclusion in the geosciences. Association for the Study of Higher and Postsecondary Education, Tampa, FL.

Chapter 4

Posselt, J., Porter, K. B., & Kamimura, A. (2018). Organizational pathways toward gender equity in doctoral education: Chemistry and civil engineering compared. *American Journal of Education, 124*(4), 383–410.

Slay, K. E., Reyes, K. A., & Posselt, J. R. (2019). Bait and switch: Representation, climate, and tensions of diversity work in graduate education. *Review of Higher Education, 42*(5), 255–286.

Chapter 5

Posselt, J. R., Reyes, K. A., Slay, K. E., Kamimura, A., & Porter, K. (2017). Equity efforts as boundary work: How symbolic and social boundaries shape access and inclusion in graduate education. *Teachers College Record, 119*(10), 1–38.

Chapter 7

Hernandez, T., & Posselt, J. R. (2018, April). *Unsupported in STEM: A negative case analysis of underrepresented students' faculty and institutional interactions.* Paper presented at the American Educational Research Association, New York, NY.

Porter, K. B., Posselt, J. R., Reyes, K., Slay, K. E., & Kamimura, A. (2018). Burdens and benefits of diversity work: Emotion management in STEM doctoral students. *Studies in Graduate and Postdoctoral Education, 9*(2), 127–143.

Posselt, J. (2018). Normalizing struggle: Dimensions of faculty support for doctoral students and implications for persistence and well-being. *Journal of Higher Education, 89*(6), 988–1013.

Notes

Chapter 1

1. Another definition of equity is "just and fair inclusion into a society in which all can participate, prosper, and reach their full potential" (Policy Link, 2015).

2. Tierney (1988), p. 3.

3. Tierney (1988), p. 8.

4. Differentiated and fragmented organizational cultures are normal and expected in heterogeneous organizations (Martin, 2001).

5. Of the forces that organizational culture exerts in higher education, William Tierney (1988) writes, "Institutions certainly are influenced by powerful, external factors such as demographic, economic, and political conditions, yet they are also shaped by strong forces that emanate from within. This internal dynamic has its roots in the history of the organization and derives its force from the values, processes, and goals held by those most intimately involved in the organization's workings. An organization's culture is reflected in what is done, how it is done, and who is involved in doing it. It concerns decisions, actions, and communication both on an instrumental and a symbolic level" (p. 3).

6. Carter, Dueñas, & Mendoza (2019); Gonzales (2013); Posselt (2016).

7. By "we," I am referring to all of us engaged in education, whom I consider responsible for shaping its trajectory.

8. Uhlmann & Cohen (2007).

9. Miller & Stassun (2014); Educational Testing Service (2018). See also Educational Testing Service (2019).

10. Posselt (2016).

11. Petriglieri & Stein (2012).

12. The need to question meritocratic foundations of current systems for allocating educational opportunity is one of the core tenets of critical race theory. See, e.g., Ladson-Billings & Tate (2016).

13. NASEM is a set of nonprofit institutions that brings together leading scholars to assess the current state of knowledge on critical topics, in order to inform policy and the investments of funding agencies and other social institutions.

14. Change agents routinely cite these reports in making the case for attention to, investment in, and reform of graduate education, for NASEM provides a high-prestige, no-questions-asked basis for any recommendation they want to make.

15. Where possible, I refer in this book to the specific race/ethnicity; however, in this case I refer to institutional data from the universities involved, which was aggregated to an underrepresented minority category.

16. American Physical Society (2018).

17. Lemieux (2008).

18. National Science Foundation (2013).

19. On socialization in doctoral education, see Austin (2002); Gopaul (2011, 2016); Margolis & Romero (1998).

20. I use the terms *ethno-racial* and *racial/ethnic* interchangeably to represent the distinctiveness of race/ethnicity as well as the tendency for some groups to be racialized on the basis of ethnicity (e.g., People of Asian descent and/or Latin American origins). The US population is 12.2 percent Black/African American, 16.4 percent Hispanic, 63.6 percent White, and 50.9 percent female (National Science Foundation, NSF, 2015). Racial stratification is less pronounced in graduate education at the master's level. See Posselt & Grodsky (2017).

21. Sowell, Allum, & Okohana (2015).

22. Stassun et al. (2011).

23. NSF (2013).

24. In addition to those discussed, there are other sociological theories that can be used to interpret the intersection of graduate education's increasing importance and inequalities. Human capital theory, for example, which constructs education as an investment in one's skills, suggests that above and beyond the general professional skills obtained by spending more time in an educational setting, graduate and professional education provides field-specific forms of human capital. However, if the skills and knowledge expected for either entry into or positive outcomes within graduate education are disproportionately found among groups who are already advantaged in society, then graduate education will prove a very slow mechanism for reducing demographic inequities in the labor market. For graduate education to do anything *but* maintain or widen inequities demands equitable criteria and processes for admissions.

Theories of closure and credentialing help explain stratification within and resulting from graduate education. Training at this level is very much intended to protect the quality and resources of professional communities—both disciplinary and occupational. The manifest or official effect of closure in graduate education is to ensure disciplinary and professional quality standards are maintained through credentialing and licensure, but the exclusion that necessarily accompanies closure also serves to reduce the supply of candidates for positions. Reduced supply drives up the value of the people and their skills and maximizes the returns to their degrees. If human capital theory highlights the potential of graduate school entry to reproduce inequalities, then closure and credentialing highlights the potential for how we educate graduate students to contribute to inequities.

25. Bowen & Rudenstine (2014); Xie & Shauman (2003).

26. It creates opportunities for advanced coursework, whose benefits include increasing the odds of earning high standardized test scores, a favorably weighting one's grade point average, developing self-confidence interacting with teachers and authority figures, and engaging in extracurricular activities that admissions offices are more likely to find impressive (Stevens, 2009).

27. Attiyeh & Attiyeh (1997); Posselt, Jaquette, Bielby, & Bastedo (2012).

28. Posselt (2020).

29. Lovitts (2001).

30. Gardner (2006); Golde (2000); Lechuga (2011); Lovitts (2001); Nettles & Millett (2006).

31. Deitch et al. (2003); Espino (2014); Felder (2010); Lovitts (2001); Nettles (1990).

32. Ray (2019).

33. Because of the available institutional data as I began the studies, I looked at department and course racial and gender composition separately.

34. In the natural sciences, *theory* means a tested set of explanatory statements about some phenomenon, and in the physical sciences, these are often reducible to equations. In the social sciences and humanities, *theory* refers to sets of propositions that may describe reality but can also operate as a way of seeing familiar phenomena with a fresh perspective.

35. Although the case studies I present do not generalize, their insights about mechanisms and underlying processes do. Social scientists have a name for this: *theoretical generalization.*

36. Freire (1970) called this combination of qualities critical consciousness.

37. Walker, Golde, Jones, Bueschel, & Hutchings (2009).

Chapter 2

1. Barad (2007).

2. Ibid.

3. Frescura & Hiley (1984).

4. This is not to say that there will not be relationships among properties. But as an example, a magnetometer can determine whether some substance is magnetic, but it cannot directly measure other properties of the same substance, such as opacity, weight, or conductivity. My thanks to Casey Miller for this example.

5. Weick (1984)

6. Correll (2017); Weick (1984).

7. Kezar (2012).

8. Barad (2007).

9. Hallett & Ventresca (2006).

10. Ibid.

11. Robert Ross, as cited in Callahan & Bhattacharya (2017), p. 5.

12. Noble (2018).

13. Prescod-Weinstein (2017); Ray (2018).

14. Barad (2007).

15. Popkin (2018).

16. This view is closely related to Giddens's (1984) structuration theory.

17. Scott & Davis (2015).

18. Posselt, Porter, & Kamimura (2018).

19. Ely & Thomas (2001).

20. Faulkner (2011).

21. Barad (2007), p. 234.

22. Barad (2007), p. 26.

23. Waters & Asbill (2013).

24. Freire (1970).

25. Berger & Luckmann (1991).

26. Francis Bacon's notion in 1621 that we best refine theory through observations, hypothesis formation, experimental design, and further observation was the product of historical and contemporary influences from Copernicus and Galileo.

27. The National Institute for Standards and Technology's activities include everything from maintaining an atomic clock that determines the official time in the United States (measurements of cesium's natural resonance frequency determine the second) to producing documents that define capacities and sizes of berry baskets and boxes, or articulating rules for rounding numerical values. The institute has also expanded its mission into physical sciences research. See the website of the National Institute for Standards and Technology, part of the Department of Commerce, at https://www.nist.gov.

28. Laced through questions like these are values and power dynamics that scientists are not always trained to perceive. In a lecture at a meeting of the American Physical Society, theoretical astrophysicist Chanda Prescod-Weinstein offered an illustration of this from history, discussing the damage done to and by institutions of German science in the name of Nazi Germany's nativism, xenophobia, racism, and authoritarianism. Physicists associated with the Deutsche Physik movement tried to impose Nazis' political orthodoxy on the conduct of science, revealing the inevitable integration of political values with the incentive structure for science. This story also reveals, she argued, the importance of scientists taking action today in the political sphere to ensure that values attributed to "science" ultimately serve the ends of justice, freedom, and humanity.

29. Close to the heart of science is elevating the value of some forms of knowledge over others. Scientists evaluate H_1 versus H_0, privilege objectivity versus subjectivity, and seek evidence versus myth.

30. In addition to the structural challenge across the disciplines of adding knowledge and skills that promote equity into our expectations for doctoral training, some STEM fields present a distinctive cultural challenge—the view that human involvement is a common source of bias (i.e., systematic error). This assumption may operate as an indirect barrier to appreciating the relevance of social identities to scientific work.

31. Posselt (2016).

32. Lamont & Molnár (2002), p. 168.

33. To understand the logic of how social exclusion emerges through the definition of symbolic boundaries, "we have to shift our analytical focus away from what members of marginalized groups (the 'other') share, and toward what members of those inside the boundary share—and what they imagine themselves to share" (Edgell, Gerteis, & Hartmann, 2006, p. 231).

34. Ibid.

35. He writes: "The very definition of 'cultivation' or, in the modern world of bureaucracies, 'merit' that predominates in a particular society expresses underlying power relations and tends, accordingly, to reflect the particular cultural ideals of those group that hold the power of cultural definition. By its very nature, the process of defining 'cultivation' and 'merit,' far from being neutral, is thus a profoundly political one" (Karabel, 2006).

36. One does not need to espouse racist or sexist views to participate in the institutionalization of racial hierarchies in science. Similarly, racial microaggressions and sexual harassment and assault are simply manifestations of a broader system of symbolic violence, "the power to impose (and even inculcate) . . . knowledge and expression of social reality, which are arbitrary but not recognized as such" (Bourdieu, 1979, p. 80).

37. As symbolic boundaries become widely agreed on as self-defining for an organization, members may also lose sight of the potential that symbolic, cultural boundaries will overlap with social boundaries (i.e., by gender, socioeconomic status, race/ethnicity, and more) so that boundaries "take on a constraining character and pattern social interactions in important ways" (Lamont & Molnár, 2002, p. 169).

38. Lamont & Molnár (2002); Anderson (2006).

39. Tyndall (1905); Gieryn (1983).

40. See Tilly (2004), Gonzales (2018), Hill (2019), and Liera & Dowd (2019), for additional examples of boundary work in relation to inequities in academia. Tilly, for example, argued that boundary change occur through a combination of a mechanisms that prompt change (e.g., conversation, borrowing, encounter) and at least one mechanism that constitutes the change itself (e.g., inscription-erasure, activation-deactivation, relocation). These combinations modify relations on either side of

a social boundary, relations across the boundary, or shared representations of the boundary itself.

41. Weick (1984).

42. Snow (2012).

43. It will help, of course, when the incentive structure in our universities rewards such boundary spanning activities, as they reward expectations for other types of professional performance.

44. hooks (1989), p. 78.

45. This use of disciplinary language to reach consensus on decisions that can encourage equity can be thought of as a different application of disciplinary logics. In research that I conducted where I identified this concept, the tendency was for strong paradigm fields like physics to use disciplinary language to justify decisions that outsiders might think of as inequitable or even discriminatory. However, there is no reason that these same logics might not also be used to enable groups to come together in developing buy-in for actions that support equity. See Posselt (2015).

46. Rovelli (2016).

Chapter 3

1. Routines and habits also embed norms.

2. St. John, Riggs, & Mogk (2016).

3. Clancy, Nelson, Rutherford, & Hinde (2014).

4. Sexton et al. (2016).

5. Additional detail can be found in the methodological references.

6. Sargent (2009).

7. I learned of this phrase at a meeting of NSF principal investigators from the geosciences. Although the people in the conversation were from a variety of geoscience disciplines (structural geology, ecology, marine sciences, oceanography), they admitted—with some chagrin—that they had each heard of this phrase.

8. The first findings of this project are presented in a paper with my colleague Anne-Marie Núñez and survey the culture of learning in both an undergraduate structural geology field camp in the Rocky Mountains and the graduate-level geoscience field course I observed.

9. Aside from adding to the intensity of the experience, standards for toughness only on rare occasion appear to benefit the science itself. That is, in most cases, geologists emphasize toughness for toughness's sake.

10. Although most of the class typically wore either long black hiking pants or khaki cargo shorts, there were as many types of hats within the group as there were people. This was exemplified within the instructional team. The lead instructor wore a safari-style nylon hat and other two professors wore a baseball cap and a Stetson, while the TAs wore a wide-brimmed straw hats, a bandanna wrap, and a fishing hat, respectively.

11. Aware that my own participation in a culture marked by alcohol consumption would bear consequences for how the group viewed me—and thus acted around me, affecting my data—but also that drinking alcohol while collecting data could compromise the quality of data collected, I did not drink anything during times that I was collecting data. However, I would occasionally have beer with the group at dinner or after the evening seminar.

12. Ridgeway (2009).

13. For this discussion, it is important to be clear about the group's composition. There were ten women in this twenty-four person group: Heidi was the one woman among three professors; Malia was the one woman among four teaching assistants (TA), and there were eight women students among the seventeen enrolled. In addition, two course coordinators (both women) were involved but not present for all activities. The lead professor introduced Marissa and Bonnie the first day as responsible for "all things non-science and, uh, some science too" (Bonnie, it is worth noting, has had a career of more than thirty years as a PhD-trained scientist.) There were also about ten additional guest instructors (two of whom were women) who joined the group for short periods to provide evening seminars.

14. Foxx et al. (2019).

15. The class was divided about half by international students and US students.

16. All names have been replaced with pseudonyms, unless otherwise indicated.

17. Dannin (2004).

18. Hefner & Eisenberg (2009); Abouserie (1994).

19. Dekker & Barling (1998), p. 7.

20. Schneider, B. E. (1987).

21. Hinsley, Sutherland, & Johnston (2017); Rios & Stewart (2015).

22. Such informality was typical for the geoscience lectures. One of the male TA's lectures included the words *barf, voodoo, fuck,* and *shit.* A white male guest lecturer compared taco trucks to the evolution of cytoskeletons, noting how tacos, gorditas, tortas, and burritos all combined similar ingredients in new ways.

23. As the class went on, I also observed that Heidi took on what feminist scholars call mom work. She cleaned up minor spills in shared spaces, reminded people to use coasters under their beer bottles, and at least once brought the guest lecturer a glass of water.

24. Scully & Creed (1997).

25. Meyer & Rowan (1977).

26. For the updated version of the AGU ethics policy, see "AGU Revises Its Integrity and Ethics Policy," https://eos.org/agu-news/agu-revises-its-integrity-and-ethics-policy.

27. Glinskis (2019).

28. Clancy et al. (2014).

29. For example, the FIELD project from which research in this chapter originated also includes a three-day professional development institute for field leaders.

30. Although I have focused in this chapter on the ways that the culture of geosciences may be driving away women, there is also a critical conversation to be had about this discipline's difficulty attracting and retaining people of color.

31. Tierney & Bensimon (1996), p. 81.

Chapter 4

1. Prichep (2013); Wade (2009).

2. Berrey (2015).

3. Goffman (1959), p. 9.

4. Stevens & Roksa (2011).

5. Slaughter, Tao, & Pearson (2015).

6. Marichal (2009); Berrey (2015); Avery & McKay (2006); Kim & Gelfand (2003); Bersola, Stolzenberg, Love, & Fosnacht (2014).

7. Weick (1976).

8. Garces & Cogburn (2015).

9. Posselt (2016).

10. Thornhill (2018).

11. See also Thornhill (2018), who found in an audit study of 517 white admissions counselors that they were "more responsive to black students who presented as deracialized and racially apolitical than they were to those who evince a commitment to antiracism and racial justice."

12. Among many possible examples, see Broido (2000); Patton & Bondi (2015); Meyerson & Tompkins (2007); Sturm (2006); Dowd & Bensimon (2015); Gurin, Nagda, & Lopez (2004).

13. For two excellent examples of research by scientists reporting on interventions in the culture of their fields, see Girod et al. (2016); Stassun et al. (2011).

14. Kimberly Reyes, Kelly Slay, Aurora Kamimura, and Kamaria Porter each contributed to the data collection and analysis for the case studies reported in this chapter. The case studies are also presented in Posselt, Porter, and Kamimura (2018); Posselt, Reyes, Slay, Kamimura, & Porter (2017); and Slay, Reyes, & Posselt (2019).

15. "ADVANCE encourages institutions of higher education and the broader science, technology, engineering and mathematics (STEM) community, including professional societies and other STEM-related not-for-profit organizations, to address various aspects of STEM academic culture and institutional structure that may differentially affect women faculty and academic administrators." National Science Foundation, "ADVANCE at a Glance," https://www.nsf.gov/crssprgm/advance/.

16. Slay et al. (2019).

17. According to Harper and Patton (2007), whites often want to avoid the risk of feeling guilty or "uncomfortable." Others lament that discussing race openly requires acknowledging also that racism exists and is likely to persist. Accepting racism's reality carries with it a responsibility for addressing racial inequalities and bringing about

changes about which they feel some ambivalence. They may feel ill equipped because it risks introducing conflict with their colleagues, or simply because such conversations may force an uncomfortable look at their privilege, biases, and complicity in systems of oppression.

18. Ahmed (2012), p. 72.

19. Solorzano, Ceja, and Yosso (2000) note that the *micro* in *microaggression* refers to their positioning in everyday discourse.

20. Slay et al. (2019).

21. Griffin, Muñiz, & Espinosa (2012).

22. Milem, Chang, & Antonio (2005).

23. Argyris (1976).

24. Ibid.

25. My thanks to Michelle Masse for this evocative phrase, which she used to describe strategies that ought to be avoided when leading a graduate school.

26. Argyris (1977).

27. Goffman (1959).

28. Avery & McKay (2006); Thomas & Wise (1999).

29. Slay et al. (2019).

30. Goffman (1959).

31. Ibid., pp. 9–10.

Chapter 5

A version of this chapter was published as Posselt, J. R., Reyes, K. A., Slay, K. E., Kamimura, A., & Porter, K. B. (2017). Equity efforts as boundary work: How symbolic and social boundaries shape access and inclusion in graduate education. *Teachers College Record, 119*(10).

1. All participants in this chapter have been given pseudonyms to protect anonymity, except the current and founding directors, and the university president at the time of the program establishment, who have given their consent to be named.

2. About labels: because of our focus on graduate education, in which departments may administer multiple academic programs whose graduate students may or may not interact, we use the language of graduate *programs* rather than academic *department* but draw on the available research about departmental cultures.

3. Disclosure statement: No member of our research team had prior relationship with members of the applied physics program before this project. We learned about it through administrative data provided by the university, in which the program stood out for its high rates of enrollment and degree attainment by people of color and women over the previous five years.

4. Although it is not the focus of this study, an adjacent mechanism for cultural change through graduate education is students' development of a critical consciousness about the academic environments in which they find themselves. As students

reflect on their experiences with disciplinary socialization, they may enter the professoriate with a commitment to resisting prevailing norms and values.

5. Knorr Cetina (1999); Hermanowicz (2009).

6. Hermanowicz (2011).

7. Merton & Zuckerman (1973), as cited in Hermanowicz (2011).

8. Knorr Cetina (1999).

9. Hermanowicz (2009); Posselt (2015).

10. Traweek (1988), p. 8.

11. Lamont & Molnár (2002). As discussed in Chapter 2, Lamont did not deny the role of status struggle in the reproduction of inequalities (or the roles of status struggle in habitus, social, and cultural capital). Rather, she added the drawing of symbolic boundaries as an additional mechanism. Other mechanisms may also be possible. One could relate these mechanisms by noting that organizations determine whom to exclude by drawing boundaries that separate those who do and do not have forms of social and cultural capital that the group has defined as valuable or desirable.

12. Rao, Monin, & Durand (2005).

13. Tilly (2004).

14. Ibid., p. 225.

15. Mulvey & Nicholson (2008).

16. Three decades later, we can see that Roy's pragmatic approach of making the diversity conversation a matter of disciplinary perspective and race, rather than race alone, enabled him to launch a program that was progressive for its time. Recent education scholars have critiqued the practice of collapsing race with additional types of diversity, however, and others question the wisdom of using a discourse of diversity to justify equity-oriented efforts. This approach risks conflating the pursuit of difference with the pursuit of equity and can stymie subsequent efforts if diversity becomes mistaken for the goal rather than a strategy in service of equity (Ahmed, 2012; Bensimon, 2005; Chang, 2002). Pushing for diversity without being explicit about race can undermine racial equity by detracting attention from it (Shiao, 2004). While progressive for its time, Roy's strategy should not be read as best practice across all contexts of time and place.

17. Roach (2006).

18. Ibid.

19. Knorr Cetina (1999).

20. Frickel (2004).

21. Traweek (1988), p. 8.

22. Patton (2009); Posselt (2018); Taylor & Antony (2000).

23. Upper administrators at the university tapped him for insight about declining shares of graduate students of color and about potential changes in the applied physics program directorship, for example.

24. Tilly (2004).

25. White (1992), p. 127.

26. Tilly (2004).

27. On the political nature of defining what should be considered within the bounds of merit, Karabel (1984) wrote: "The very definition of 'cultivation' or, in the modern world of bureaucracies, 'merit' that predominates in a particular society expresses underlying power relations and tends, accordingly, to reflect the particular cultural ideals of those group that hold the power of cultural definition. By its very nature, the process of defining 'cultivation' and 'merit,' far from being neutral, is thus a profoundly political one" (p. 2). On gatekeeping activities, see Posselt (2015); Lamont (2009).

28. Lamont & Molnár (2002), p. 188.

29. Lamont (1992), p. 10.

30. Weick (1976).

31. Although our paper adopts a cultural sociological perspective, a closely related tenet from social psychology asserts that individuals define themselves (i.e., their identities) in relation to others. Cultural sociologists do note, however, that boundaries tend to be rooted in identities and have amassed a rich body of scholarship that discusses the patterns of norms and behaviors associated with specific social identities.

32. Carter (2006), p. 324.

33. Gardner & Holley (2011); Margolis & Romero (1998).

Chapter 6

1. Abbott (2015).

2. Ibid., p. 126.

3. Binder & Abel (2019).

4. Although the notion of a hierarchy of disciplines is today controversial, various scholars have proposed them over time. Medieval scholars understood theology to be the queen of the disciplines. In 1303, for example, the theologian and philosopher Ramon Llull captured a hierarchy of disciplines in *De nova logica*, portraying the disciplines as a staircase to heaven beginning with the study of rocks and flames, stepping up to the study of animals and humans, then up further to understand the sky, space, and angels, and ultimately heaven (i.e., theology). More recently, Daniele Fanelli proposed a hierarchy of disciplines centered on the "hardness" of research, defined as "the extent to which research questions and results are determined by data and theories as opposed to non-cognitive factors" (as cited in Trabesinger, 2010; see also Fanelli, 2010).

5. Instrumentation is closer to physics than other subfields of astronomy. As one astronomer whom I member checked my findings with put it, instrumentation within astronomy "is much closer to physics than any other part of astronomy, since building an instrument to make measurements really doesn't differ between the two fields. In fact, the techniques and technologies are often shared and swapped between fields. The way many physicists cross over to astronomy is by bringing their instrument building skills to an astronomical problem."

6. Greenwood, Suddaby, & Hinings (2002), p. 59.

7. DiMaggio & Powell (1983).

8. Professional associations often differ from disciplinary societies in having a more explicit regulatory function, particularly insofar as professional associations may be tasked with establishing standards for program accreditation.

9. A final illustration of coercive isomorphism's potential for positive socio-intellectual change is the NSF's establishment of "broader impacts" (i.e., for society and the scientific community) in 1997 as a merit review criterion alongside "intellectual merit" for all proposed projects' evaluation. Some scientists, especially those already working in STEM education and outreach, easily incorporated these interests. Others resisted the notion on principle—that disciplinary research should exist for its own sake. A third group resisted this evaluation criterion because they had never been trained to design or engage in projects to those ends and thus struggled to reframe their works. Nevertheless, NSF's director Rita Colwell issued this directive: "Effective October 1, 2002, NSF will return without review proposals that do not separately address both merit review criteria." Years later, the effects of coercive isomorphism via NSF's redefinition of merit for scientific proposal are clear. Although it would be far too much to say that this requirement has engendered equity, and in some cases has appeared to harden scientists against it, it has no doubt forced scientists to attend to the social implications of their work.

10. Greenwood, Suddaby, & Hinings (2002).

11. These projects include the Inclusive Graduate Education Network (IGEN) Design and Development Launch Pilot, IGEN Alliance, Cal-Bridge, Sci-Steps Design and Development Launch Pilot, and the American Astronomical Society's Task Force on Equity and Inclusion in Graduate Education.

12. I heard one astronomer tell the same story twice to colleagues about a point early in his career that "crystallized a lot of other observations I had made over the years about the cultures of physics [versus] astronomy." Both fields had professional society meetings set to take place in January. The physicists had chosen to meet in Alaska because hotel rooms would be inexpensive, whereas "astronomers don't go to meetings in crummy places" and would be meeting in Hawaii. He went to Hawaii. The first time he shared the story, it bears noting, was at a physics conference in the context of a group discussing the meager breakfast provided to attendees. The second time he told the story, another astronomer in the conversation backed up this assessment of astronomers' appreciation for meeting in desirable locales. He noted that when brown dwarf stars were discovered, leaders of the effort chose to meet every two years for some time on a different Mediterranean island. Through member checking, I learned that any pattern of "astronomers don't go to meetings in crummy places" is likely related to the field's history of traveling to telescopes for observation.

13. Hodapp & Brown (2018); Hodapp & Woodle (2017); Stassun et al. (2011).

14. In addition to managerial and advocacy cultures, Bergquist and Pawlak (2008) identify collegial, developmental, virtual, and tangible cultures.

15. Bergquist & Pawlak (2008).

16. Ibid., p. 121.

17. See Meyerson and Scully (2001, 2003) on the role of faculty as "tempered radicals" who also participate in the advocacy culture.

18. According to AAS, "Once every ten years, the astronomical communities gather panels of experts to set community-wide priorities for the coming decade. These surveys are facilitated by the National Academies and commissioned by the Federal agencies. The most recent surveys were completed between 2010 and 2013." See the American Astronomical Society's Decadal Surveys, at https://aas.org/advocacy/decadal-surveys.

19. For a full description of the motivation, design, and initial outcomes of this program, see Stassun et al. (2011).

20. Bridge and postbaccalaureate programs are also common in psychology and biomedical sciences.

21. According to NSF, "The objective of PAARE is to enhance diversity in astronomy and astrophysics research and education by stimulating the development of formal, long-term, collaborative research and education partnerships among minority-serving institutions and partners at research institutions, including academic institutions, private observatories, and NSF Division of Astronomical Sciences (AST)-supported facilities." See Partnerships in Astronomy and Astrophysics Research and Education, at https://www.nsf.gov/pubs/2013/nsf13566/nsf13566.htm.

22. Bourdieu (1968/1974) wrote, "By operating a selection procedure which, although apparently formally equitable, endorses real inequalities, schools help both to perpetuate and legitimize inequalities" (p. 42).

23. Miller & Stassun (2014).

24. In what can be described only as a truly outlying moment for the movement toward inclusion in STEM, a person spoke up during the final town-hall question-and-answer period at the Women in Astronomy IV meeting with a plea not to forget the lactose intolerant in the population whose needs should be accommodated.

25. The full list of recommendations is available at American Astronomical Society (2017).

26. Ibid.

27. Ibid.

28. Ibid.

29. American Astronomical Society (2015).

30. GRE policies in 163 astronomy and physics departments are listed at https://bit.ly/2uINkl6.

31. The movement for a more inclusive astronomy combines pragmatism and politics, and this balance of interests is reflected on smaller scales as well—within conferences, within a single day of a conference, and within single conference sessions. The workshops of which I was part, the sessions of conferences I attended, and the proceedings of the Women in Astronomy meetings all emphasized practical, day-to-day work associated with implementing the recommendations. The discourse of the meetings' introductory and concluding sessions, however, underscored the moral and political dimensions of the work. At the concluding session of the 2017 Women

in Astronomy meeting, for example, speakers emphasized tactics for bringing new people on board, a need to "enforce these values" of social justice as they plays out in science, the importance of "signing on" to and acquiring "endorsement" of specific recommendations, and "getting rid of" people who impede a more inclusive scientific enterprise. They strategized around managing their colleagues' ambivalence and resistance and how the decentralized community of activists might maintain connections to sustain the movement's momentum.

32. Committees like the APS Panel on Public Affairs that has been considering a statement about the GRE are stacked with faculty and lab scientists who are selected for their status in the field. Their success and stature are products of the field as it has been, and they are therefore less likely to be sources of advocacy for change as they are bodies for the wider society to keep a pulse on the consensus view of leading scientists in the field.

33. I served as a senior advisor of the AAS graduate education task force and also advised its working group on admissions. In 2019–2020, I will be a member of the National Academies of Science, Engineering, and Medicine's Astro2020 Decadal Survey panel study on the state of the profession.

34. These documents, respectively, are known to insiders as the Baltimore Charter, Pasadena Recommendations, and Nashville Recommendations.

35. See "About the Bridge Program," at the American Physical Society's website, at https://www.apsbridgeprogram.org/about/.

36. At this conference, I counted five men look me up and down within my first twenty-four hours and wondered how long it took for the male gaze to feel normal for women in the field. It was also at that first meeting that I observed the cultural importance of the women's bathroom—that women were using it as a place to vent, cry, or receive a hug or a kind word from a colleague or stranger. There is, to be clear, no such routine use of the women's bathroom at education conferences.

37. Posselt (2016); Posselt et al. (2017).

38. The workshop series had two parts. The first was a two-hour, lecture-based seminar presenting current research and data about inequities in STEM, the legal landscape for admissions, current research about admissions in selective PhD programs (especially physics), and problems with the current approach. It was open to anyone in the university with an interest in attending. The second part was a closed three-hour session for admissions committee members and other leaders in the PhD program, and it involved a series of interactive activities to encourage reflection about their current process, discussion about its adequacy in identifying the students they want, and how to develop and implement more holistic and equitable evaluation practices. We were careful not to be overly prescriptive, recognizing that the evidence for specific practices is not directly generalizable to these contexts, and the best means of generating support for new processes is for current members to develop their own evaluation norms.

39. To better understand the structure of admissions priorities in these programs in the first year of the project, one of the research studies used nested multivariate

logistic regression to compare predictors of making the short list for admission to predictors of receiving an admissions offer. We found that, on average, PhD admissions processes emphasized academic metrics for the purposes of filtering their pool, shifting their focus to a combination of academics and student demographic characteristics when evaluating those who had made a short list. This pattern was consistent with a finding in my previous qualitative research on selective PhD admissions, summed up by the notion of metrics first, diversity later. See Posselt, Hernandez, Cochran, & Miller (2019).

40. Kania (2011).

41. Dr. Martin Luther King Jr. wrote about creative tension in "Letter from a Birmingham Jail": "I just referred to the creation of tension as a part of the work of the nonviolent resister. This may sound rather shocking. But I must confess that I am not afraid of the word 'tension.' I have earnestly worked and preached against violent tension, but there is a type of constructive nonviolent tension that is necessary for growth." Retrieved from https://kinginstitute.stanford.edu/king-papers/documents/letter-birmingham-jail.

42. Neumann (1991).

43. Page (2008).

44. Harding (2004).

45. Traweek (1988).

46. This interdependence resembles a process dubbed "complementary schismogenesis" by Bateson in 1936: "a process of differentiation in the norms of individual behavior resulting from cumulative interaction between individuals" (p. 175).

47. Bergquist & Pawlak (2008).

48. Traweek (1988).

Chapter 7

1. Worse, the eagerness to hold up indicators of progress may obscure continued power asymmetries and persistent ethno-racial and gender hierarchies.

2. They also are deployed to legitimate certain approaches to change efforts.

3. Posselt (2016), p. 174.

4. Meyerson & Tompkins (2007).

5. Labaree (2012).

6. As Confucius is quoted as saying, "The mechanic who would perfect his work must first sharpen the tools."

7. Swidler (1986) noted that it is common for people to set goals and strategies for which their existing knowledge and perspectives are sufficient and well suited rather than the goals and strategies that enable long-term success.

8. Molinsky (2013).

9. Depending on the organizational culture in which one aims for change, the specific strategies and tactics that fall into reform versus retooling may vary.

10. I mentioned in the early pages of this text that organizational culture is rarely unified. I found that at least a few people within each organization I worked with either held or developed a critical consciousness and advocacy orientation. That orientation came with eagerness for change with which others in their organization were uncomfortable.

11. For a powerful example of work in this area, see Mack, Winter, & Soto (2019).

12. Translation presents an additional boundary change mechanism to those that Tilly (2004) proposed. Recall that he argued that boundary change occurs through a combination of at least two mechanisms: one that prompts change (e.g., conversation, borrowing, encounter) and at least one that constitutes the change itself (e.g., inscription-erasure, activation-deactivation, relocation). These combinations modify interpersonal and power relations on either side of a social boundary, the relations that take place across the boundary, or how the boundary itself is represented. Cultural translation perhaps best can be thought of as an additional prompting mechanism, with the understanding that emerges from translation a useful basis for inscription, erasure, (de)activation, or relocation of an existing boundary.

13. Guinier (2004) defines racial literacy as "the capacity to decipher the durable racial grammar that structures racialized hierarchies and frames the narrative of our republic" (p. 100). See Szasz (2001) for perhaps the definitive source on cultural brokering in anthropology and history.

14. The absence of such members may explain difficult relationships across difference, and leaders can think about both how to develop these qualities in current members and how to recruit and select for them in future hiring endeavors.

15. On such emails, see Milkman (2015). On bureaucratic systems, one PhD program chair associated with IGEN off-handedly summed up what he had learned: "It's really pretty simple. Figure out the admissions issue and figure out how to treat the students well so they stick around."

16. Byars-Winston et al. (2018); Fries-Britt & Snider (2015).

17. See Navigating Holistic Admissions for a Stronger Graduate Program (http://www.holisticadmissions.org) for the website ETS has developed on holistic admissions.

18. Page (2008); Phillips (2008); Freeman & Huang (2014).

19. Victoroff & Boyatzis (2013); Boyatzis, Boyatzis, & Saatcioglu (2008).

20. In a recent version of their Guide to the Use of Scores, ETS writes about the GRE, "It is an inexact measure; only score differences that exceed the standard error of measurement of a given score can serve as a reliable indication of real differences in applicants' academic knowledge and developed abilities."

21. Miller and Stassun (2014).

22. Bastedo, Bowman, Glasener, & Kelly (2018).

23. Posselt (2016).

24. My usual recommendation is that programs explain the general categories of criteria they will be looking for (e.g., academic preparation, scholarly potential, contributions to diversity, alignment with program mission, noncognitive competen-

cies), but to avoid undue gaming of the system that they do not make public the actual rubric they will use.

25. In psychology, there was some variation across concentrations in how GRE score reliance changed over time.

26. When scores are optional to admit, more people apply, but it raises the average scores of test scores that are submitted. US News and World Report's current algorithm for rankings has tried to counter this risk by applying a weight to the mean GRE scores reported, in programs for whom less than half of enrolled students submit scores.

27. Posselt et al. (2019).

28. Posselt (2018c).

29. Hernandez & Posselt (2018).

30. Ibid.

31. Porter, Posselt, Reyes, Slay, & Kamimura (2018).

32. Ibid.

33. Taylor & Antony (2000).

34. Dweck (2007).

35. Austin (2009); Maher, Gilmore, Feldon, & Davis (2013).

36. Walker et al. (2009).

37. See, for example, the training and other mentoring resources offered by the Center for the Improvement of Mentored Experiences in Research (https://cimer project.org).

38. Ahmed (2012) notes that members who are most dedicated to transformation are also most likely to find themselves up against the wall, and may develop a more critical orientation toward the institutions they are working to transform (p. 174).

39. Some scholars call this phenomenon whiteness or masculinity as credential.

40. Saini (2017).

41. The tone of claims that we have insufficient evidence to justify trying new methods eerily resembles the tone of claims that we have an insufficient supply of students of color.

42. Experiments are needed, although to be clear, social science experiments come with different requirements and assumptions than do experiments in the lab. I highly encourage any natural scientists wanting to conduct an experiment on a social process within their department to consult a social scientist with relevant expertise.

43. Studies of the GRE's validity, the most common topic of research on graduate admissions, come to differing conclusions about its associations with different metrics of success. This variation is likely due to differences in settings where the research is carried out, differences in the methodologies that scholars are using, and tweaks to the test over time by ETS. See also Council of Graduate Schools (2010).

44. The notion of consilience introduced by nineteenth-century philosophers of science, for example, was used to describe deep interconnections among disciplines through shared laws. E. O. Wilson's (1999) book *Consilience* is perhaps the most famous of recent treatises on this topic, arguing for the unity of all knowledge and

rooting his position in the Ionian enchantment "that the world is orderly and can be explained by a small number of natural laws."

45. National Science Foundation, *Convergence Research at NSF*, https://www.nsf.gov/od/oia/convergence/index.jsp.

46. Multidisciplinarity draws on knowledge from different disciplines but stays within the boundaries of each. Interdisciplinarity analyzes, synthesizes, and harmonizes links between disciplines into a coordinated and coherent whole. Transdisciplinarity integrates the natural, social, and health sciences in a humanities context and transcends their traditional boundaries.

47. National Science Foundation, *Convergence Research at NSF*, https://www.nsf.gov/od/oia/convergence/index.jsp.

48. Martin (2000); Ray (2019).

49. Martin (2000), p. 208.

50. Harding (2015).

51. Ibid.

52. Collins & Bilge (2016).

53. Freire (1970), p. 60.

54. Wilson (1999).

55. Tilly (2004), p. 213.

56. Ricoeur (1976), p. 43, as cited in Maitland (2017).

57. Tilly (2004); Maitland (2017).

58. For a summary of equity-mindedness, see "Equity Mindedness: What Is Equity-Mindedness?" https://cue.usc.edu/about/equity/equity-mindedness/. See also Freire (1970).

59. Rorty (1983), p. 562.

60. Carter (2006).

61. National Academies of Science, Engineering, and Medicine (2018).

62. Perez, Robbins, Harris, & Montgomery (2019).

63. After all, if the training graduate education provides is aimed at developing future stewards of our disciplines, and if we would like our disciplines and departments to become more equitable, then shouldn't our standards for quality explicitly consider contributions and impediments to equity (Walker et al., 2009)?

64. Recognizing that humans wrote the rules allows us to see more clearly the embedded purposes of a game or the terms of engagement, who is positioned well to advance, and our potential to rewrite rules or even transform the game itself.

References

Abbott, A. (2010). *Chaos of disciplines*. Chicago, IL: University of Chicago Press.

Abouserie, R. (1994). Sources and levels of stress in relation to locus of control and self-esteem in university students. *Educational Psychology, 14,* 323–330.

Ahmed, S. (2012). *On being included: Racism and diversity in institutional life*. Durham, NC: Duke University Press.

Alexander, J. C. (2003). *The meanings of social life: A cultural sociology*. Oxford, England: Oxford University Press.

American Astronomical Society. (2015, December). *President's column*. Retrieved from https://aas.org/posts/news/2015/12/presidents-column-rethinking-role-gre

American Astronomical Society. (2017). *Inclusive Astronomy Nashville Recommendations*. Retrieved from https://aas.org/posts/news/2017/02/inclusive-astronomy -nashville-recommendations

American Astronomical Society. (2019). *Decadal surveys*. Retrieved from https://aas .org/policy-resources/decadal-surveys

American Geophysical Union (2018). *AGU revises its integrity and ethics policy*. Retrieved from https://eos.org/agu-news/agu-revises-its-integrity-and-ethics-policy

American Physical Society. (2018). *Permanent jobs elusive for recent physics PhDs*. Retrieved from https://www.aps.org/publications/apsnews/201208/phdjobs.cfm

American Physical Society. (2020). *About the Bridge Program*. Retrieved from https:// www.apsbridgeprogram.org/about/

Anderson, B. (2006). *Imagined communities: Reflections on the origin and spread of nationalism*. New York, NY: Verso Books.

Argyris, C. (1976). Single-loop and double-loop models in research on decision making. *Administrative Science Quarterly, 21*(3), 363–375.

Argyris, C. (1977). Double loop learning in organizations. *Harvard Business Review, 55*(5), 115–125.

Attiyeh, G., & Attiyeh, R. (1997). Testing for bias in graduate school admissions. *Journal of Human Resources, 32*(3), 524–548.

Austin, A. E. (1996). Institutional and departmental cultures: The relationship between teaching and research. *New Directions for Institutional Research,* (90), 57–66.

Austin, A. E. (2002). Preparing the next generation of faculty: Graduate school as socialization to the academic career. *Journal of Higher Education, 73*(1), 94–122.

Austin, A. E. (2009). Cognitive apprenticeship theory and its implications for doctoral education: A case example from a doctoral program in higher and adult education. *International Journal for Academic Development, 14*, 173–183.

Avery, D. R., & McKay, P. F. (2006). Target practice: An organizational impression management approach to attracting minority and female job applicants. *Personnel Psychology, 59*(1), 157–187.

Barad, K. (2007). *Meeting the universe halfway: Quantum physics and the entanglement of matter and meeting.* Durham, NC: Duke University Press.

Bell, E. L. E., Meyerson, D., Nkomo, S., & Scully, M. (2003). Interpreting silence and voice in the workplace: A conversation about tempered radicalism among Black and white women researchers. *Journal of Applied Behavioral Science, 39*(4), 381–414.

Bensimon, E. M. (2005). Closing the achievement gap in higher education: An organizational learning perspective. *New Directions for Higher Education,* (131), 99–111.

Berger, P. L., & Luckmann, T. (1991). *The social construction of reality: A treatise in the sociology of knowledge.* London, England: Penguin UK.

Bergquist, W. H., & Pawlak, K. (2008). *Engaging the six cultures of the academy* (Rev. and expanded ed. of *The Four Cultures of the Academy*). Mahwah, NJ: Wiley.

Berrey, E. (2015). *The enigma of diversity: The language of race and the limits of racial justice.* Chicago, IL: University of Chicago Press.

Bersola, S. H., Stolzenberg, E. B., Love, J., & Fosnacht, K. (2014). Understanding admitted doctoral students' institutional choices: Student experiences versus faculty and staff perceptions. *American Journal of Education, 120*(4), 515–543.

Bielby, R., Posselt, J. R., Jaquette, O., & Bastedo, M. N. (2014). Why are women underrepresented in elite colleges and universities? A non-linear decomposition analysis. *Research in Higher Education, 55*(8), 735–760.

Binder, A. J., & Abel, A. R. (2019). Symbolically maintained inequality: How Harvard and Stanford students construct boundaries among elite universities. *Sociology of Education, 92*(1), 41–58.

Bourdieu, Pierre. (1974). The school as a conservative force. In J. Eggleston (Ed.), *Contemporary research in sociology of education* (pp. 32–46). London, England: Methuen. (Originally published 1968)

Bourdieu, P. (1977). Cultural reproduction and social reproduction. In J. Karabel & A. H. Halsey (Eds.), *Power and ideology in education* (pp. 487–511). Oxford, England: Oxford University Press.

Bourdieu, P. (1979). Symbolic power. *Critique of Anthropology, 4*(13–14), 77–85.

Broido, E. M. (2000). The development of social justice allies during college: A phenomenological investigation. *Journal of College Student Development, 41*(1), 3–18.

Bowen W. G., & Rudenstine, N. L. (2014). *In pursuit of the PhD*. Princeton, NJ: Princeton University Press.

Bastedo, M. N., Bowman, N. A., Glasener, K. M., & Kelly, J. L. (2018). What are we talking about when we talk about holistic review? Selective college admissions and its effects on low-SES students. *Journal of Higher Education, 89*(5), 782–805.

Boyatzis, R., & Saatcioglu, A. (2008). A 20-year view of trying to develop emotional, social and cognitive intelligence competencies in graduate management education. *Journal of Management Development, 27*(1).

Byars-Winston, A., Womack, V. Y., Butz, A. R., McGee, R., Quinn, S. C., Utzerath, E., Saetermore, C. L., & Thomas, S. B. (2018). Pilot study of an intervention to increase cultural awareness in research mentoring: Implications for diversifying the scientific workforce. *Journal of Clinical and Translational Science, 2*(2), 86–94.

Callahan, R., & Bhattacharya, D. (2017). *Public health leadership: Strategies for innovation in population health and social determinants*. New York, NY: Routledge.

Carter, D. F., Dueñas, J. E. R., & Mendoza, R. (2019). Critical examination of the role of STEM in propagating and maintaining race and gender disparities. In M. B. Paulsen & L. W. Perna (Eds.), *Higher education: Handbook of theory and research* (pp. 39–97). Cham, Switzerland: Springer.

Carter, P. L. (2006). Straddling boundaries: Identity, culture, and school. *Sociology of Education, 79*(4), 304–328.

Chang, M. J. (2002). Perservation or transformation: Where's the real educational discourse on diversity? *Review of Higher Education, 25*(2), 125–140.

Clancy, K. B., Nelson, R. G., Rutherford, J. N., & Hinde, K. (2014). Survey of academic field experiences (SAFE): Trainees report harassment and assault. *PLoS One, 9*(7), e102172.

Clark, B. R. (1987). *The academic life: Small worlds, different worlds* (A Carnegie Foundation special report). Princeton, NJ: Princeton University Press.

Cochran, G. (2018). The problem with diversity, inclusion, and equity. *Scholarly Kitchen*. Retrieved from https://scholarlykitchen.sspnet.org/2018/06/22/problem-diversity-inclusion-equity/

Corbin, J. M., & Strauss, A. L. (2008). *Basics of qualitative research: Techniques and procedures for developing grounded theory* (3rd ed.). Los Angeles, CA: Sage.

Collins, P. H., & Bilge, S. (2016). *Intersectionality*. Mahwah, NJ: Wiley.

Correll, S. J. (2017). SWS 2016 Feminist Lecture: Reducing gender biases in modern workplaces: A small wins approach to organizational change. *Gender & Society, 31*(6), 725–750.

Council of Graduate Schools. (2010). *PhD completion and attrition: Policies and practices to promote student success*. Washington, DC: Council of Graduate Schools.

Creswell, J. W. (2013). *Research design: Qualitative, quantitative, and mixed methods approaches*. Los Angeles, CA: Sage.

Dannin, E. (2004). Teaching labor law within socioeconomic framework. *San Diego Law Review, 41*(1), 93–108.

Deitch, E. A., Barsky, A., Butz, R. M., Chan, S., Brief, A. P., & Bradley, J. C. (2003). Subtle yet significant: The existence and impact of everyday racial discrimination in the workplace. *Human Relations, 56*(11), 1299–1324.

Dekker, I., & Barling, J. (1998). Personal and organizational predictors of workplace sexual harassment of women by men. *Journal of Occupational Health Psychology, 3*(1), 7–18.

DiMaggio, P. J., & Powell, W. W. (1983). The iron cage revisited: Institutional isomorphism and collective rationality in organizational fields. *American Sociological Review*, 147–160.

Dowd, A. C., & Bensimon, E. M. (2015). *Engaging the "race question": Accountability and equity in US higher education*. New York, NY: Teachers College Press.

Dweck, C. S. (2007). *Mindset: The new psychology of success*. New York, NY: Ballantine.

Eagly, A. H., & Carli, L. L. (2007). *Through the labyrinth: The truth about how women become leaders*. Cambridge, MA: Harvard Business.

Edgell, P., Gerteis, J., & Hartmann, D. (2006). Atheists as "other": Moral boundaries and cultural membership in American society. *American Sociological Review, 71*(2), 211–234.

Ely, R. J., & Thomas, D. A. (2001). Cultural diversity at work: The effects of diversity perspectives on work group processes and outcomes. *Administrative Science Quarterly, 46*(2), 229–273.

Espeland, W. N., & Sauder, M. (2007). Rankings and reactivity: How public measures recreate social worlds. *American Journal of Sociology, 113*(1), 1–40.

Espino, M. M. (2014). Exploring the role of community cultural wealth in graduate school access and persistence for Mexican American PhDs. *American Journal of Education, 120*(4), 545–574.

Fanelli, D. (2010). "Positive" results increase down the hierarchy of the sciences. *PLoS One, 5*(4), e10068.

Felder, P. (2010). On doctoral student development: Exploring faculty mentoring in the shaping of African American doctoral student success. *Qualitative Report, 15*(3), 455–474.

Finkelstein, M. J., Conley, V. M., & Schuster, J. H. (2016). *The faculty factor: Reassessing the American academy in a turbulent era*. Baltimore, MD: Johns Hopkins University Press.

Fitzgerald, L. F., Gelfand, M. J., & Drasgow, F. (1995) Measuring sexual harassment: Theoretical and psychometric advances. *Basic and Applied Social Psychology, 17*(4), 425–445.

Freeman, R. B., & Huang, W. (2014). Collaboration: Strength in diversity. *Nature News, 513*(7518), 305.

Freire, P. (1970). *Pedagogy of the oppressed*. New York, NY: Continuum Press.

Frescura, F. A. M., & Hiley, B. J. (1984). Algebras, quantum theory and prespace. *Revista Brasileira de Fisica, 70*, 49–86.

Frickel, S. (2004). Building an interdiscipline: Collective action framing and the rise of genetic toxicology. *Social Problems, 51*(2), 269–287.

Fries-Britt, S., & Snider, J. (2015). Mentoring outside the line: The importance of authenticity, transparency, and vulnerability in effective mentoring relationships. *New Directions for Higher Education*, (171), 3–11.

Garces, L. M. (2012). Racial diversity, legitimacy, and the citizenry: The impact of affirmative action bans on graduate school enrollment. *Review of Higher Education*, 36(1), 93–132.

Garces, L. M., & Cogburn, C. D. (2015). Beyond declines in student body diversity: How campus-level administrators understand a prohibition on race-conscious postsecondary admissions policies. *American Educational Research Journal*, 52(5), 828–860.

Gardner, S. K. (2006). "I heard it through the grapevine": Doctoral student socialization in chemistry and history. *Higher Education*, 54(5), 723–740.

Gardner, S. K., & Holley, K. A. (2011). "Those invisible barriers are real": The progression of first-generation students through doctoral education. *Equity & Excellence in Education*, 44(1), 77–92.

Gasman, M., Gerstl-Pepin, C., Anderson-Thompkins, S., Rasheed, L., & Hathaway, K. (2004). Negotiating power, developing trust: Transgressing race and status in the academy. *Teachers College Record*, 106(4), 689–715.

Giddens, A. (1984). *The constitution of society: Outline of the theory of structuration*. Berkeley, CA: University of California Press.

Gieryn, T. F. (1983). Boundary-work and the demarcation of science from non science: Strains and interests in professional ideologies of scientists. *American Sociological Review*, 781–795.

Girod, S., Fassiotto, M., Grewal, D., Ku, M. C., Sriram, N., Nosek, B. A., & Valantine, H. (2016). Reducing implicit gender leadership bias in academic medicine with an educational intervention. *Academic Medicine*, 91(8), 1143–1150.

Glinskis, E. (2019, January 15). STEM students are asking more of the #MeToo movement. *The Nation*. Retrieved from https://www.thenation.com/article/stem-students-are-asking-more-of-the-metoo-movement/

Goffman, E. (1959). *The presentation of self in everyday life*. London, England: Doubleday.

Golde, C. M. (2000). Should I stay or should I go? Student descriptions of the doctoral attrition process. *Review of Higher Education*, 23(2), 199–227.

Golde, C. M. (2005). The role of the department and discipline in doctoral student attrition: Lessons from four departments. *Journal of Higher Education*, 76(6), 669–700.

Golde, C. M., & Dore, T. (2001). *At cross purposes: What the experiences of today's doctoral students reveal about doctoral education*. Philadelphia, PA: Pew Charitable Trusts.

Gonzales, L. D. (2013). Faculty sensemaking and mission creep: Interrogating institutionalized ways of knowing and doing legitimacy. *Review of Higher Education*, 36(2), 179–209.

Gonzales, L. D. (2018). Subverting and minding boundaries: The intellectual work of women. *Journal of Higher Education*, 89(5), 677–701.

Gopaul, B. (2011). Distinction in doctoral education: Using Bourdieu's tools to assess the socialization of doctoral students. *Equity & Excellence in Education, 44*(1),
10–21.

Gopaul, B. (2012). *The practice of doctoral education: A Bourdieusian analysis of the
socialization of doctoral students* (Unpublished doctoral dissertation). University
of Toronto, Toronto, ON.

Gopaul, B. (2016). Applying cultural capital and field to doctoral student socialization. *International Journal for Researcher Development, 7*(1), 46–62.

Griffin, K. A., & Muñiz, M. M. (2011). The strategies and struggles of graduate diversity officers in the recruitment of doctoral students of color. *Equity & Excellence
in Education, 44*(1), 57–76.

Griffin, K. A., Muñiz, M. M., & Espinosa, L. (2012). The influence of campus racial
climate on diversity in graduate education. *Review of Higher Education, 35*(4),
535–566.

Guinier, L. (2004). From racial liberalism to racial literacy: *Brown v. Board of Education*
and the interest-divergence dilemma. *Journal of American History, 91*(1), 92–118.

Gumport, P. J. (1993). Graduate education and organized research in the United States.
In B. Clark (Ed.), *The research foundations of graduate education: Germany, Brit-
ain, France, United States, Japan* (pp. 225–260). Berkeley, CA: University of California Press.

Gurin, P., Nagda, B. R. A., & Lopez, G. E. (2004). The benefits of diversity in education
for democratic citizenship. *Journal of Social Issues, 60*(1), 17–34.

Hallett, T., & Ventresca, M. J. (2006). Inhabited institutions: Social interactions and
organizational forms in Gouldner's patterns of industrial bureaucracy. *Theory
and Society, 35*(2), 213–236.

Harding, S. G. (Ed.). (2004). *The feminist standpoint theory reader: Intellectual and
political controversies.* London, England: Psychology Press.

Harding, S. (2015). *Objectivity and diversity: Another logic of scientific research.* Chicago, IL: University of Chicago Press.

Harper, S. R. (2012). Race without racism: How higher education researchers minimize racist institutional norms. *Review of Higher Education, 36*(1), 9–29.

Harper, S. R., & Patton, L. D. (Eds.). (2007). *Responding to the realities of race on campus.* New directions for student services 120. San Francisco, CA: Jossey-Bass.

Hefner, J., & Eisenberg, D. (2009). Social support and mental health among college
students. *American Journal of Orthopsychiatry, 79*, 491–499.

Hermanowicz, J. C. (2009). *Lives in science: How institutions affect academic careers.*
Chicago, IL: University of Chicago Press.

Hermanowicz, J. C. (2011). Anomie and the academic profession. In J. C. Hermanowicz (Ed.), *The American academic profession: Transformation in contemporary
higher education* (pp. 216–237). Baltimore, MD: John Hopkins University Press.

Hernandez, T., & Posselt, J. R. (2018, April). *Unsupported in STEM: A negative case
analysis of underrepresented students' faculty and institutional interactions.* Paper
presented at the American Educational Research Association, New York.

Hinsley, A., Sutherland, W. J., & Johnston, A. (2017). Men ask more questions than women at a scientific conference. *PLoS One, 12*(10), e0185534.

Hodapp, T., & Brown, E. (2018). Making physics more inclusive. *Nature, 557,* 629–632.

Hodapp, T., & Woodle, K. S. (2017). A bridge between undergraduate and doctoral degrees. *Physics Today, 70*(2), 50–56.

Holley, K. A., & Gardner, S. (2012). Navigating the pipeline: How socio-cultural influences impact first-generation doctoral students. *Journal of Diversity in Higher Education, 5*(2), 112–121.

hooks, b. (1989). *Talking back: Thinking feminist, thinking black.* Boston, MA: South End Press.

Hurtado, S., Eagan, M. K., Tran, M. C., Newman, C. B., Chang, M. J., & Velasco, P. (2011). "We do science here": Underrepresented students' interactions with faculty in different college contexts. *Journal of Social Issues, 67*(3), 553–579.

Karabel, J. (1984). Status-group struggle, organizational interests, and the limits of institutional autonomy. *Theory and Society, 13*(1), 1–40.

Karabel, J. (2006). *The chosen: The hidden history of admission and exclusion at Harvard, Yale, and Princeton.* Boston, MA: Houghton Mifflin Harcourt.

Kim, S. S., & Gelfand, M. J. (2003). The influence of ethnic identity on perceptions of organizational recruitment. *Journal of Vocational Behavior, 63*(3), 396–416.

Knorr Cetina, K. (1999). *Epistemic cultures: How the sciences make knowledge.* Cambridge, MA: Harvard University Press.

Kreutzer, K., & Boudreaux, A. (2012). Preliminary investigation of instructor effects on gender gap in introductory physics. *Physical Review Special Topics—Physics Education Research, 8*(1), 010120.

Labaree, D. F. (2012). *Someone has to fail.* Cambridge, MA: Harvard University Press.

Ladson-Billings, G., & Tate, W. F. (2016). Toward a critical race theory of education. In A. D. Dixson, C. K. Rousseau Anderson, & J. K. Donnor (Eds.), *Critical race theory in education: All God's children got a song* (pp. 10–31). New York, NY: Routledge.

Lamont, M. (1992). *Money, morals, and manners: The culture of the French and the American upper-middle class.* Chicago, IL: University of Chicago Press.

Lamont, M., & Molnár, V. (2002). The study of boundaries in the social sciences. *Annual Review of Sociology, 28,* 167–195.

Lattuca, L. R. (2002). Learning interdisciplinarity: Sociocultural perspectives on academic work. *Journal of Higher Education, 73*(6), 711–739.

Lechuga, V. M. (2011). Faculty-graduate student mentoring relationships: Mentors' perceived roles and responsibilities. *Higher Education, 62,* 757–771.

Lee, J. J. (2007). The shaping of the departmental culture: Measuring the relative influences of the institution and discipline. *Journal of Higher Education Policy and Management, 29*(1), 41–55. https://doi.org/10.1080/1360080060117577

Lemieux, T. (2008). The changing nature of wage inequality. *Journal of Population Economics, 21*(1), 21–48.

Liera, R., & Dowd, A. C. (2019). Faculty learning at boundaries to broker racial equity. *Journal of Higher Education, 90*(3), 462–485.

Lovitts, B. E. (2001). *Leaving the ivory tower: The causes and consequences of departure from doctoral study.* New York, NY: Rowman & Littlefield.

Lovitts, B. E., & Nelson, C. (2000). The hidden crisis in graduate education: Attrition from PhD programs. *Academe, 86*(6), 44–50.

Mack, K. M., Winter, K., & Soto, M. (Eds.). (2019). *Culturally responsive strategies for reforming STEM higher education: Turning the TIDES on inequity.* New York, NY: Emerald.

Maher, M. A., Gilmore, J. A., Feldon, D. F., & Davis, T. E. (2013). Cognitive apprenticeship and the supervision of science and engineering research assistants. *Journal of Research Practice, 9*(2), art. M5.

Maitland, S. (2017). *What is cultural translation?* London, England: Bloomsbury.

Margolis, E., & Romero, M. (1998). "The department is very male, very white, very old, and very conservative": The functioning of the hidden curriculum in graduate sociology departments. *Harvard Educational Review, 68*(1), 1–33.

Marichal, J. (2009). Frame evolution: A new approach to understanding changes in diversity reforms at public universities in the United States. *Social Science Journal, 46*(1), 171–191.

Martin, J. (2000). Hidden gendered assumptions in mainstream organizational theory and research. *Journal of Management Inquiry, 9*(2), 207–216.

Mattern, K., & Radunzel, J. (2015). *Who goes to graduate school? Tracking 2003 ACT®-tested high school graduates for more than a decade.* ACT Research Report Series (Vol. 2). Iowa City, IA: ACT.

Merriam, S. B. (2009). *Qualitative research: A guide to design and implementation.* San Francisco, CA: Jossey-Bass.

Meyer, J. W., & Rowan, B. (1977). Institutionalized organizations: Formal structure as myth and ceremony. *American Journal of Sociology, 83*(2), 340–363.

Meyerson, D., & Tompkins, M. (2007). Tempered radicals as institutional change agents: The case of advancing gender equity at the University of Michigan. *Harvard Journal of Law & Gender, 30*, 303–322.

Milem, J. F., Chang, M. J., & Antonio, A. L. (2005). *Making diversity work on campus: A research-based perspective.* Washington, DC: Association of American Colleges and Universities.

Milkman, K. L., Akinola, M., & Chugh, D. (2015). What happens before? A field experiment exploring how pay and representation differentially shape bias on the pathway into organizations. *Journal of Applied Psychology, 100*(6), 1678–1712.

Miller, C. W. (2013, March). Diversity in physics: Impact of using minimum acceptable GRE scores for graduate admissions. *APS Meeting Abstracts, 1*, 38003.

Miller, C., & Stassun, K. (2014). A test that fails. *Nature, 510*(7504), 303–304.

Molinsky, A. L. (2013). The psychological processes of cultural retooling. *Academy of Management Journal, 56*(3), 683–710.

Mulvey, P. J., & Nicholson, S. (2008). *Enrollments and degree report, 2006* (No. R-151.43). College Park, MD: American Institute of Physics Statistical Research Center.

Museus, S. D. (2014). The culturally engaging campus environments model: A new theory of college student success among racially diverse student populations. In

M. B. Paulsen (Ed.), *Higher education: Handbook of theory and research* (pp. 189–227). New York, NY: Springer.

National Academies of Science, Engineering, and Medicine. (2018). *Graduate STEM education for the 21st century.* Washington, DC: National Academies Press.

National Science Foundation. (2013a). *National survey of college graduates.* Alexandria, VA: Author.

National Science Foundation. (2013b). *Women, minorities, and persons with disabilities in science and engineering* (NSF 13-304). Arlington, VA: National Center for Science and Engineering Statistics. Retrieved from http://www.nsf.gov/statistics/wmpd/2013/race.cfm

Nettles, M. T. (1990). Success in doctoral programs: Experiences of minority and white students. *American Journal of Education, 98*(4), 494–522. https://doi.org/10.1086/443974

Nettles, M. T., & Millett, C. M. (2006). *Three magic letters: Getting to PhD.* Baltimore, MD: Johns Hopkins University Press.

Neumann, A. (1991). The thinking team: Toward a cognitive model of administrative teamwork in higher education. *Journal of Higher Education, 62*(5), 485–513.

Noble, S. U. (2018). *Algorithms of oppression: How search engines reinforce racism.* New York, NY: New York University Press.

Ong, M., Wright, C., Espinosa, L. L., & Orfield, G. (2011). Inside the double bind: A synthesis of empirical research on undergraduate and graduate women of color in science, technology, engineering, and mathematics. *Harvard Educational Review, 81*(2), 172–209.

Page, S. E. (2008). *The difference: How the power of diversity creates better groups, firms, schools, and societies.* Princeton, NJ: Princeton University Press.

Patton, L. D. (2009). My sister's keeper: A qualitative examination of mentoring experiences among African American women in graduate and professional schools. *Journal of Higher Education, 80*(5), 510–537.

Patton, L. D., & Bondi, S. (2015). Nice white men or social justice allies? Using critical race theory to examine how white male faculty and administrators engage in ally work. *Race Ethnicity and Education, 18*(4), 488–514.

Patton, S. (2014, October 27). Black man in the lab. *Chronicle of Higher Education.* Retrieved from http://chronicle.com/article/Black-Man-in-the-Lab/149565?cid=cp8

Perez, R. J., Robbins, C. K., Harris, L., Jr., & Montgomery, C. (2019). Exploring graduate students' socialization to equity, diversity, and inclusion. *Journal of Diversity in Higher Education, 12*(3).

Phillips, K. W. (Ed.). (2008). *Diversity and groups.* New York, NY: Emerald.

Policy Link. (2015). *The equity manifesto.* Retrieved from https://www.policylink.org/about-us/equity-manifesto

Popkin, G. (2018, April 25). Einstein's "spooky action at a distance" spotted in objects almost big enough to see. *Science.* Retrieved from https://www.sciencemag.org/news/2018/04/einstein-s-spooky-action-distance-spotted-objects-almost-big-enough-see

Porter, K. B., Posselt, J. R., Reyes, K., Slay, K. E., & Kamimura, A. (2018). Burdens and benefits of diversity work: Emotion management in STEM doctoral students. *Studies in Graduate and Postdoctoral Education, 9*(2), 127–143.

Posselt, J. R., Jaquette, O., Bielby, R., & Bastedo, M. N. (2012). Access without equity: Longitudinal analyses of institutional stratification by race and ethnicity, 1972–2004. *American Educational Research Journal, 49*(6), 1074–1111.

Posselt, J. R. (2015). Disciplinary logics in doctoral admissions: Understanding patterns of faculty evaluation. *Journal of Higher Education, 86*(6), 807–833.

Posselt, J. (2016). *Inside graduate admissions: Merit, diversity, and faculty gatekeeping.* Cambridge, MA: Harvard University Press.

Posselt, J. (2018a). Rigor and support in racialized learning environments: The case of graduate education. *New Directions for Higher Education, 181,* 59–70.

Posselt, J. R. (2018b). Trust networks: A new perspective on pedigree and the ambiguities of admissions. *Review of Higher Education, 41*(4), 497–521.

Posselt, J. (2018c). Normalizing struggle: Dimensions of faculty support for doctoral students and implications for persistence and well-being. *Journal of Higher Education, 89*(6), 988–1013.

Posselt, J. (2020). *Discrimination, support, and competitiveness in graduate student mental health* (Race and Ethnicity Report). Washington, DC: American Council on Education.

Posselt, J. R., Hernandez, T. E., Cochran, G. L., & Miller, C. W. (2019). Metrics first, diversity later? Making the shortlist and getting admitted to physics PhD programs. *Journal of Women and Minorities in Science and Engineering, 25*(4).

Posselt, J. R., Jaquette, O., Bielby, R., & Bastedo, M. N. (2012). Access without equity: Longitudinal analyses of institutional stratification by race and ethnicity, 1972–2004. *American Educational Research Journal, 49*(6), 1074–1111.

Posselt, J. R., Reyes, K. A., Slay, K., Kamimura, A., & Porter, K. (2017). Equity efforts as boundary work: How symbolic and social boundaries shape access and inclusion in graduate education. *Teachers College Record, 199*(10), 1–38.

Potvin, G., Chari, D., & Hodapp, T. (2017). Investigating approaches to diversity in a national survey of physics doctoral degree programs: The graduate admissions landscape. *Physical Review Physics Education Research, 13*(2), 020142.

Prescod-Weinstein, C. (2017). Curiosity and the end of discrimination. *Nature Astronomy, 1*(6), 0145.

Prichep, D. (2013). A campus more colorful than reality: Beware that college brochure. *Weekend Edition Sunday.* Retrieved from https://www.npr.org/2013/12/29/257765543/a-campus-more-colorful-than-reality-beware-that-college-brochure

Rao, H., Monin, P., & Durand, R. (2005). Border crossing: Bricolage and the erosion of categorical boundaries in French gastronomy. *American Sociological Review, 70*(6), 968–991.

Ray, V. (2018). A theory of racialized organizations. *American Sociological Review, 84*(1), 26–53.

Ridgeway, C. L. (2009). Framed before we know it: How gender shapes social relations. *Gender & Society, 23*(2), 145–160.

Rios, D., & Stewart, A. J. (2015) Insider and outsider-within standpoints: The experiences of diverse faculty in science and engineering fields. *Journal of Women and Minorities in Science and Engineering, 21*(4).

Roach, R. (2006, August 24). Remembering the Michigan Mandate. *Diverse: Issues in Higher Education.* Retrieved from http://diverseeducation.com/article/6264/

Rogers, M. R., & Molina, L. E. (2006). Exemplary efforts in psychology to recruit and retain graduate students of color. *American Psychologist, 61*(2), 143.

Rorty, A. O. (1983). Experiments in philosophic genre: Descartes' "Meditations." *Critical Inquiry, 9*(3), 545–564.

Rovelli, C. (2016). *Seven brief lessons on physics.* New York, NY: Riverhead Books.

Saini, A. (2017). *Inferior: How science got women wrong—and the new research that's rewriting the story.* Boston, MA: Beacon Press.

St. John, K., Riggs, E., & Mogk, D. (2016). Sexual harassment in the sciences: A call to geoscience faculty and researchers to respond. *Journal of Geoscience Education, 64*(4), 255–257.

Sargent, C. (2009). Playing, shopping, and working as rock musicians: Masculinities in "de-skilled" and "re-skilled" organizations. *Gender & Society, 23*(5), 665–687.

Sauder, M., & Espeland, W. N. (2009). The discipline of rankings: Tight coupling and organizational change. *American Sociological Review, 74*(1), 63–82.

Schneider, B. E. (1987). Graduate women, sexual harassment, and university policy. *Journal of Higher Education, 58*(1), 46–65.

Scott, W. R., & Davis, G. F. (2015). *Organizations and organizing: Rational, natural and open systems perspectives.* New York, NY: Routledge.

Scully, M., & Creed, D. (1997, August). *Stealth legitimacy: Employee activism and corporate response during the diffusion of domestic partner benefits.* Paper presented at the Academy of Management annual meeting, Boston, MA.

Sexton, J. M., Newman, H., Bergstrom, C., Pugh, K., Riggs, E., & Phillips, M. (2016). Mixed methods study to investigate sexist experiences encountered by undergraduate geoscience Students. *Geological Society of America Abstracts with Programs, 48*(7). Retrieved from https://gsa.confex.com/gsa/2016AM/webprogram/Paper278443.html

Shiao, J. L. (2004). *Identifying talent, institutionalizing diversity: Race and philanthropy in post–civil rights America.* Durham, NC: Duke University Press.

Slaughter, J. B., Tao, Y., & Pearson, W., Jr. (Eds.). (2015). *Changing the face of engineering: The African American experience.* Baltimore, MD: Johns Hopkins University Press.

Slay, K., Reyes, K., & Posselt, J. (2019). Bait and switch? Representation, climate, and the tensions of diversity in graduate education. *Review of Higher Education, 42*(5), 255–286.

Snow, C. P. (2012). *The two cultures.* Cambridge, England: Cambridge University Press.

Solorzano, D., Ceja, M., & Yosso, T. (2000). Critical race theory, racial microaggressions, and campus racial climate: The experiences of African American college students. *Journal of Negro Education*, 69(1), 60–73.

Sowell, R., Allum, J., & Okohana, H. (2015). *Doctoral initiative on minority attrition and completion*. Washington, DC: Council of Graduate Schools.

Stassun, K. G., Sturm, S., Holley-Bockelmann, K., Burger, A., Ernst, D. J., & Webb, D. (2011). The Fisk-Vanderbilt Master's-to-PhD Bridge Program: Recognizing, enlisting, and cultivating unrealized or unrecognized potential in underrepresented minority students. *American Journal of Physics*, 79(4), 374–379.

Stevens, M. L. (2009). *Creating a class*. Cambridge, MA: Harvard University Press.

Stevens, M. L., & Roksa, J. (2011). The diversity imperative in elite admissions. In L. M. Stulberg & S. L. Weinburg (Eds.), *Diversity in American higher education: Toward a more comprehensive approach* (pp. 63–73). New York, NY: Routledge.

Stewart, D.-L. (2017, March 30). The language of appeasement. *Inside Higher Education*. Retrieved from https://www.insidehighered.com/views/2017/03/30/colleges -need-language-shift-not-one-you-think-essay

Sturm, S. (2006). The architecture of inclusion: Advancing workplace equity in higher education. *Harvard Journal of Law & Gender*, 29, 247–334.

Swidler, A. (1986). Culture in action: Symbols and strategies. *American Sociological Review*, 51(2), 273–286.

Szasz, M. (2001). *Between Indian and white worlds: The cultural broker*. Norman, OK: University of Oklahoma Press.

Taylor, E., & Antony, J. S. (2000). Stereotype threat reduction and wise schooling: Towards the successful socialization of African American doctoral students in education. *Journal of Negro Education*, 69(3), 184–198.

Thomas, K. M., & Wise, P. G. (1999). Organizational attractiveness and individual differences: Are diverse applicants attracted by different factors? *Journal of Business and Psychology*, 13(3), 375–390.

Thornhill, T. (2018). We want Black students, just not you: How white admissions counselors screen Black prospective students. *Sociology of Race and Ethnicity*, 5(4), 456–470.

Tierney, W. G. (1988). Organizational culture in higher education: Defining the essentials. *Journal of Higher Education*, 59(1), 2–21.

Tierney, W. G., & Bensimon, E. M. (1996). *Promotion and tenure: Community and socialization in academe*. New York, NY: SUNY Press.

Tierney, W. G., & Sallee, M. W. (2008). Do organizational structures and strategies increase faculty diversity? A cultural analysis. *American Academic*, 4(1), 159–184.

Tilly, C. (2004). Social boundary mechanisms. *Philosophy of the Social Sciences*, 34(2), 211–236.

Trabesinger, A. (2010). Hierarchy of sciences: How hard is physics? *Nature Physics*, 6(5), 327.

Traweek, S. (1988). *Beamtimes and lifetimes: The world of high energy physicists*. Cambridge, MA: Harvard University Press.

Trowler, P. (2008). *Cultures and change in higher education: Theories and practices.* New York, NY: Palgrave Macmillan.

Tyack, D. B., & Cuban, L. (1995). *Tinkering toward utopia.* Cambridge, MA: Harvard University Press.

Tyndall, J. (1905). *Fragments of science.* New York, NY: Collier.

Uhlmann, E. L., & Cohen, G. L. (2007). "I think it, therefore it's true": Effects of self-perceived objectivity on hiring discrimination. *Organizational Behavior and Human Decision Processes, 104*(2), 207–223.

Valletta, R. (2015). Higher education, wages, and polarization. *Federal Reserve Bank of San Francisco Economic Letter, 2,* 1–5.

Victoroff, K. Z., & Boyatzis, R. E. (2013). What is the relationship between emotional intelligence and dental student clinical performance? *Journal of Dental Education, 77*(4), 416–426.

Wade, L. (2009, September 2). Doctoring diversity: Race and Photoshop. *Sociological Images.* Retrieved from https://thesocietypages.org/socimages/2009/09/02/doctoring-diversity-race-and-photoshop/

Walker, G. E., Golde, C. M., Jones, L., Bueschel, A. C., & Hutchings, P. (2009). *The formation of scholars: Rethinking doctoral education for the twenty-first century* (Vol. 11). Mahwah, NJ: Wiley.

Waters, A., & Asbill, L. (2013). Reflections on cultural humility. *CYF News.* Retrieved from https://www.apa.org/pi/families/resources/newsletter/2013/08/cultural-humility.

Weick, K. E. (1976). Educational organizations as loosely coupled systems. *Administrative Science Quarterly, 21*(1), 1–19.

Weick, K. (1984). Small wins: Redefining the scale of social problems. *American Psychologist 39*(1), 40–49.

Wellmon, C. (2015). *Organizing enlightenment: Information overload and the invention of the modern research university.* Baltimore, MD: Johns Hopkins University Press.

White, H. C. (1992). *Identity and control: A structural theory of social action.* Princeton, NJ: Princeton University Press.

Wilson, E. O. (1999). *Consilience: The unity of knowledge.* New York, NY: Vintage Books.

Xie, Y., & Shauman, K. A. (2003). *Women in science: Career processes and outcomes.* Cambridge, MA: Harvard University Press.

Yin, R. K. (2003). *Case study research: Design and methods* (3rd ed.). Thousand Oaks, CA: Sage.

Zerubavel, E. (1991). *The fine line.* New York, NY: Free Press.

Index

AAS (American Astronomical Society),
111, 115, 118, 120, 124, 126–128, 130, 138,
141–143, 190n11, 191n18
Abbott, Andrew, 112
academic communities. *See* community
academic cultures. *See* culture
activation in boundary processes, 91
activism, 120
admissions: about, 162, 192–193n39; GRE
in, 154–156; holistic review in, 152–157,
160; as an inclusive practice in high-
diversity STEM PhD programs, 147;
racial equality and graduate, 72–73;
reinventing, 95–97, 154–157; to universities, 64–65
ADVANCE, 186n15
advanced coursework, 181n26
advocacy culture: about, 118–120; agenda
and, 141–142; in astronomy, 120–130;
barriers to implementation in the,
129–130; coordinated, 128–129; disciplinary cultural tools and, 142–143;
by leaders, 62; in physics, 130–138;
relationship between managerial
culture and, 139–141; rise of, 120; sup-

port of activism by, 120; top-down,
126–128
advocate role, 1–2
agency: about, 19; view of, 24–25
agendas, 141–142
agential realism, 18
AGU, 59, 114, 141
Agüeros, Marcel, 128
Ahmed, Sarah, 79, 161, 195n38
alcohol, 35–36, 41–42, 185n11
alienation, 120
American Astronomical Society (AAS),
111, 115, 118, 120, 124, 126–128, 130, 138,
141–143, 190n11, 191n18
American Center for Physics, 133
American Chemical Society (ACS), 127,
141
American Geophysical Union (AGU),
59, 114, 141
American Institute of Physics, 141
American Physical Society (APS), 93, 96,
111, 115, 117, 118, 127, 128, 131, 132, 134, 137,
138, 142, 182n28, 192n32
American Psychological Association
(APA), 114